Classifying the

Zhuangzi Chapters

T0341890

Michigan Monographs in Chinese Studies, no. 65

To John B. Elliotte

Classifying the

Zhuangzi Chapters

Liu Xiaogan

Center for Chinese Studies • The University of Michigan

Open access edition funded by the National Endowment for the Humanities/ Andrew W. Mellon Foundation Humanities Open Book Program.

MICHIGAN MONOGRAPHS IN CHINESE STUDIES
SERIES ESTABLISHED 1968

Published by Center for Chinese Studies
The University of Michigan
Ann Arbor, 48104–1608

© 1994 by Center for Chinese Studies

Translated by William E. Savage
Cover design by Heidi Dailey

Printed and bound by CPI Group (UK) Ltd, Croydon, CR0 4YY

♾ The paper used in this publication meets the requirements of the American National Standard for Information Sciences—Permanence for Publications and Documents in Libraries and Archives ANSI/NISO/Z39.48—1992.

Library of Congress Cataloging-in-Publication Data

Liu Xiaogan, 1947–
 Classifying the Zhuangzi chapters / by Liu Xiaogan.
  p. cm.—(Michigan monographs in Chinese Studies ; no. 65)
 Includes bibliographic references and index.
 ISBN 978-0-892-64164-2 (paper)
 1. Chuang-tzu. Nan-hua ching. 2. Lao-tzu. Tao te ching.
 I. Title. II. Series.
 BL1900.C576L5863   1994
 299'.51482—dc20
                                                          93-50079
                                                          CIP

ISBN 978-0-89264-106-2 (hardcover)
ISBN 978-0-89264-164-2 (paper)
ISBN 978-0-472-12739-9 (ebook)
ISBN 978-0-472-90134-0 (open access)

Contents

Foreword

by Donald J. Munro

The historian must have a reliable fulcrum that he can use to pry up items and separate them from other items. Thus begins Liu Xiaogan early in his first chapter, citing an idea of Fung Yu-lan. Continuing the use of the image, Liu enumerates various chapters of various texts that scholars have used as fulcrums to study the *Zhuangzi*. His own position, which describes the orientation of the present work, is this:

> Since our present fulcrums are insufficient to distinguish between Zhuangzi's writings and those of his followers, and since we can find no more satisfactory evidentiary basis outside of the book *Zhuangzi*, are we then able to search only within its confines for the evidence we need? The answer is very simple. If the distinctions between the Inner chapters and the Outer and Miscellaneous chapters are historical distinctions, then objective differences must exist between them. If these objective differences indicate a temporal succession between two portions of the text, then our problems are easily resolved. On the other hand, if the differences between the Inner chapters and the Outer and Miscellaneous chapters are the result of Guo Xiang's arbitrary arrangements, then it will be impossible for us to find objective differences between them. So the crux of the question is, Are there any objective differences between the Inner chapters and the Outer and Miscellaneous chapters, and can these objective distinctions be used to acertain

their chronological relationship? What follows below are the results from our examination of this "crux."

Liu Xiaogan himself uses four different fulcrums in considering whether or not there is any objective evidence of differences between these sets of chapters: technical terms that may appear as individual characters or as two-character compounds; *Zhuangzi* passages quoted in the *Lüshi chunqiu* and *Hanfeizi*; statements by the Han historians Sima Tan and Sima Qian; and statements or phrases repeatedly used in certain chapters that he groups together.

This work is not for the general reader. It is basic research intended for those already familiar with the text of the *Zhuangzi*. It focuses on certain issues that normally come across as mere guesses, assertions, or assumptions in lectures and writings for the undergraduate and general reader and tries to get them straight. These issues are the dating of the chapters and their relations to one another. The plausibility of claims about the content of the text often depends on these more basic matters of dating and classification. This is why, in his book *Zhuangzi zhexue ji qi yanbian*, Liu Xiaogan begins with these problems. The present monograph represents a translation by William E. Savage of the first three chapters of that work.

In these introductory pages, I want to describe Liu's approach and some of his conclusions. I will also compare them with those of Angus Graham, the most prominent Western scholar of Zhuangzi, pointing to their disagreements and convergences. I will then say something about where I think the strengths and weaknesses lie in the conclusions of both authors.

Liu's approach here is to provide brief sections of similar passages from different chapters and sets of chapters in the *Zhuangzi*. Because he does not provide the full text of the passages, they are not accessible to the non-specialist. However, a person having some familiarity with the text and knowing what kind of questions to ask will find Liu's juxtapositions provocative. They offer rich factual material concerning the evolution of ideas and the development of speech patterns.

Angus Graham deals with some of the dating and classification issues in his works on the Zhuangzi, large sections of which are accessible to the general reader. These works include, "How Much of *Chuang-tzu* Did Chuang-tzu Write?" and *Chuang-tzu: The "Inner Chapters."* Graham and Liu produced their findings independently, and neither their methods nor their conclusions always agree. The large strokes in their classification portraits do converge. Comparing the two works provides an opportunity for a critical look at the respective standards used in the most exacting and helpful Chinese and Western textual scholarship.

Liu's method includes identifying single-character technical terms that also appear in compounds: *dao* 道, *de* 德, *xing* 性, *ming* 命, *jing* 精, and *shen* 神, and also the compounds *daode* 道德, *xingming* 性命, and *jingshen* 精神. Their philosophical centrality needs no defense here. He separates out the chapters in which they respectively appear in these forms and states that the compounds appeared later than the single terms.

In this way, Liu has one tool for differentially dating *Zhuangzi* chapters. And such a division permits him to identify other terms characteristic of the author of the early chapters of the work (for example, *lai* 來 functioning as an auxiliary at the end of a sentence, *xiaoyao* 逍遙, and *you* 遊).

The other primary feature of his dating method is to make statistical counts of the *Zhuangzi* passages quoted in the *Lüshi chunqiu*, a work of around 240 B.C. that collects from other sources, and in the *Hanfeizi* (together, the two works quote 14 of the present 33 chapters). From this information, Liu is able to make inferences about the date when the combined Inner, Outer, and Miscellaneous chapters became a book. He believes that the book's chapter headings were gradually assigned over a period of time.

Liu's method in classifying the Outer and Miscellaneous chapters is to tabulate all similarities in linguistic expression and doctrine between these chapters and the Inner chapters. He lists the pertinent passages side-by-side, so the reader can see and compare the varying, similar, or identical phrasings and descriptions.

For example, in one set of 12 Outer and Miscellaneous chapters (17–27) he finds about 90 passages that are identical to or correspond to passages in the Inner chapters, an average of approximately 7.5 instances per chapter. Also, within this group are to be found 23 of the total of 25 records of Zhuangzi's activities in the Outer and Miscellaneous chapters. The Inner chapters contain 4, appended at the ends of chapters, whereas these 23 are mainly at the beginnings or in the middles of chapters. And no important ideas different from those of the Inner chapters are introduced in this set. Liu attributes these chapters to the school of "Transmitters."

Applying these methods throughout, Liu comes to the following conclusions. The seven Inner chapters are mid–Warring States period. They share sufficient vocabulary style and thought to constitute a single body or complete unit. Within them, there appears to be development of Zhuangzi's thought from minimal disdain for the world to seeking complete transcendence from it. The Outer and Miscellaneous chapters were completed by the last years of the Warring States period, before 235 B.C. when Lü Buwei, compiler of the *Lüshi chunqiu*, died. To argue for a compilation date before the final Qin conquest goes against the prevailing opinion of Chinese scholarship, namely that the Outer and Miscellaneous chapters are creations of the early Han.

Liu Xiaogan concludes that all of the Outer and Miscellaneous chapters were written by followers of Zhuangzi. They are not a melange of materials from disparate Daoist schools. However, these chapters do divide according to three schools of Zhuangzi's followers. Clarity about terminology is important. Zhuangzi had followers, but there is no evidence presented about an *organized* school continuing after his death.

One of these groups of followers is the transmitters or expositors who lived nearest in time to Zhuangzi and whose thought most closely resembles that of the Inner chapters. Their works replicate such Inner chapter themes as the relativity of perspectives. Liu calls them the "Transmitter school" 述莊派, cites "Qiushui" (chapter 17) as a good example of their writing, and assigns to them chapters 17–27 and 32. Angus Graham's closest counterpart is the "school of Zhuangzi," to which he assigns chapters 17–22.[1]

The second set of chapters is writings left by those of Zhuangzi's later followers who adopted the Huang-Lao teachings that became popular in the late Warring States period. Liu calls these writers the "Huang-Lao school" 黃老派. A telltale mark of the late Warring States is the attempt to draw strength through comprehensiveness. Thus the Huang-Lao writers synthesize Confucian, Daoist, and Legalist ideas. And they revere the arts of the Yellow Emperor (mentioned in the later *Zhuangzi* chapters) and Laozi. In the Han, Sima Tan associated a certain eclecticism with Daoism: "They selected the good parts of Confucianism and Moism and gathered the essentials of the School of Names and the Legalists."[2] These chapters discuss human nature, social rank or divisions, and inaction and treat Heaven as equal to the Dao or even superior to it. Their style involves parable and conversation. Liu considers "Tiandao" (chapter 13) an apt example of these Huang-Lao writings, and attributes to these writers chapters 12–16, 33, and the latter part of 11. Graham's closest match is the "Syncretists," to whom he attributes chapters 12–14, the tail end of 11, 15, and 33.[3]

Liu's classification system highlights some ideas in these Outer and Miscellaneous chapters that are not found in the Inner chapters. For example, where the Inner chapters reveal no political interest, those of the Huang-Lao school advocate non-action by rulers and zealous action by ministers. On this point they converge with Legalist writings. Where the Zhuangzi of the Inner chapters repudiates Confucian virtues such as be-nevolence/goodwill and doing what is proper, the Huang-Lao chapters are tolerant of them. At the same time, the Huang-Lao author(s) subscribes to certain important ideas in the Inner chapters. These include forgetting one's bodily identity so as to join in great unity with the boundless. Liu finds 14 passages in the Huang-Lao chapters that resemble passages in the Inner chapters.

The third group of chapters Liu assigns to the "school of No Sovereign" or "Anarchists" 無君派. These chapters consider hearing and sight, and they discuss the essentials of the inborn nature *(xingming zhi qing)*. In opposing benevolence, propriety, ritual, and ceremony, they differ from some of the more tolerant Huang-Lao chapters. They long for a time prior to the emergence of the civilizing arts. "Pianmu" (chapter 8) well illustrates their approach, which is found in chapters 8–10, 28–29, 31 and the first part of 11. Graham's counterpart is the "Primitivist" group (chapters 8–10 and the first part of 11)[4] and the "Yangist" group (chapters 28–31),[5] is a non-Daoist set containing the ideas of Yang Zhu. In other words, Graham divides Liu's "Anarchist" set into two units.

While establishing the ties of the Anarchist chapters to the Inner chapters, Liu also points out their differences. The former use short arguments rather than allegories. They state that man's goal should be to liberate his nature from controls, where the earlier chapters emphasize experiencing the Dao. On this basis we can probe in more depth the differences between Liu's work and Graham's.

Angus Graham differs from Liu Xiaogan in holding that the Inner chapters are mutilated and that it is possible to repair them with scraps from other chapters. Liu finds no justification for this. We now see that they also diverge on matters of classification.

Liu treats all Outer and Miscellaneous chapters as Daoist (except perhaps chapter 30) and as written by the followers of Zhuangzi. Graham maintains that while some are Daoist, such as the passages that relate directly to the Inner chapters and selections that Graham terms "school of Zhuangzi," there are, in addition, three other classes of writings, divided by topical differences. The second and third of these, he believes, are non-Daoist.

The first is the essays (chapters 8–10 and part of 11) of a single author, the "Primitivist," whom Graham dates to the interregnum between Qin and Han (209–202 B.C.) They idealize the tribal utopia in which men live as spontaneously as animals, there are no social distinctions, and no moralizing as Confucius and Mozi came to do. The Primitivist believes that punishments, reasoning, and moralizing disrupt spontaneity. His interests are social and political, not mystical. In short, these essays in spirit amplify the Daoist *Laozi,* chapter 80, though they are written from the citizen's viewpoint, not that of the ruler.

Graham's second class, and one that he considers non-Daoist, is the "Yangist" miscellany (chapters 28–31). These writings prize the individual caring for his body and avoiding risk so as to live out his term. They disdain involvement with material things and prefer private life to life in office. Their debate is with the moralist who advocates taking office even at risk to his life. These chapters date from just after 200 B.C.

Graham's third class, also not fully Daoist, is the "Syncretist" documents (chapters 12–15), which lay out a political philosophy in which the way of Heaven and earth provides guidelines for government. These chapters reflect many hands and can be considered the ideas of a school. Graham suspects that the members of this school edited *Zhuangzi* and placed chapter 33 at the end. The themes in these chapters include the Daoist concept of the king who does nothing, Confucian benevolence and propriety, and Legalist administrative techniques. These writings idealize the Yellow Emperor and the Emperors Yao and Shun (designers of moral codes and administrative hierarchy); such emperors were disdained by the Primitivist and Yangist.

There are some crucial issues that divide Graham and Liu. I would like to present Liu's case on two such matters, because I find it convincing. One is his position that among Zhuangzi's later followers who authored certain of the chapters were people who belonged to the Huang-Lao school, an appellation he prefers to Graham's "Syncretists." The other is his rejection of the thesis about "Yangist" chapters. In discussing these issues, I must draw on some points in Liu's original book that are not translated in the present monograph.

The *Zhuangzi* chapters that Liu identifies as Huang-Lao contain three stories about the Yellow Emperor. One of these takes him to be a Daoist master and the other two treat him as a follower of Daoist teachings. They contain eight stories about Laozi, all of which treat him as the master of Daoism. There are also some isolated sentences with either praise or criticism for the Yellow Emperor. (It is curious that a school that came to be designated as Huang-Lao manifests so little devotion to the Yellow Emperor in the extant texts.)

The term "Huang-Lao" is a Han expression. There is no evidence that the Zhuangzi followers in question called themselves that, no evidence indeed as to what they called themselves. However, Sima Qian in the *Shiji* does refer to Shen Dao and Han Feizi studying Huang-Lao doctrine in the Warring States period.[6] He also speaks of Shen Dao studying "Huang-Lao *daode*."[7] This means that a Han commentator applies the term "Huang-Lao Daoism" to that earlier time. In his writings, Sima Qian uses the terms *daojia* (Daoist school), *Huang-Lao*, and *daode (jia)* interchangeably.[8]

There is a description by Sima Tan of what the Daoists (i.e. Huang-Lao followers) believed. Liu takes this as the most authentic existing standard for categorizing something of the Warring States Period as Daoist or Huang-Lao:

> Daoism teaches people to be in spiritual concentration, moving in accordance with the formless, keeping tranquil and spreading it over all things.
>
> The art of Daoism is following the great concords of the Yin and Yang [schools], adopting the advantage of Confucianism and Moism, and applying the essence of the School of Names and Legalism.
>
> It lets people act according to the movement of time, respond to the change of things, establish custom and inspire things, without anything imperfect. Yet the key [of the art of Daoism] is concise and easy to employ, the effort is little and the achievement is great.
>
> However, Confucians are different. They think that a sovereign is the model and example of the whole world. Hence, the sovereign makes proposals and then ministers respond to it. A sovereign moves first, then ministers follow him. Therefore the sovereign exhausts himself, and ministers take it easy.[9]

Using Sima Tan as the ultimate standard, Liu finds that the chapters of the *Zhuangzi* that he terms "Huang-Lao" match the characteristics in this passage. First, when it describes the Daoist amalgamation of other doctrines (Daoism, Confucianism, Legalism) the passage appears to lay out a *system* in which there is a hierarchy of doctrine. In *Zhuangzi*, ("Tiandao," chapter 13), there is a statement describing the teaching of the men of old:

> The men of old who made clear the great Way first made Heaven clear [explaining Daoism]. And the moral path and virtue *(daode)* were next: and when the moral path and virtue were clear, humaneness and duty *(renyi* 仁義) were next: and when humaneness and duty were clear, status and responsibilities were next [explaining Confucianism]. And when status and responsibilities were clear, title and performance were next: and when title and performance were clear, putting the suitable man in charge was clear, inquiry and inspection were next: and when inquiry and inspection were clear, judging right or wrong was next: and

when judging right or wrong was clear, reward and punishment were next [explaining Legalism]. Cleverness and strategy were unused, they invariably referred back to what was from Heaven in them. It is this that is meant by supreme tranquillity, the utmost in government.[10]

So the fact that the *Zhuangzi* chapters in question put forth a hierarchical synthesis corresponding to that described by Sima Tan is the first piece of evidence in support of designating them as Huang-Lao.

Liu's reason for taking "the great Way" and "Heaven" in the passage above as referring to Daoism is that in the Huang-Lao chapters, both Heaven and the Dao/Way are exalted, and sometimes Heaven is ranked even higher than Dao. He regards the interpretation of *daode* as the Confucian moral path and virtue, rather than Daoism's *Dao* and *de*, as probable, not certain. There are other examples in *Zhuangzi* in which *daode* means "moral path and virtue" or "morality," rather than meaning the Daoist *dao* and *de* (*de* as the *Dao* within individual things).[11] *Daode* and *renyi* both describe the content of Confucianism (along with *fenshou*, status and responsibilities), Liu believes, because many characteristics of Legalism follow (*xingming*, title and performance; *yuanxing*, inquiry and inspection; *shifei*, right or wrong; and *shangfa*, reward and punishment). In terms of style, it is unlikely that the writer would attribute only one or two characteristics to Confucianism and four to Legalism when the former is ranked higher than the latter.

Sima Tan criticizes the Confucians, saying that according to their teachings, "The sovereign exhausts himself, and the ministers take it easy"[12] Knowing that the Daoists insisted that the ruler should practice doing nothing and that the ministers should exert themselves, we can count as the second piece of evidence the convergence on this point between Sima's description and the pertinent Daoist chapters. It is true that Laozi and Zhuangzi say that the sovereign should practice *wuwei*. But not until the Huang-Lao disciples of Zhuangzi does the addition appear that the minister should take action (*youwei*). In "Tiandao" it says,

> The *de* in the emperor or king ... has Doing Nothing as its norm. Doing nothing, one has more than enough to be employer of the world. If one keeps doing something, he will keep being employed by the whole

world, and nothing will be enough to satisfy the world. . . . The man above must do nothing and be employer of the world, the men below must do something and be employed by the world; this is the irreplace-able Way.[13]

Confucians had said the ruler should observe humaneness or good-will (*ren*) and duty (*yi*). The Legalists wanted the ruler to control rewards and punishments. Non-action is first of all a Daoist principle for the ruler.

Third, Sima Tan stresses timeliness ("It shifts with the times and changes in response to things"). This idea appears in *Xunzi* and *Hanfeizi*. Laozi and Zhuangzi speak about according with nature, not about timeli-ness itself. It was the Huang-Lao followers of Zhuangzi, however, who defined "according with nature" in terms of timeliness. This means, as Sima Tan says, that whether there are laws or not, a person should do what is appropriate to the circumstances.

Fourth, Sima Tan talks about concentration and spiritual tranquillity. These ideas also occur in the relevant chapters of the *Zhuangzi*.

Several points follow from Liu's use of Sima Tan as the ultimate standard. One is that the reader can now describe what it means to be a Huang-Lao follower of Zhuangzi, using the above list of four items. I would add that it also means respecting the Yellow Emperor and Laozi as having achieved the highest level of the cultivation of Daoist principles. This takes the form of: equanimity towards life and death, *wuwei* with respect to popular goals such as wealth and status, and disdain for custom-ary standards.

Liu would not use Graham's term "Syncretist writings" when there is a suitable alternative available, because there was no syncretist school in Chinese history. But there were people who came to be described as Huang-Lao followers. In view of the evidence Liu provides of conver-gence between the Han depiction of Huang-Lao teachings and those in the relevant chapters, and of the fact that Huang-Lao is an actual school designation, I find that Liu's terminology is preferable to that of Graham.

Finally (and very controversially), Liu would say that the Mawangdui silk manuscripts may be Huang-Lao, but they are not typical Huang-Lao. They have too much Legalism in them and too little Confucianism (as required by the Sima Tan standard).

Angus Graham identifies chapters 28–31 as "Yangist." This means that he associates them with Yang Zhu's teaching that the individual's preservation and nurturance of his own life is the supreme value. This marks the other major split between Liu and Graham on the matter of classification. For with the exception of chapter 30, which to Liu does not seem to contain any Daoist words, ideas, or style, these chapters are simply Daoist, and there is no legitimate reason for introducing the term "Yangist."

For example, there are similarities in wording between four statements in chapters 28 and 29 and four places in the Inner chapters. Further, each of the three chapters contains the saying "Our Master [or Confucius] was twice driven out of Lu" a passage also contained in the unquestionably Daoist chapter 20. Next, Daoist terminology in chapter 28 includes the statement, "Wander free and easy between heaven and earth." Chapter 29 includes the names "Never-Enough" *(Wuzu* 無足 *)* and "Sense-of-Harmony" *(Zhihe* 知和 *)*, which are both person's names and also descriptions of Zhuangzi's manner. This chapter also includes criticisms of the sages Yao and Shun, Tang and Wu. In chapter 31 the Daoist terminology includes the statement, "The Truth is that which is received from Heaven. By nature it is the way it is and cannot be changed. Therefore, the sage patterns himself on Heaven, and prizes the Truth."[14]

The principal arguments against a Yangist attribution hinge on the association of Yangism with prizing the self and emphasizing life. Now there certainly are some stories in chapter 28 that do treasure these things. However, in the same chapter nearly an equal number prize just the opposite: Bian Sui throws himself into the river and drowns; Wu Guang loads a stone on his back and drowns himself; and Bo Yi and Shu Qi starve themselves to death.[15] Graham asserts that the suicides are only examples of the absurdity of sacrificing one's life in vain.[16] Furthermore, there are lots of themes in this and the other two chapters, including the transcendence of traditional values and commonplace life. The reader may wonder on what basis Graham selects prizing self or life rather than these other themes as revealing the core. In the end, there is no evidence to say that Yang Zhu gave birth to a school. Perhaps he did. But there is no evidence that convincingly links these chapters to Yangism.

There is general agreement between Liu and Graham on the look of the trees in the forest. The great sweeps of their classification schemes are harmonious. They differ on the species that exist in the forest and on how many instances there are of each.

Liu Xiaogan has provided us with an enormous amount of data that different scholars can use in their own ways. For example, there is a list of 29 activities of Zhuangzi that appear to be recorded by later followers. (Graham provided translations of 15 such stories.) Liu lists all passages that are similar between the different sets of chapters. In this way the reader can spot patterns, such as the frequency with which the chapter "Qiwulun" was cited. It had a powerful impact on Zhuangzi's successors. There are lists of terms in the Outer and Miscellaneous chapters not found in the Inner chapters. And there are summaries of the views of the major commentators over the centuries on the relations of the Outer and Miscellaneous to the Inner chapters. These include Gui Youguang, Wang Fuzhi, Lin Yunming, Lu Shuzhi, and modern commentators such as Luo Genze, Zhang Hengshou, and Wang Shumin.

One weak link in Dr. Liu's analysis concerns an assumption that followers of Zhuangzi at least formed themselves into a kind of line, with implications that they speak for the founder. For example, in discussing three chapters that he assigns to the Anarchist school, Liu says, "Though these three chapters are not products of the legitimate branch of Zhuangzi's later followers, they were influenced by Zhuangzi and the Zhuangzi school" (p.137). The reader does not have the evidence to substantiate the existence of legitimate and illegitimate lines of descent.

The other weak link has to do with what constitutes "similarity" between chapters. The analyst should make a convincing case for the reader as to why certain features that are selected for comparison are significant. Many of Liu's selections are significant. But some are not. In justifying grouping seven chapters together as "Anarchist," among other evidence Liu points to the fact that they habitually use the phrases "from the Three Dynasties on down" and "Let me try explaining what I mean." We are not told why these phrases constitute noteworthy evidence of philosophical coherence between the different chapters that share their usage.

Angus Graham's work at times provokes comparable questions in the reader's mind. The "similarities" he looks for are between passages in the Outer and Miscellaneous chapters and those in the Inner chapters, so that he can use such Outer and Miscellaneous chapter fragments to repair gaps that he sees in the Inner chapters. He assumes that one author wrote the fragments and the relevant Inner chapters. The similarities that he finds are in words or patterns of words, such as: *you ya* 有涯, *wu ya* 無涯 ; *dai* 殆 ; *ke bu* 可不 ; *yi hu yi hu* 已乎已乎; *zhi yi* 至矣; *bu yi bei hu* 不亦悲乎 ; *an zhi* 安知; *zao hua* 造化; *qi* 其.[17] However, these are common words. Graham does not provide us with evidence as to why these words or the actual frequency with which they are used are significant enough for textual analysis. So there is certainly not enough guidance as to why we should take them as evidence that certain fragments were written by a certain author. Liu Xiaogan makes softer claims for his evidence, namely that there are certain relations between certain Outer and Miscellaneous chapters and the Inner chapters, but not that specific fragments and Inner chapters were by the same author.

Finally, there is an assumption in Graham's work similar in spirit to Liu's assertions about philosophical coherence. Graham says that every Inner chapter has a certain coherence or structure. This permits inferences about where scraps from Outer and Miscellaneous chapters belong. But he does not develop an argument to rebut the thesis that many chapters are little more than collections of anecdotes, fables, and proverbs.

Like the work of Angus Graham, this treatise by Liu Xiaogan greatly advances our knowledge of the *Zhuangzi*. The reader can imagine a dialogue between Liu and Graham. In the challenges and responses in both directions, standards are examined, terminology revised or clarified, and arguments tightened. There are not necessarily any final interpretive truths, fixed for all times. But the level of analysis rises accordingly.

Notes

1   Graham, *Chuang-tzu: The Inner Chapters*, 116–99.

2   Sima Tan, "Tai shi gong zixu" in Sima Qian, *Shiji*, 3288.

3   Graham, *Chuang-tzu: The Inner Chapters*, 259–85.

4   Graham, *Chuang-tzu: The Inner Chapters*, 200–17.

5   Graham, *Chuang-tzu: The Inner Chapters*, 224–53.

6   "Laozi Han Fei liezhuan" in *Shiji* 7: 63, 2146.

7   "Mengzi Xun Qing liezhuan" in *Shiji* 7:74, 2346.

8   Liu Xiaogan, *Zhuangzi zhexue jiqi yanbian*, 299–300.

9   Translation by Liu Xiaogan, personal communication.

10   Translation by Liu Xiaogan, personal communication.

11   One example is in the Huang-Lao chapter, "Tianxia" (chapter 33). See Qian Mu, ed., *Zhuangzi zuanjian*, "Tianxia," 270, line 7: "The world is in chaos, sages and worthies are unclear, and *dao* and *de* are not one."

12   Sima Tan, "Tai shi gong zixu" in *Shiji*, 3288.

13   Translated by Liu Xiaogan, building on and modifying substantially the translation by Graham in *Chuang-tzu: The Inner Chapters*, 260–61.

14   Watson, trans., *Complete Works of Chuang Tzu*, 350.

15   These stories can be found in Watson, trans., 320–322.

16   Graham, "How Much of *Chuang-tzu* Did Chuang-tzu Write?" 484.

17   Graham, "How Much of *Chuang-tzu* Did Chuang-tzu Write?" 472–73.

Acknowledgments

Many thanks are due to some of my friends and colleagues for help in the publication of this book. It was Professor Donald J. Munro who first proposed translating this book, and he has been very helpful in every way. His scholarship and friendship are always a great encouragement. Professors Shuen-fu Lin and Kenneth J. DeWoskin, as well as the Director of the Asia Library at the University of Michigan, Mr. Weiying Wan, were also very kind and active in supporting this project. I am grateful to Dr. William E. Savage, who translated this dull and difficult book during the evenings and over the weekends over a period of several years when he was head of his department at University Microfilms International and was traveling around the world. All friends at the Center for Chinese Studies at the University of Michigan will also be remembered warmly.

I will never forget that Dr. Quan Ruxian worked all night long to translate an outline of this book and send it to me before dawn, when I was to leave for America. Unfair but not uncommon imprisonment in China took twenty years from him, and he has spent most of his remaining time helping young people, although his solid scholarship and great personality could have made him a prominent scientist and well-known professor.

True compliments should also be paid to one of my closest friends, Professor Leo S. Chang, who helped me to come to the United States and has remained helpful both academically and personally since we met at Beijing University in 1984. I can never convey enough appreciation to him.

I should also mention Professor Tu Wei-ming. His kindness facilitated my working at Harvard for two years. Also Professor Ying-shi Yu invited me to come to Princeton to continue my career. Their concern and help have offered me an excellent opportunity to promote my academic work.

Regarding my comparison between the *Laozi* and the *Shijing,* I owe Professor Yu-gung Kao a great debt of thanks. He is an expert in Chinese literature and poetry, and his scholarship and encouragement have been crucial to my study. Without his suggestions, I might not yet have reached my conclusions.

This is also an opportunity to express my gratitude to all of my American friends and colleagues, young and old, men and women. Their generosity and kindness have given me many good impressions of the American people and academic community. Among them, I have to mention Professor Fritz Mote, who is a model scholar in the Chinese tradition—erudite, humble, and enthusiastic. The same is true of my respected mentor, Professor Kenneth Morgan, who conveys the finest expression of American friendship towards other nationalities. I have been deeply moved when they have offered thoughtful help, which I did not expect.

Last but not least, I wish to thank Mr. Walter Michener, the editor at the Center for Chinese Studies, for his unfailing support and minute attention to various technical issues.

Liu Xiaogan

1

Dating the Inner Chapters of the *Zhuangzi*

Background of the Problem

The three questions concerning the Inner chapters of the *Zhuangzi*—their date, their authorship, and whether we should rely on them when studying Zhuangzi's philosophy—are, in fact, a single question: that is, are the Inner chapters earlier than the Outer and Miscellaneous chapters? The world of learning basically has four points of view concerning this question.

1) The first holds that the Inner chapters of the *Zhuangzi* are earlier than the Outer and Miscellaneous chapters and assents to the proposition that the Inner chapters were written by Zhuang Zhou. From Wang Fuzhi (1619–92) on, most scholars have supported this view.

2) The second holds that the Inner chapters are later than the Outer and Miscellaneous chapters and that the Outer and Miscellaneous chapters were written by Zhuangzi. This position is represented by Ren Jiyu.[1]

3) The third holds that because the Inner, Outer, and Miscellaneous chapters have been jumbled by Guo Xiang (252?–312), the first two chapters, "Xiaoyaoyou" and "Qiwulun," should be used as the basis for classifying the other chapters, disregarding the division into Inner, Outer, and Miscellaneous. This position is represented by Fung Yu-lan;[2] however, he has never indicated how to do this or what other chapters would in fact be identified as Zhuangzi's work.

4) The fourth holds that the *Zhuangzi* was fundamentally authored by Zhuang Zhou and that it is unnecessary to draw distinctions among the Inner, Outer, and Miscellaneous chapters.[3]

A general summary of the above four points of view is that: (1) the Inner chapters were written by Zhuangzi; (2) the Outer and Miscellaneous chapters were written by Zhuangzi; (3) the Inner chapters as well as the Outer and Miscellaneous chapters each contain portions written by Zhuangzi; or (4) the Inner chapters and the Outer and Miscellaneous chapters were all written by Zhuangzi. Admitting the premise that *Zhuangzi,* the book, is related to Zhuangzi, the person, the above four positions are the only possible ones concerning his works. This divergence of opinion indicates that traditional methods of textual analysis have fallen short in explaining the significance of the distinction among the Inner, Outer, and Miscellaneous chapters, as well as in identifying those chapters written by Zhuangzi himself.

Traditional methods of textual criticism require the use of certain pieces of text as the basis for determining which of the writings in the book are Zhuangzi's. Fung Yu-lan once said,

> When studying history, of no matter what period, one must employ some texts that everyone recognizes as reliable to act as a fulcrum, which one uses to distinguish a certain category of historical materials from others; otherwise there is no way research will make progress.[4]

Accordingly, we can designate traditional methods of textual research as a method of fulcrums.

At present, there are about five fulcrums to use in the textual examination of the *Zhuangzi*.

1) Fung Yu-lan employs chapter 33, "Tianxia," which contains an important section describing Zhuangzi's spirit and doctrine.[5]

2) Ren Jiyu uses the short biography of Zhuangzi by Sima Qian in *Shiji*.[6]

3) Zhang Hengshou uses texts from before the second century B.C. (early Han dynasty) that clearly state, "Zhuangzi said"; for example, one passage from chapter 13 of *Zhuangzi*, "Tiandao," one from the "Quyou" chapter of the *Lüshi chunqiu*, the other from the "Daoying" chapter of the *Huainanzi*.[7]

4) We can take the two brief criticisms of Zhuangzi in *Xunzi* as support materials.[8]

5) Finally, the 29 passages in the *Zhuangzi* that record Zhuangzi's activities can also be used.[9]

However, the fulcrums mentioned above are all quite simple and brief, and the understanding of a fulcrum differs from one person to the next; thus it is difficult to draw identical conclusions.

Since our present fulcrums are insufficient to distinguish between Zhuangzi's writings and those of his followers, and since we can find no more satisfactory evidentiary basis outside of the book *Zhuangzi*, are we then able to search only within its confines for the evidence we need? The answer is very simple. If the distinctions between the Inner chapters and the Outer and Miscellaneous chapters are historical distinctions, then objective differences must exist between them. If these objective differences indicate a temporal succession between two portions of the text, then our problems are easily resolved. On the other hand, if the differences between the Inner chapters and the Outer and Miscellaneous chapters are the result of Guo Xiang's arbitrary arrangements, then it will be impossible for us to find objective differences between them. So the crux of the question is, Are there any objective differences between the Inner chapters and the Outer and Miscellaneous chapters, and can these objective distinctions be used to acertain their chronological relationship? What follows below are the results from our examination of this "crux."

The Priority of the Inner Chapters: Linguistic Evidence

While performing a comparative study on several fronts, we have discovered that clear differences exist between the ways compounds are used in the Inner chapters and in the Outer and Miscellaneous chapters. Though the Inner chapter use words such as *dao* 道, *de* 德, *ming* 命, *jing* 精, and *shen* 神, the compounds *daode* 道德, *xingming* 性命, and *jingshen* 精神 are not used, while in the Outer and Miscellaneous chapters *daode, xingming,* and *jingshen* all appear repeatedly, 36 times in all.

Daode

In the seven Inner chapters the character *dao* appears 42 times; the character *de* appears 34 times. The expressions or compounds formed from the character *dao* are *dadao* 大道, *miaodao* 妙道, *rendao* 人道, *daoshu* 道術; the expressions formed from *de* include *quande* 全德, *dade* 大德, etc. For example:

> Fish forget each other when swimming in rivers and lakes; men forget each other in the arts of the Way *(daoshu).* ("Dazongshi," 210)[10]
>
> I take this to be the working of the mysterious Way *(miaodao).* ("Qiwulun," 97)
>
> A Virtue that increases daily would not succeed, much less a great display of Virtue *(dade).* ("Renjianshi," 141)
>
> If so much care is taken to keep himself intact, how much more in the case of a man whose Virtue is whole *(quande)*? ("Dechongfu," 210)

However, the Inner chapters are absolutely without examples of the combined use of the two characters *dao* and *de,* while in the Outer and Miscellaneous chapters *dao* and *de* are used together in a habitual phrase (the Way and its Virtue) in 16 places. Needless to say, the meaning of *daode* varies in different contexts. However, for the sake of linguistic comparison, it is translated simply as "the Way and its Virtue," disregarding the complication of its meaning in specific texts. In other words, we sacrifice fluency for literal accuracy. (The same difficulty arises with *xingming, jingshen,* and other terms used in our analysis.)

1) Men overly reliant on benevolence and righteousness try to practice them, even to the extent that they align them with the five organs! This negates the truth of the *Way and its Virtue.* ("Pianmu," 312)

2) Why then do they come with benevolence and righteousness, tangled and tied with strings and line, glue and lacquer, and try to wander within the *Way and its Virtue*? ("Pianmu," 321)

3) I am fearful before the *Way and its Virtue.* Hence I dare not present myself on high with deeds of benevolence and righteousness, or dare to lower myself with debasing deeds. ("Pianmu," 327)

4) If the *Way and its Virtue* had not been discarded, how would anyone seek benevolence and righteousness?" ("Mati," 336)

5) Destroying the *Way and its Virtue* to create benevolence and righteousness—these are the errors of the sage. ("Mati," 336)

6) Emptiness, stillness, softness, silence, inaction—these are the level of Heaven and Earth, the ultimate of the *Way and its Virtue.* ("Tiandao," 457)

7) The virtue of emperors and kings relies on Heaven and Earth as its ancestor, the *Way and its Virtue* as the principle, inaction as a constant rule. ("Tiandao," 465)

8) Therefore the men of ancient times who understood the Great Way first made Heaven manifest, followed by the *Way and its Virtue.* ("Tiandao," 471)

9) Having made manifest the *Way and its Virtue,* they followed with benevolence and righteousness. ("Tiandao," 471)

10) Hence, it is said, softness, silence, emptiness, and inaction—these are the level of Heaven and Earth and the substance of the *Way and its Virtue.* ("Keyi," 538)

11) If you climb upon the *Way and its Virtue* and go drifting and wandering. . . . ("Shanmu," 668)

12) Remember this my students, it is only the realm of the *Way and its Virtue*. ("Shanmu," 668)

13) When a man possesses the *Way and its Virtue* but is unable to put them into practice, he is exhausted. ("Shanmu," 688)

14) The person who has the *Way and its Virtue* cannot control himself, much less one who simply mimics the Way in his actions. ("Gengsangchu," 783)

15) When the *Way and its Virtue* are present, then destitution or prosperity are simply the alternation of cold and heat, wind and rain. ("Rangwang," 983)

16) The world is in great disorder; the worthies and sages are not influential, and the *Way and its Virtue* are no longer consistent. ("Tianxia," 1069)

Xingming

In the Inner chapters, the character *ming* appears in a total of 16 places. There are no instances of the character *xing* nor the compound *xingming* (inborn nature). In the Outer and Miscellaneous chapters, *xing* and *ming* are used together 12 times, as shown below.

1) He who holds to complete rightness does not lose the essentials of his *inborn nature*. ("Pianmu," 317)

2) Men of no benevolence cut short the essentials of their *inborn nature* as they lust for rank and wealth. ("Pianmu," 319)

3) What I call expertness has nothing to do with benevolence or righteousness; it is relying on the essentials of your *inborn nature,* nothing more. ("Pianmu," 327)

4) From the Three Dynasties on, there has been nothing but fuss over this business of rewards and punishments. How could anyone have the leisure to rest in the essentials of his *inborn nature?* ("Zaiyou," 365)

5) Should the world rest in the essentials of its *inborn nature,* then these eight delights could exist or pass away with no consequence. ("Zaiyou," 367)

6) But when the world does not rest in the essentials of its *inborn nature,* these eight delights become untrue and wild, bringing confusion to the world. ("Zaiyou," 367)

7) When there is inaction, one may then rest in the essentials of his *inborn nature.* ("Zaiyou," 369)

8) When the Great Virtue was no longer unitary, the *inborn nature* was scattered and dissolved. ("Zaiyou," 373)

9) Carriages and caps are but physical regalia, they are not part of the *inborn nature.* ("Zaiyou," 558)

10) Nothing was able to rest in the essentials of its *inborn nature.* Still, they thought themselves sages! Was it not shameful! ("Tianyun," 527)

11) If you set out to sate your appetites and desires and cater to your likes and dislikes, then you harm the essentials of your *inborn nature.* ("Xu Wugui," 818)

12) Your *inborn nature* is not yours to possess; it is something entrusted to you by Heaven and Earth. ("Zhibeiyou," 739)

Jingshen

In the seven Inner chapters, the character *jing* appears twice while the character *shen* appears 20 times. While the phrase *shenming* 神明 is formed from the character *shen,* there are no instances of the two characters *jingshen* (pure spirit) used together. In the Outer and Miscellaneous chapters, there are 8 instances where the two characters *jingshen* are used together:

1) Still water is so clear, how much more so must *pure spirit* be. ("Tiandao," 457)

2) These five trifling things require the movement of *pure spirit* and the impetus of the mind's art; and afterwards there will be those who will follow them. ("Tiandao," 468)

3) *Pure spirit* flows simultaneously into the four directions; there is no place it does not reach. ("Keyi," 544)

4) You must fast; cleanse your mind and wash your *pure spirit*. ("Zhibeiyou," 741)

5) Dazzling brightness arises from deep darkness; regularity arises from formlessness; *pure spirit* arises from the Way. ("Zhibeiyou," 741)

6) The Perfect Man returns his *pure spirit* to that which has no beginning and rests in the outlying areas of nothing-at-all. ("Lieyukou," 1047)

7) The little man's understanding does not go beyond his gifts and wrappings and calling cards. He harms his *pure spirit* in trivialities. ("Lieyukou," 1098)

8) His *pure spirit* came and went alone with Heaven and Earth; yet he did not approach the ten thousand things with disdain. ("Tianxia," 1098)

These observations are summarized in table 1.1. Use of the compounds *daode, xingming,* and *jingshen* clearly distinguishes the Outer and Miscellaneous chapters from the Inner chapters. How, then, do we interpret the significance of this distinction?

The history of the development of Chinese vocabulary tells us that simple, single-character terms appeared first and that only later did compound phrases gradually appear. With the passage of time, the frequency of the use of compounds gradually increased.[11] According to this analysis, among literary materials from different time periods, as long as each is adequately represented, those which use comparatively fewer compounds must have appeared earlier while those which use more must have appeared later. From this we can tentatively conclude that the Inner chapters of the *Zhuangzi* were written first and that the Outer and Miscellaneous chapters were written later.

The above is only a general inference; advancing a step to examine the actual historical process by which the compounds *daode, xingming,* and *jingshen* evolved can help determine the proper chronology of the Inner, the Outer, and the Miscellaneous chapters.

Table 1.1. Distribution of Compounds among the Inner, Outer, and Miscellaneous Chapters

Chapters	Compounds			
	daode	*xingming*	*jingshen*	**Total**
Inner				
1–7	0	0	0	0
Outer				
8	3	3	0	6
9	2	0	0	2
11	0	5	0	5
13	4	0	2	6
14	0	1	0	1
15	1	0	1	2
16	0	1	0	1
20	3	0	0	3
22	0	1	2	3
Miscellaneous				
23	1	1	0	2
28	1	0	0	1
32	0	0	2	2
33	1	0	1	2
Total	16	12	8	36

1) In the *Zuozhuan*, *dao* appears in over 100 places, while the character for *de* appears in over 150 places. However, *dao* and *de* are not used together. *Xing* appears 5 times in the *Zuozhuan* while *ming* appears over 200 times. However, there is not a single example of the compound *xingming*. *Jing* is found twice in the *Zuozhuan* while the character for *shen* is found over 30 times. But, there is not a single instance of the combined use of *jing* and *shen*.

2) In the *Analects*, the character *dao* appears approximately 100 times while the character *de* appears nearly 40 times. But there is simply no instance in which *dao* and *de* are used together. The character *xing* appears twice in the *Analects*, while the character *ming* appears over 150 times; the character *jing* appears once, while the character for *shen* appears 6 times. Yet there are no compounds *xingming* or *jingshen*.

3) In the *Mozi,* the character *dao* appears over 160 times, while the character *de* appears over 30 times. But there is no example of *dao* and *de* being used together. The character *xing* appears twice, while the character *ming* appears in over 150 places. There is no compound *xingming.* The character for *jing* appears in the *Mozi* 2 or 3 times, while *shen* appears in approximately 100 places. Yet we do not find the compound *jingshen.*

4) In the *Laozi,*[12] the character for *dao* appears over 70 times, while the character for *de* appears over 40 times. Yet there are no instances of the compound *daode.* The character for *ming* appears only 3 or 4 times, and there is no character for *xing.* Hence, there is no compound *xingming.* The character *jing* appears 3 or 4 times in the *Laozi,* and there are 7 or 8 instances of the character *shen.* But there is no compound *jingshen.*

5) In the *Mencius,* the character *dao* is used about 150 times while the character *de* is used around 40 times. Yet, there is no compound *daode.* Mencius was the first philosopher who paid attention to *xing,* nature. In his book, the frequency of instances of the character *xing* surpasses that of any previous book. It appears over 30 times, and there are also about 50 instances of *ming.* Yet there is no example of the combination *xingming.* The character for *jing* is not used in the *Mencius,* while the character for *shen* appears 4 or 5 times. There is, of course, no compound *jingshen.*

In the works cited above, there are many compounds or combined expressions formed from *dao, de, xing, ming, jing,* or *shen* combined with another character. However, none of these books uses the compounds *daode, xingming,* or *jingshen.* This is not a coincidence. Taking our inquiry one step further, we find that these three also do not occur in the *Shijing, Shangshu, Guoyu,* or other works produced prior to the mid–Warring States period. From this, we can be sure that prior to the mid–Warring States, before Mencius, these three compounds had yet to appear. It is possible that some of these texts may have been altered after the mid–Warring States, but this certainly won't affect our conclusion.

In chronological sequence, we will examine first the *Xunzi,* where the terms *daode, xingming,* and *jingshen* all occur, as well as later texts, such as the *Hanfeizi, Lüshi chunqiu,* and others.

Xunzi

In the *Xunzi, daode* appears 11 times:

1) Therefore, learn until you begin to work on the *Rites*, for this is the pinnacle of the *Way and its Virtue.* ("Quanxue," X 122)[13]

2) When requesting instruction on the *Way and its Virtue,* do not regard later kings as different from those of remote antiquity. ("Ruxiao," X 160)

3) To make complete the *Way and its Virtue,* to set the exalted on high, to order the patterned fabric of the world . . . these are the tasks of the heavenly kings. ("Wangzhi," X 168)

4) . . . there is no other reason for it, when the *Way and its Virtue* are made fully manifest, advantage and benefit are rich and liberal. ("Wangba," X 189)

5) . . . thereupon, the people would acquire the ability of transforming goodness, self-cultivation, and correct action, accumulating propriety and righteousness, honoring the *Way and its Virtue . . . .* ("Yibing," X 211)

6) There are three kinds of awe: There is the awe of the *Way and its Virtue,* the awe of robbers and brigands, and the awe of the violent and arrogant. ("Qiangguo," 212)

7) So, when the people are exhorted without employing rewards, and awe-inspiring conduct takes place without employing punishments, this is called the awe of the *Way and its Virtue.* ("Qiangguo," X 213)

8) The awe of the *Way and its Virtue* is accomplished through resting in strength. The awe of robbers and brigands is accomplished through intimidating the weak. . . . ("Qiangguo," X 213)[14]

9) When the *Way and its Virtue* are pure and in order, wisdom is most clear. ("Zhenglun," X 227)

10) When the *Way and its Virtue* are pure and complete, slanderous speech is cast away. ("Fu," X 281)

11) The gentleman is fond of employing the *Way and its Virtue,* hence, his people cleave to the Way. ("Yaowen," X 304)

In the *Xunzi, xingming* appears once:

> 1) When action already has its source, then it is unchangeable like the *inborn nature* or flesh. ("Aigong," *X* 300)

In the *Xunzi, jingshen* appears twice:

> 1) When *pure spirit* accumulates through turning back on itself, it becomes unitary, not a multiplicity, and constitutes the sage. ("Chengxiang," *X* 275)

> 2) Extending his *pure spirit,* he returns to the clouds. ("Fu," *X* 279)

Hanfeizi

In the *Hanfeizi, daode* appears twice:

> 1) When the sage is the model for the state, he must act contrary to what the world desires and accord with the *Way and its Virtue.* ("Jianjie shichen," *H* 639)[15]

> 2) Men of high antiquity struggled for the *Way and its Virtue.* Men of the middle ages followed with their knowledge and stratagems. Men of today wrangle about their strength and spirit. ("Wudu," *H* 799)

Xingming is found once:

> 1) Now the *inborn nature* is not something that can be learned from other men. ("Xianxue," *H* 787)

Jingshen is found 10 times:

> 1) Those who are sparing, love their *pure spirit* and are sparing of their knowledge. ("Jielao," *H* 654)

> 2) All evil influences are when the souls are dispersed and the *pure spirit* is scattered. ("Jielao," *H* 655)

> 3) When *pure spirit* is scattered, Virtue is no more. ("Jielao," *H* 655)

> 4) When the Souls are not dispersed, then the *pure spirit* is not scattered. ("Jielao," *H* 655)

> 5) When the *pure spirit* is not scattered, this is called possessing Virtue. ("Jielao," *H* 655)

6) When the rulers are replete in their Virtue and their souls do not scatter their *pure spirit,* then the fullness of their Virtue extends to the people ("Jielao," *H* 655)

7) For this reason, the sage loves his *pure spirit* and honors resting in quietude. ("Jielao," *H* 657)

8) If he does not love his *pure spirit* or honor living in quietude, the harm will be greater than that caused by the tiger and rhinoceros. ("Jielao," *H* 657)[16]

9) Now, if you govern yourself and keep objects at a distance, you will not scatter your *pure spirit.* ("Jielao," *H* 659)

10) When the *pure spirit* is exhausted on external appearances, there is no internal ruler. ("Yulao," *H* 664)

Lüshi chunqiu

In the *Lüshi chunqiu, daode* appears twice:

1) Display the precious jade of the Ho clan and the finest expressions of the *Way and its Virtue* to the worthies. ("Yibao," *L* 347)[17]

2) As for the *Way and its Virtue,* they are not so. There is neither complaining nor abusing. ("Biji," *L* 383)

Xingming is found 9 times:

1) There are those who are so cautious it may eventually harm them; they do not achieve the essentials of their *inborn nature.* ("Zhongji," *L* 282)

2) If they do not achieve the essentials of their *inborn nature,* what use is cautiousness? ("Zhongji," *L* 282)

3) The ability to decide on the basis of what is heard rests in the essentials of the *inborn nature.* ("Jinting," *L* 367)

4) Those who are deluded do not know this rests in the essentials of the *inborn nature.* ("Jinting," *L* 367)

5) First view their changes and move afterward, this is achieving the essentials of the *inborn nature.* ("Guanshi," *L* 401)

6) Therefore those who are good at acting as lords carefully serve the essentials of *inborn nature* and the various officers are governed. ("Wugong," *L* 417)

7) The lord serves the essentials of *inborn nature* and dispels feelings of love and hate. ("Zhidu," *L* 418)

8) The key of the art of government must conform to *inborn nature*. ("Zhidu," *L* 418)

9) Those who are firm in their comprehension of the essentials of *inborn nature* act without partiality. ("Youdu," *L* 492)

Jingshen appears twice:

1) Therefore *pure spirit* accords with form, and longevity obtains its span therein. ("Jinshu," *L* 296)

2) When the enemy is full of fear and dread and is unsettled and disturbed, his *pure spirit* is exhausted. ("Lunwei," *L* 331)

In time, the three compounds *daode, xingming,* and *jingshen* became even more common in Han dynasty texts such as the *Xinyu, Huainanzi,* and *Lunheng.*

During the mid–Warring States period, or more specifically, during the time of Mencius (372?–289? B.C.) and just prior to Mencius, no one employed the terms *daode, xingming,* and *jingshen.* It was only during the later Warring States period, probably during Xunzi's lifetime (325?–235 B.C.), that these compounds began to appear and circulate. From a logical point of view, we certainly cannot deny the possibility that someone prior to Xunzi used these three compounds. Yet, while that may be true, it is impossible that they were employed frequently or that they were used very early. Otherwise, there would be traces in some pre-Xunzi texts. Thus differences in the use of compounds between the Inner chapters and the Outer and Miscellaneous chapters in the *Zhuangzi* are, in fact, objective distinctions of the years left for us by history. These lines of demarcation tell us that the Outer and Miscellaneous chapters cannot be the products of the mid–Warring States period. Only the Inner chapters can be the literature of that period, and Zhuangzi was in fact a man of the mid–Warring States. Thus, if we are willing to assume that the contents of the *Zhuangzi* include the writings of Zhuangzi himself, then we must believe that the Inner chapters essentially were written by Zhuangzi and that the Outer and Miscellaneous chapters could only have been written by later followers of various schools.

In the case of classical literature and accompanying commentaries, the commentaries were certainly written later. We can be sure that the "Xingshi" commentary in the *Guanzi* is later than the canonical text of the "Xingshi" chapter. Just as expected, the compounds *daode* and *xingming* do not occur in the canonical text of the "Xingshi" chapter, but do appear in the "Xingshi" commentary. This also demonstrates that when comparing two samples of literary material, that containing the compounds *daode, xingming,* and *jingshen* is reliably later.

It may be objected that not all of the Outer and Miscellaneous chapters contain the compounds *daode, xingming,* or *jingshen.* Can we not assert that these chapters are also products of the mid–Warring States period? The question can be answered from three directions. First, we should make clear that if we wish to undertake vocabulary analysis, we must rely on a sufficient amount of literary material. The smaller the scope of the analysis, the greater the chance of coincidence and the less the degree of reliability. This is very similar to observing the age and style of architecture. You must begin analysis from the totality of the structure. If you only base your analysis on a window or a door, the results are unreliable. This is to say that only in a study of proper scope and possessing reasonably complete literary materials are we able to come to a reasonably reliable conclusion. We cannot take certain sections from a certain chapter of the *Zhuangzi* and proceed with a comparison of compounds. We can only compare different kinds of material. For example, the chapter "Dasheng" does not contain the three compounds. However, as soon as we recognize that it belongs to the same group as chapters such as "Shanmu," then we have no reason to take "Dasheng" alone as a product of the mid–Warring States period.

Next, we have uncovered an important difference in the use of compounds between the Inner chapters and the Outer and Miscellaneous chapters. But, we cannot formulate specific conditions under which these differences can be universally applied to determine the dating of any chapter or any group of works. Since it is possible that in several later works the content or style would preclude use of *daode, xingming,* or *jingshen,* one cannot prove that these are works that appeared prior to the mid–Warring States period.

Finally, we will point out from other perspectives why essays in the Outer and Miscellaneous chapters that do not contain *daode, xingming,* or *jingshen* are later than the Inner chapters. Several additional ways to demonstrate this appear below.

The Priority of the Inner Chapters: Evidence from Other Areas

Looking to the flowing relations of thought as we continue our comparison of the Inner with the Outer and Miscellaneous chapters, we observe that the author of the Inner chapters repeatedly described the perfect man as one who cannot drown, cannot be burned, and cannot be harmed. For example:

> The true men of ancient times . . . could scale the heights without fear, enter water and not get wet, enter fire and not be burned. ("Dazongshi," 226)

> The perfect man is spirit-like. The great swamps may blaze, but they cannot burn him. The great rivers may freeze, but they cannot chill him. Though thunder and lightning shatter the mountains and wild winds roil the oceans, they cannot frighten him. ("Qiwulun," 96)

> Nothing can harm this man. Though floods fill the heavens, he will not drown. Though burning drought melts metal and stone and scorches the earth and mountains, he will not be burned. ("Xiaoyaoyou," 30)

What is worthy of notice here is that though the Inner chapters expend a great deal of effort describing how the perfect man is spirit-like and transcendent, they never explain exactly what this combination of not burning, drowning, or being harmed is. However, the authors of the Outer and Miscellaneous chapters do explain and expand upon it. "Qiushui" says,

> As for a man of perfect virtue, fire cannot burn him, water cannot drown him, hot and cold cannot harm him, birds and beasts cannot injure him.

This is not to say that he disregards them. In fact, he discriminates between safety and danger, shelters himself in fortune or misfortune, and is circumspect coming and going. Therefore nothing can harm him. (588)

This equates the reason for not burning or drowning with knowledge and perspicacity. However, "Dasheng" explains:

Master Liezi asked of the Gate Keeper Yin, "The perfect man walks under water without distress, walks on fire without being burned, and travels above the ten thousand things without fear. May I ask, how has he come to this?" Gate Keeper Yin replied, "This is because he preserves the pure breath; it does not concern wisdom, skill, resolve, or daring. . . . When a drunken man falls from a carriage, though it may be speeding along, he won't be killed. He has bones and joints like other men, and yet he differs from them in the harm he suffers. This is because his spirit is whole. . . . If he can maintain this integrity through wine, how much more can one do so through Heaven! The sage hides himself in Heaven; hence, nothing can harm him." (634)

The author of "Dasheng" denies the explanation of "Qiushui" and holds that the perfect man's imperviousness to harm results not from knowledge or daring but from being entirely dependent on what is natural (his "spirit is whole," he "hides in Heaven").

The author of "Tianzifang" then somewhat simply states that for the true man of old, "Life and Death are important, but they are not change to him. . . . The spirit of such a man may soar over Mount Tai without being bothered, may dive into the deepest springs and not get wet." As it turns out, not burning or drowning merely indicated that one's spirit transcended heat and wetness. Clearly, the authors of the Outer and Miscellaneous chapters were consciously explaining the content of the Inner chapters from different perspectives and according to their own understanding.

Logic and the progression of history both tell us that a theme is generally raised by a teacher, and afterward his students separately proceed to explain or develop it. Hence, the first appearance of a theme indicates an earlier essay by the teacher, while individual and various explanations of this theme must be the later works of students. On this basis, I believe that since the Inner chapters raise themes such as not burning or drowning, they must be earlier than the Outer and Miscellaneous chapters that explain and develop these themes. Hence it is tenable to hold that the Inner chapters were written by Zhuangzi. At the same time, we can reliably conclude that although "Qiushui," "Dasheng," and "Tianzifang" do not use the compounds *daode, xingming,* or *jingshen,* they too are later than the Inner chapters.

Further evidence for Zhuangzi's authorship of the Inner chapters can be found in a comparative study of the order and arrangement of essays within the individual Inner, Outer, and Miscellaneous chapters. Generally speaking, a student can only append records of a teacher's activities at the end of the teacher's essays. Only in the student's own work can he place them at the front or middle of the chapter. In the entire *Zhuangzi* there are a total of 29 sections that are records directly mentioning Zhuangzi's activities. Excluding those few sections from the Inner chapters, such as Zhuangzi's dream of the butterfly, which are possibly Zhuangzi's own stories, generally they all can be seen as records of Zhuangzi's activities by his followers. Below are all the important contents of those 29 records:

1) Huizi said to Zhuangzi, "The king of Wei gave me some seeds of a huge gourd." ("Xiaoyaoyou," 36)

2) Huizi said to Zhuangzi, "I have a big tree of the kind men call *chu.*" ("Xiaoyaoyou," 39)

3) Once Zhuang Zhou dreamt he was a butterfly. ("Qiwulun," 112)

4) Huizi said to Zhuangzi, "Can a man really be without feelings?" ("Dechongfu," 220–22)

5) Zhuangzi said, "This teacher of mine, this teacher of mine." ("Tiandao," 462)

6) Dang, the Prime Minister of Shang, asked Zhuangzi about benevolence. ("Tianyun," 497–99)

7) Gongsun Long heard the words of Zhuangzi and was bewildered by their strangeness. ("Qiushui," 597)

8) Once, when Zhuangzi was fishing in the Pu River, the king of Chu sent two officials to go and invite him. ("Qiushui," 603)

9) When Huizi was Prime Minister in Liang, Zhuangzi set off to visit him. ("Qiushui," 605)

10) Zhuangzi and Huizi were strolling along the bridge of the Hao River. ("Qiushui," 606)

11) Zhuangzi's wife died and he pounded on a tub and sang. ("Zhile," 614)

12) When Zhuangzi went to Chu, he saw an old skull. ("Zhile," 617)

13) Zhuangzi was walking in the mountains when he saw a great tree. ("Shanmu," 667)

14) Zhuangzi wore a robe of coarse cloth and hemp shoes and went calling on the King of Wei. ("Shanmu," 687)

15) Zhuang Zhou was wandering in Diaoling when he spied a different kind of crow. ("Shanmu," 695)

16) Zhuangzi went to see Duke Ai of Lu and said, "Lu has few Confucians." ("Tianzifang," 717)

17) Master Dong Guo asked Zhuangzi, "This thing called the Way— where does it exist?" ("Zhibeiyou," 749)

18) Zhuangzi said, "Suppose an archer without taking aim hits the mark..." ("Xuwugui," 838)

19) Zhuangzi was accompanying a funeral when he passed by the grave of Huizi. ("Xuwugui," 843)

20) Zhuangzi heard the words of the border guard at Changwu and said, "People of today, when it comes to ordering their bodies..." ("Zeyang," 897–99)

21) Zhuang Zhou's family was very poor and so he went to borrow some grain from the Marquis of Jianho. ("Waiwu," 924)

22) Huizi said to Zhuangzi, "Your words are useless." ("Waiwu," 936)

23) Zhuangzi said, "If you have the capacity to wander, how can you keep from wandering?" ("Waiwu," 936)

24) Zhuangzi said to Huizi, "Confucius has been going along for sixty years and he has changed sixty times." ("Yuyan," 952)

25) Zhuangzi said, "To know the Way is easy; to keep from speaking about it is hard." ("Lieyukou," 1045)

26) Zhuangzi said to the man of Song, Cao Shang, "When the king of Qin falls ill, he calls for his doctors." ("Lieyukou," 1049)

27) There was a man who had an audience with the king of Song and received from him a gift of ten carriages. With his ten carriages, he went bragging and strutting to Zhuangzi. ("Lieyukou," 1061)

28) Someone sent gifts to Zhuangzi with an invitation to office. Zhuangzi replied to the messenger, "Have you ever seen a sacrificial ox?" ("Lieyukou," 1062)

29) When Zhuangzi was about to die, his disciples expressed a desire to give him a sumptuous burial. ("Lieyukou," 1063)

In addition to these references, there is a section in chapter 33, "Tianxia," that clearly comments on Zhuangzi's thought. Because the general form of this chapter differs from the others, however, we are unable to compare it to similar essays, and we will not include it in our comparative figures.

It is easy to see from table 1.2 that of the 25 stories recording Zhuangzi's activities in the Outer and Miscellaneous chapters, only 2 appear in the latter parts of chapters. Of the 12 chapters involved, 7 contain this type of narrative in the first or second position. The 4 such passages that appear in Inner chapters, on the other hand, are all placed at the ends of the chapters. Regarding this clear distinction in the pattern of distribution, we can offer only one explanation: The Inner chapters are the teacher's own compositions. Anecdotes about Zhuangzi himself could only be appended at the ends of his compositions. The Outer and Miscellaneous chapters are his students' compositions; consequently, records of Zhuangzi's activities were placed in the most important positions of these essays. The teacher's works are arranged at the front; the students' works follow. This is a general principle of chapter organization in ancient Chinese books. In the *Mozi*, for example, the theories Mozi expounded were arranged in the front chapters, and the works of his followers are found afterward. In the *Guanzi*, the chapters "Explaining Guanzi" ("Guanzi Jie") appear after

Table 1.2. Passages Featuring Zhuangzi in the Inner, Outer, and Miscellaneous Chapters

Chapter	No. of sections	Sections featuring Zhuangzi	Position within chapter
Inner			
"Xiaoyaoyou" (1)	5	#4, #5	end
"Qiwulun" (2)	10	#10	end
"Dechongfu" (5)	6	#6	end
Outer			
"Tiandao" (13)	10	#2	beginning
"Tianyun" (14)	7	#2	beginning
"Qiushui" (17)	7	#4, #5, #6, #7	middle, end
"Zhile" (18)	7	#2, #4	beginning, middle
"Shanmu" (20)	9	#1, #6, #8	beginning, middle
"Tianzifang" (21)	10	#5	middle
"Zhibeiyou" (22)	11	#6	middle
Miscellaneous			
"Xuwugui" (24)	15	#5, #6	middle
"Zeyang" (25)	12	#6	middle
"Waiwu" (26)	11	#2, #7, #8	beginning, middle
"Yuyan" (27)	7	#2	beginning
"Lieyukou" (32)	12	#2, #4, #10–12	throughout

canonical chapters ("Jingyan") and similar sections presumably written by Guanzi.

These observations further support our contention that those of the Outer and Miscellaneous chapters lacking the compounds *daode, xing-ming,* and *jingshen,* such as "Zhile," "Xuwugui," "Zeyang," "Waiwu," and "Yuyan," are nonetheless the work of later students.

From the application of certain phrases, we can also discover some fine lines or traces of information as we continue to compare the Inner chapters with the Outer and Miscellaneous chapters. First, we shall look at the circumstances under which the character *lai* is used as an auxiliary at the end of a sentence.

The character *lai* 來 is a common word meaning "come." In classical Chinese, however, *lai* may be used as an auxiliary at the end of a sentence as an exclamation. This usage is not very common, but we find 4 instances in 3 locations in the Inner chapters where *lai* is used in this way. Because there is no corresponding grammatical form in English, we have translated *lai* as "Ah" and put it at the beginning of sentences, sometimes disregarding fluency or accuracy.

1) Ah! Sang-hu! Ah! Sang-hu! You have returned to your true form. ("Dazongshi," 266)

2) You must have some plan in mind. Ah! Please tell me now! ("Renjianshi," 141)

3) Ah! Have you some advice you can give me? ("Renjianshi," 153)

In the Outer and Miscellaneous chapters, there is only one example of this usage.

1) I [Zhuangzi] asked the fish, "Ah! Fish! What are you doing here?" ("Waiwu," 924)

Among the 17 occurrences of *lai* in the Inner chapters (excluding personal names) there are 4 in which *lai* functions as an auxiliary at the end of a sentence, but there is only one such among the 60 occurrences of *lai* in the Outer and Miscellaneous chapters. Interestingly, this single instance is in a quotation of Zhuangzi. Is this merely fortuitous? We can offer only the following explanation: Among the many authors of the various chapters of the *Zhuangzi,* only the author of the Inner chapters was accustomed to using *lai* as an auxiliary at the end of a sentence. This author was Zhuangzi. Consequently, while recording Zhuangzi's words, the author of "Waiwu" consciously copied this grammatical pattern to make them appear that much closer to reality. Of course, *lai* is used in this way in the *Mencius* and other ancient texts, so we cannot say that this is a linguistic habit peculiar to Zhuang Zhou. Nevertheless with reference to the *Zhuangzi,* we are unlikely to find another explanation for the circumstances mentioned above.

The consideration of other words used in the *Zhuangzi* can also answer some questions. The most essential of these terms are *you* 遊 and *xiaoyao* 逍遙, which may be the most characteristic words in the *Zhuangzi.* The

Table 1.3. *You* and *Xiaoyao* in Works of Pre-Qin Philosophers

Work	Occurences of *You*	Occurences of *Xiaoyao*
Lunyu	5	0
Mengzi	8	0
Mozi	1	0
Xunzi	4	0
Zhouyi	2	0
Hanfeizi	39*	0
Lüshi chunqiu	4	0
Zhuangzi	96	6

* excluding personal names

Zhuangzi is the first work in which these terms are commonly used; they rarely appear in the works of other pre-Qin philosophers.

From table 1.3 it is easily seen that the majority of ancient classical philosophical texts do not use *xiaoyao* at all. (The *Shijing* and *Chuci* are separate matters.) The character *you* appears in the *Zhuangzi* far more frequently than in the texts of other philosophers. Hence, we see that *you* and *xiaoyao* are words with quite a special character in the *Zhuangzi*. In the *Zhuangzi, you* not only means *jiaoyou* 交遊 (to have friendly contact with people), *youshui* 遊説 (to visit and try to persuade people), and *youwan* 遊玩 (to ramble), but also encompasses the idea of a spirit-like free and easy composure, a usage quite different from that in the texts of other philosophers. In fact, this peculiar usage is the precise reason why the character *you* is used so many times in the *Zhuangzi*. It is worth noting that these characteristic terms appear a total of 32 times in the *Zhuangzi's* Inner chapters; an average of 20 times for each 10,000 characters or 4.6 times in each chapter. In the 26 Outer and Miscellaneous chapters they appear a total of 69 times;[18] an average of only 11 times per 10,000 characters or only 2.7 times in each chapter. Whether averaged according to the number of characters or according to the number of chapters, the frequency with which these two terms are used in the Inner chapters is 1.8 times greater than in the Outer or Miscellaneous chapters. If we admit that *you* and *xiaoyao* are the two most characteristic vocabulary elements in the *Zhuangzi*, then we must admit that the Inner chapters are more characteristic than the Outer and Miscellaneous chapters and also that they more closely coincide with the special features of Zhuangzi's thought.

Above, we have already mentioned most of the essays in the Outer and Miscellaneous chapters. Now we can briefly examine several chapters we have yet to mention, such as "Tiandi," "Quqie," "Daozhi," and "Yufu."

The fourth section in "Tiandi" relates the story that "Yao's teacher was Xu You, Xu You's teacher was Nie Que, Nie Que's teacher was Wang Ni, Wang Ni's teacher was Bei Yi" (415). Since these five dissimilar characters are linked together in a single story, this already borders on the unsettling. However, in the later parts of the chapter, there is absolutely no mention of Bei Yi, and it seems unnecessary that the story make explicit the order in which the five learned from one another. This is even more unsettling. What is the reason for this? In point of fact, chapter 1 in the Inner chapters, "Xiaoyaoyou," contains a story concerning how Xu You instructed Yao (24), while in chapter 3, "Qiwulun" and chapter 7, "Yingdiwang," there appears the story of Nie Que questioning Wang Ni and talking with Pu Yi Zi (91, 287). According to Cheng Xuanying (c. 663),[19] Pu Yi Zi is Bei Yi.[20] Obviously the author of "Tiandi" strung together characters from several parables in the Inner chapters. Hence, it is impossible that "Tiandi" be earlier than the Inner chapters. Why would its author fabricate an unfounded scholastic genealogy, then having done so, totally disregard it?

"Quqie" relates that "Viscount Tiancheng one morning murdered the Lord of Qi," and that subsequently "for twelve generations his family possessed the state of Qi" (343). Since the events in this story extend beyond the Warring States period, it is impossible for this chapter to have been a product of the mid–Warring States. "Daozhi" and "Yufu" are somewhat removed in thought and literary style from the description of Zhuangzi that appears in chapter 33, "Tianxia," in which "he argued strange and unsettling theories, using bold and reckless language, free and unfettered phrases. He abandoned himself to the times without partiality and did not look at things from a single perspective" (1098). Moreover, those chapters do not completely coincide with what is said in "Yuyan," "Imputed words make up nine tenths of it; weighted words make up seven tenths of it; goblet words daily issue forth" (947). Hence, it does not appear possible that "Yufu" and "Daozhi" were written by Zhuangzi. Sima Qian stated in his "Laozi Han Fei liezhuan" (Biography of Laozi and Han Fei) that Zhuangzi wrote "Yufu," "Daozhi," and "Quqie" to slander the followers of Confucius; however, this statement does not prove that these three chapters were written by Zhuangzi. By the same token, one cannot prove that writings not mentioned by Sima Qian are not the work of Zhuangzi. Sima Qian held that Zhuangzi "wrote a book of 100,000 words." In other words, Sima Qian was under the impression that the original *Zhuangzi* was entirely written by Zhuangzi. (The present text is only some 70,000 words.) He had simply never questioned that all of the chapters were written by Zhuangzi. We are unable to surmise that Sima Qian could answer questions he was fundamentally unable to recognize. It is difficult to establish the inference that the material mentioned by Sima Qian was written by Zhuangzi and what went unmentioned was not.

To sum up, we have conducted a comparative examination of the Inner chapters and Outer and Miscellaneous chapters from several perspectives: from the application of compounds, the sources of thought, literary style, and the use of characteristic vocabulary. They all demonstrate that of the Inner, Outer, and Miscellaneous chapters, only the Inner chapters could have been written by Zhuangzi. Although there may be fragments of Zhuangzi's lost works in the Outer and Miscellaneous chapters, these chapters are not Zhuangzi's work.

Relationships and Differences among the Seven Inner Chapters

Our comparative analysis of vocabulary and other aspects of the *Zhuangzi* indicates that the distinction among the Inner, Outer, and Miscellaneous chapters was not meaningless. Still, there are some philosophic points of view in the Inner chapters that are by no means completely consistent. Hence, some scholars are of the opinion that "Renjianshi," or the first three sections of it, is neither part of the Inner chapters nor the work of Zhuangzi. To resolve this issue, we must examine for a moment some of the relationships and differences among the seven Inner chapters. In the seven Inner chapters there exist quite a few obvious consistencies. We will set out the clearly similar or related linguistic styles and philosophic points of view in the seven Inner chapters. Basically, we will not offer an explanation but simply let the facts speak for themselves. We will try to avoid materials in which there is a real philosophical connection but for which the linguistic relationship is not obvious.

Ideally, a single Chinese phrase should be translated into different English expressions according to the specific context and nuance. To show the linguistic similarities in Chinese, however, this has not been done in the following quotations, which have been translated more for comparison than for accuracy of meaning.

1) "Xiaoyaoyou" says,

> *He mounts the clouds and mist,* rides a flying dragon, and *wanders beyond the four seas.* (28)

A passage from "Qiwulun" relates,

> *He mounts the clouds and mist,* rides the sun and moon, and *wanders beyond the four seas.* (96)

2) "Xiaoyaoyou" says,

> *Pacing up and down,* do nothing at its side, or lie down to rest *free and easy* beneath it. (40)

"Dazongshi" says,

> *Pacing up and down* beyond the dust and dirt, they pursue a career of *free and easy* wandering in having no-action." (268)

3) "Xiaoyaoyou" says,

> Plant it in the *realm of nothing whatsoever, in the wild expanses that go on forever.* (40)

"Yingdiwang" also says,

> Wander in the *realm of nothing whatsoever to live in the broad, borderless expanses.* (293)

4) "Xiaoyaoyou" contains a conversation in which *"Jianwu said to Lianshu,* 'I heard from *Jieyu.'"*(26). In "Yingdiwang" we find, *"Jianwu met the madman Jieyu"* (289). And in "Renjianshi" we find, *"Jieyu the madman of Chu* wandered in front of his gate" (183).

5) "Xiaoyaoyou" says,

> Nothing can harm this man. Though floods fill the heavens, *he will not drown.* Though burning drought melts metal and stone and scorches the earth and mountains, *he will not be burned.* (30)

"Qiwulun" says,

> The perfect man is spirit-like. The great swamps may blaze, but *they cannot burn him.* The great rivers may freeze, but *they cannot chill him.* Though thunder and lightning shatter the mountains and wild winds roil the oceans, *they cannot frighten him.* (96)

"Dazongshi" says,

> The true men of ancient times . . . could scale the heights *without fear,* enter water and *not get wet,* enter fire and *not get burned.* (226)

6) "Xiaoyaoyou" says, "Who could *be willing to exert himself for the things of this world?*" (31). "Dechongfu" says, "How could he *be willing to exert himself for the things of this world?*" (193).

7) "Xiaoyaoyou" says,

> I have a *great tree,* . . . its trunk is so twisted and rough, *it cannot be plumbed with a measuring line. Its branches are so bent and crooked, they will not accept the measuring rod or square.* (39)

"Renjianshi" relates,

> Looking up he saw *its branches were all crooked; twisted and bent, they could not be used for beams or timbers.* He looked down and saw *its trunk was rotted and crumbling and was unsuited for coffins.* (176)

8) "Xiaoyaoyou" describes a big tree that

> *is completely useless* —how will you suffer or be distressed because of it? (40)

"Renjianshi" makes the statement,

> *I [the big tree] have sought to be completely useless* for some time now. (172)

9) "Qiwulun" says,

> *Day and night alternate before our very eyes,* yet no one knows from whence they arise. (51)

In "Dechongfu" we find,

> *Day and night alternate before our eyes,* yet our wisdom cannot delineate their beginnings. (212)

10) "Qiwulun" says,

> *Nie Que asked Wang Ni,* "Do you know what all things agree upon as true?" (91)

In "Yingdiwang" we find,

> *Nie Que asked Wang Ni*; he questioned him four times and four times he did not know. (287)

11) "Qiwulun" says,

> *How do I know* what I call knowing is not really not knowing? *How do I know* what I call not knowing isn't really knowing? (92)

"Dazongshi" says,

> *How do I know* what I call Heaven is not really man and what I call man isn't really Heaven? (225) ... *How do I know* what I call myself isn't really someone other than myself? (275) [21] ... *How do I know* the creator of things won't remove my branded face and repair my disfigured nose? (280)

"Renjianshi" says,

> Outwardly, some seem to agree; within they do not consider it at all. *How do I know* it is all right? (141)

12) "Qiwulun" says,

> Your plans lead to great expectations. You see an egg and *expect a rooster; you see a crossbow bolt and expect a roast owl.* (99)

In "Dazongshi" we find,

> Perhaps my left arm gradually will be transformed into a *rooster and I will have him keep watch* 'til dawn. Perhaps my right arm *gradually*

will become a crossbow bolt, and I will use it for roast owl at dinner.
(260)

13) "Yangshengzhu" says, "In antiquity, this was called hiding *from
Heaven's punishment"* (128). In "Dechongfu" we find, "How can he be
released *from Heaven's punishment?"* (205).

14) "Yangshengzhu" says,

> *when one follows the times and dwells accordingly, distress and
> pleasure cannot enter.* The ancients called this *release from the bonds
> of* di. (128)

In "Dazongshi" we find,

> *when one follows the times and dwells accordingly, distress and
> pleasure cannot enter.* The ancients called this *release from the bonds.*
> (260)

15) "Renjianshi" says, "Ride along with things to *let your mind wander"*
(160). In "Dechongfu" we find, *"Let your mind wander* in the harmony of
Virtue" (191). And in "Yingdiwang" we find, *"Let your mind wander* in
indifference" (294).

16) "Renjianshi" says,

> when men call you The Child, this is called *being a follower of Heaven*
> . . . when men find no fault in you, this is called *being a follower of
> man.* (143)

"Dazongshi" says,

> When complete, he is a *follower of Heaven;* when incomplete, he is a
> *follower of man.* (234)

17) "Renjianshi" says,

> Make oneness your abode, *reside in the inevitable* and you will be close
> to it (148) . . . *Put your trust in the inevitable* to nurture your core, this
> is perfection. (160)

"Dazongshi" says,

> Hard pressed, *he did the inevitable.* . . . He assumed wisdom was
> doing the timely, *so there was an inevitability to his works.* (234)

18) In "Renjianshi" we find,

> *To know what you cannot change and rest in it as if it were fated,* this is perfect Virtue. (155)

A similar statement is found in "Dechongfu":

> *To know what you cannot change and rest in it as if it were fated,* only men of perfect Virtue can accomplish this. (199)

19) In "Renjianshi" we find, "How can you leisurely arrive at *loving life and hating death?*" (155). In "Dazongshi" we find, "He did not know to *love life,* nor did he know *to hate death*" (229).

20) "Renjianshi" says,

> Their utility brings harm to their lives, so they *do not complete the years Heaven granted them but are stopped prematurely in mid-course.* (172)

There we also find,

> *So they could not complete the years Heaven granted them, but were stopped prematurely in mid-course* by the woodsman's axe. (177)

"Dazongshi" says,

> He completed the years Heaven granted him and was not stopped prematurely in mid-course. This is called knowing completion. (224)

21) "Renjianshi" says,

> And then there is Cripple Shu—*with his chin pushed into his navel, shoulders higher than the crown of his head, the back of his head pointing to the sky, and his five organs lodged above* two thighs that are more like ribs. (180)

In "Dazongshi" we find,

> Crooked, twisted over and hunch backed, *his five organs lodged on top, his chin pushed down into his navel, shoulders higher than the crown of his head, while the back of his head pointed to the sky.* (258)

22) "Dechongfu" says,

> He *constantly accords with what is natural* and does not add anything extra to life. (221)

In "Yingdiwang" we find,

> *Accord with things and what is natural,* leave no room for selfishness. (294)

23) "Dazongshi" says,

> *A blind eye does not have the ability to appreciate* the shading of an eyebrow or the rouge of a cheek. *An eye without a pupil has no means of perceiving* the green and yellow of embroidered robes. (280)

In "Xiaoyaoyou" we find,

> *An eye without a pupil has no means of perceiving* badges distinguishing rank. *A deaf ear does not have the ability to hear* the sound of bells and drums. (30)

24) "Dazongshi" says, "I am about to become a man *along with the maker of things*" (268). In "Yingdiwang" we find, "I am about to become a man *along with the maker of things*" (293).

25) "Yingdiwang" says, "What do you think you are doing *troubling your mind with schemes of ruling the world?*" (293). In "Xiaoyaoyou" a similar idea is expressed: "Now, why should we *struggle over the affairs of the world?*" (30).

26) In "Qiwulun" we find, *"Enough. Enough.* We have it morning and evening. It is that from which life derives" (51). This phrasing of "enough" also appears in "Renjianshi": *"Enough. Enough.* You observe men through Virtue" (183).

The materials listed above indicate that clear relations exist among the seven Inner chapters. The above materials, totaling 26 pairs (or groups), average approximately 3.7 pairs per chapter. Among the Outer and Miscellaneous chapters, the most mutual relations only average 2.3 pairs per chapter.[22] The material of the seven Inner chapters is obviously more interrelated than that in any group of essays in the Outer and Miscellaneous chapters. This demonstrates that among the 33 chapters of the *Zhuangzi,* the essays in the seven Inner chapters most easily form a single type; they are the most closely related and their philosophic content is the most concentrated. Therefore, we allow that the Inner chapters are, generally

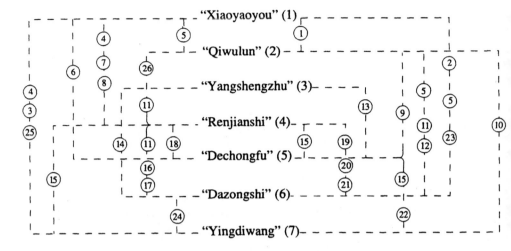

Figure 1.1. Connections among the Inner Chapters in Terms of Syntactic Similarities (Numbers correspond to examples enumerated in the text.)

speaking, a complete unit. Based on the 26 pairs above, we can diagram the relations among them (figure 1.1). The dotted lines represent relations between essays; the numbers of the dotted lines indicate the items listed above. The relationships presented above and represented in the diagram should make it apparent that the Inner chapters are a single unit.

Now we will examine the rather heavily disputed fourth chapter, "Renjianshi." Ye Guoqing first raised questions concerning "Renjianshi" in his book *Zhuangzi yanjiu* (A study of Zhuangzi).[23] However, he never drew any detailed conclusions. Zhang Hengshou's *Zhuangzi xintan* (A new examination of Zhuangzi) developed Ye Guoqing's point of view and argued that "the important sections of the chapter [the first three sections] are not the work of Zhuangzi."[24] Zhang's argument is somewhat more detailed. However, Zhang is unable to dispose of the possibility that "Renjianshi" belongs to the Inner chapters or that it was written by Zhuangzi because there are still more and clearer connections between those three sections and the Inner chapters than between those three sections and other chapters or the writings of other thinkers.

1) In the first three sections of "Renjianshi" we find,

> *To know what you cannot change and rest in it as if it were fated,* this is perfect Virtue. (155)

A similar statement is found in "Dechongfu":

> *To know what you cannot change and rest in it as if it were fated,* only men of perfect Virtue can accomplish this. (199)

2) In the first three sections of "Renjianshi" we find,

> When men call you The Child, this is called *being a follower of Heaven* ... when men find no fault in you, this is called *being a follower of man.* (143)

"Dazongshi" says,

> When complete, he is a *follower of Heaven:* when incomplete, he is a *follower of man.* (234)

3) Another topic of the first three sections is "Ride along with things to *let your mind wander*" (160). The phrase also appears in "Dechongfu": *"Let your mind wander* in the harmony of Virtue" (191). And in "Yingdiwang": *"Let your mind wander in indifference"* (294).

4) The first three sections contain the statement

> When he wants to be a child, act the child with him. When he wants to deny the boundaries of fields and states, join him in denial of those boundaries and lines. (165)

A similar attitude of changeableness is found in "Yingdiwang":

> Sometimes, he took himself to be a horse, sometimes he was a cow. (287)

5) In the first three sections we find,

> And do you also know what it is that dissipates Virtue, and what brings forth knowledge? *Virtue is dissipated by names; knowledge arises from contention.* (135)

According to the punctuated text of Wang Xiaoyu, a passage of "Waiwu" reads,

> Zhuangzi said . . . *"Virtue is dissipated by names,* names are made abundant by tyranny, plans accumulate in perilous times and *knowledge arises from contention."* (942)

This indicates that the author of "Waiwu" attributed authorship of "Renjianshi" to Zhuangzi.

6) The first sections say,

> Make oneness your abode, *reside in the inevitable* and you will be close to it (148) . . . *Put your trust in the inevitable* to nurture your core, this is perfection. (160)

"Dazongshi" says,

> Hard pressed, *he did the inevitable.* . . . He assumed wisdom was doing the timely, *so there was an inevitability to his works.* (234)

7) In the first three sections of "Renjianshi" we find,

> To have no calamity befall him *whether he succeeds or not,* only a man of Virtue can do this. (153)

"Shanmu" records,

> Zhuangzi laughed and said, "Now I would assume a position between *utility and inutility.* But between the two, though there seems to be some place, in fact there is none. Hence, you would not avoid getting trapped in it. But then if you were to ascend on the Way and its Virtue to float and wander freely, that would be different, wouldn't it." (668)

It seems that there is some similarity between *utility and inutility* and *being successful or unsuccessful.* And while "Shanmu" denies a position between utility and inutility, it also proceeds to advocate a more developed position of ascending the Way and its Virtue to float and wander freely. This demonstrates that the words of Zhuang Zhou recorded in "Renjianshi" are earlier than those found in "Shanmu."

8) The first three sections raise the topic of the *fasting of the mind.* "Yan Hui said, 'Now that there has never begun to be Hui, can this be called

emptiness?'" The condition of "never having begun to be a Hui" is consistent with a passage from "Qiwulun," where we find, "I, the person presently before you, have lost myself." This is also consistent with what is found in "Dazongshi": "After nine days he was able to remove life from himself." In another section, Yan Hui says he can "throw off this physical body and discard intelligence." This indicates that the fasting of the mind, quiet sitting, and meditation are all consistent with one another. Thus it is simply unfounded to say that the fasting of the mind is not one of Zhuangzi's methods of self-cultivation.

9) In the first three sections we find, "Ah (*lai*)! Please tell me now! . . . Ah (*lai*)! Have you some advice for me?" In these two examples, the character *lai* is used as a verbal auxiliary at the end of a phrase. It also appears in "Dazongshi," in a section describing the attempts of two men to hail the spirit of a departed friend, "Ah! (*lai*) Sang-hu. Ah! (*lai*) Sang-hu." "Waiwu" records a comment by Zhuangzi, "Ah (*lai*)! Fish! What are you doing here?" Hence, Yang Shuda says Zhuangzi habitually used the character *lai* as an auxiliary at the end of a phrase.[25]

10) In the first three sections we find the phrase "And how much more so for those of lesser standing." The usage of the character *san* to mean "lesser, worthless" also appears in the later four sections of "Renjianshi." For example, "You, a *worthless* man about to die, how can you know I am a *worthless* tree?"

11) Zhang Hengshou says,

> From the perspective of linguistic usage, it appears that these three sections show certain traces of similarity with the works of the Zhuangzi school. For example, the interrogative phrase *yongju* 庸詎 (how *or* what use) and the temporal phrase *weishi* 未始 (not yet beginning to be) and the use of the character *wu* 惡 as an interrogative (how) are all commonly found in "Qiwulun" and "Dazongshi."[26]

In sum, though there are some differences between the first three sections of "Renjianshi" and the remainder of the Inner chapters, there are a good many unequivocal similarities. These relations clearly are more numerous than those between this chapter and the Outer or Miscellaneous chapters or books such as the *Guanzi*. Hence, it is entirely possible that these sections belong to the Inner chapters, and it is also possible that they are the work of Zhuangzi himself.

How then, do we explain the discrepancies between the first three sections of this chapter and the rest of the Inner chapters? We must first dispel the insistence on consistency, the assumption that a person may only have a single kind of thought. Doing philosophy, or thinking, must involve a process of development and cannot be frozen and unchanging. Thus, points of view that are not entirely consistent will appear in the work of one man. This is nothing to marvel at. Confucius, for example, asserted that human nature was constant; it was learning and practice that set certain men apart. At the same time, he reiterated the unchanging principle that the wise are above and the unintelligent are below. The Moists expended a great deal of energy denying that fate controlled human life, yet they believed that heavenly spirits meted out rewards and punishments. Han Feizi advocated totalitarianism, yet took pleasure in Laozi's doctrine of *wuwei,* or no forced action. Liu Zongyuan was a materialist; yet he revered Buddhism. Rich and penetrating a thinker as Zhu Xi was, we find that he asserted both that principle was prior to ether and that there could be no question of priority between principle and ether. Incomplete consistency is common in the history of thought. So why is it not allowed in the case of Zhuangzi?

The important differences between "Renjianshi" and the other literature of the Inner chapters lie in its attitude toward reality, including the rulers of the world. As Zhang Hengshou has said,

> The attitude that summarizes "Xiaoyaoyou," "Qiwulun," and other chapters is one of extreme disillusion over the future of man and society; it is an attitude that seeks subjective freedom and pleasure in insubstantial imagination. On this account, in each chapter there is displayed a disdain and uncaring disposition toward questions of general social ethics. And yet the central question of the first three sections of "Renjianshi" consists in how to serve one's father and one's ruler, how not to fail carrying out one's ruler's orders and how to

maintain one's life intact. There are points that are not addressed in "Xiaoyaoyou" or other chapters.[27]

Since Zhuangzi's general disposition is characterized as an "extreme disillusion over the future of man and society," people have reasonably asked whether Zhuangzi was disillusioned from his youth? Clearly not. To a naive youth who had just set out on his own, the entire world would be full of newness and secrets. It would be impossible for him to be "extremely disillusioned" at this time. But, if we consider his disposition at a later time, when he had seen more of society's imperfections or when he wished to escape it all and was unable to do so, or when he desired to change something and was unsuccessful, then perhaps he would think of cleansing himself and finding what was good for himself. Further along, it is possible that he could become extremely disillusioned and seek a spiritual life completely transcending the common. There must have been a process of development from naivete to extreme disillusionment with reality to using *xiaoyaoyou* 逍遙遊. At a certain stage in this process, Zhuangzi certainly may have recognized that society had its darker aspects but may not yet have been completely disillusioned. Thus, it is entirely possible that he hoped "not to fail to carry out one's lord's orders and to be able to maintain one's person intact." Hence, the argument that the important sections of "Renjianshi" were not written by Zhuangzi because they show an insufficient attitude of "disdain toward the world and leaving the common" does not stand. In fact, the emphasis of "Renjianshi" is not on how to insure that one's lord's orders are carried out; it is on maintaining one's life intact. And on this issue the first three sections of "Renjianshi" are in complete agreement with all the other important points of the chapter.

In fact, the stories in the other Inner chapters concerning "disdain for the world and leaving the common" are not completely similar. "Tianxia" says that

> he came and went alone with the *pure spirit* of Heaven and earth; yet he did not approach the ten thousand things with disdain. He did not accuse on the basis of right and wrong, but resided in the times with their vulgarity. . . . Above he wandered with the creator of all things;

below he befriended those who spend their days outside of life and death and beyond beginning or end. (1098–99)

The Inner chapters most representative of this style are "Xiaoyaoyou," "Qiwulun," and "Dazongshi." "Dechongfu" and "Yingdiwang" exhibit this to a lesser extent, followed by "Yangshengzhu" and "Renjianshi." These are differences of degree and not of substance among generally consistent assumptions. If, in fact, Zhuangzi's thought does show a developmental process and if the sequence of this development is consistent with the actual process of history, then we can say that "Renjianshi" and "Yangshengzhu" are both works from the first period in Zhuangzi's thought. "Yingdiwang" and "Dechongfu" derive from the period approaching maturity, while "Dazongshi," "Qiwulun," and "Xiaoyaoyou" are representative of the mature period. The contents of the first three sections of "Renjianshi" and the sense of what is found in "Tianxia" ("He did not accuse on the basis of right and wrong, but resided in the times with their vulgarity") match exactly. Hence "Renjianshi" should also be considered one of Zhuangzi's works.

To summarize, among the *Zhuangzi*'s seven Inner chapters, there are some differences but greater similarities; basically, they are the work of the same system of thought.

The Confusion Surrounding the Inner, Outer, and Miscellaneous Chapters

We have shown above that the Inner chapters are fundamentally a single body and that they date from an earlier period than the Outer and Miscellaneous chapters. However, there are still some scholars who deny the differences between the Inner chapters and the Outer and Miscellaneous chapters and contend that the current divisions reflect a jumbling that occurred in Guo Xiang's compilation of the text in the Jin dynasty. Consequently, these scholars deny the possibility that the Inner chapters are fundamentally the work of Zhuangzi. To respond to this, it will be necessary to make some analytic distinctions concerning the circumstances in which the Inner chapters were mistakenly intermingled with the Outer and Miscellaneous chapters. We will principally analyze several representative arguments of Wang Shumin, the most forceful proponent of this theory.

1) Wang points out that

> in the second chapter, "Qiwulun," there is a passage that reads "Now there have never been boundaries in the Dao." Below this is a comment from Cui Zhuan [fl. 290] that says, "There are seven sections in this chapter. This passage is connected to the above section, while Ban Gu [32–92] explains that it appears in the Outer chapters." From this we know that Ban Gu saw the fifty-two-chapter edition of the book and that the section beginning with the phrase of "Now there have never been boundaries in the Dao" was originally in the Outer chapters.[28]

Now, the meaning of the statement by Ban Gu (32–92) cited by Cui Zhuan (fl. 290)[29] is really not that clear. "Ban Gu explains that it appears in the Outer chapters" possibly indicates that Ban Gu saw this section in the text of the Outer chapters. The reliability of the text could also be called into question. In addition, it is possible that the sense of this passage is that Ban Gu considered that the content of this section belongs with the Outer chapters, an interpretation proposed by Jiang Xichang:

> Ban Gu explains that it appears in the Outer chapters. Now this passage states that in Ban Gu's edition, this section was also in the original chapter. But Ban Gu analyzed according to the meaning of the passage; he considered that it belonged in the Outer chapters.[30]

The famous annotation of the *Zhuangzi* by Sima Biao (?–305) was lost sometime after the seventh century. However, Sun Fengyi (c. 1799) assembled *Sima Biao Zhuangzi zhu* (Sima Biao's annotations to the *Zhuangzi*) from the many quotations from Sima Biao's work found in the writings of other scholars. Below the sentence "Now there have never been boundaries in the Dao and words have never had constancy" there is the annotation "Constancy means lasting a long time." If the text Sun Fengyi has collected is reliable, then it explains that the section containing the phrase was originally in the Inner not the Outer chapters. To sum up, even if we suppose that "Now there have never been boundaries in the Dao" is actually part of the contents of the Outer chapters, this only demonstrates that certain sections from the Inner chapters fell into and were mixed with the Outer and Miscellaneous chapters. It does not show that "Qiwulun" does not belong to the Inner chapters and even less that the Inner chapters are not essentially the work of Zhuangzi.

(2) Wang Shumin says,

> Another example is the first part of chapter 1 of the *Bailun Shu* by the Sui Dynasty Buddhist, Ji Zang [548–623]. There it says, "In the Outer chapters of the *Zhuangzi,* there is the story of Cook Ding, who had not seen a whole ox for twelve years." In the present edition, this story is in the third chapter, "Yangshengzhu," in the Inner chapters.[31]

In fact, the sentence "Cook Ding had not seen a whole ox for twelve years" does not appear in the present edition. The only passages related to the sense of this sentence are "After three years, I no longer saw the whole ox" and "Now, I have used my knife for nineteen years." Neither is very similar in either form or content to what Ji Zang quoted. If that sentence were to appear in the modern edition, it would be repetitive and incongruous. As we cannot be sure that the phrase "did not see a whole ox for twelve years" was derived from the extant version of "Yangshengzhu," there is no way to be sure that this chapter was originally in the Outer chapters. In fact, it is very possible that this fragment is an entirely different record in the Outer chapters. Because it was redundant, it was deleted from the shortened edition produced by Guo Xiang and others.

This kind of confusion is not difficult to understand. In the modern edition, a similar situation appears in "Qiwulun" in the Inner chapters and "Xuwugui" in the Miscellaneous chapters. Both chapters contain stories relating how "Nanguo Ziqi sat leaning on his armrest, staring up at the sky." Their contents appear to be the same when, in fact, they are not. If, in a commentary relying upon the single chapter "Xuwugui" it was recorded that "the Miscellaneous chapters say that Nanguo Ziqi sat leaning on his armrest, staring up at the sky," later students would be unable to decide if the story in "Qiwulun" concerning Nanguo Ziqi originated in the Miscellaneous chapters or in the Inner chapters. Similar situations arise with the parables of the great tree; of the fish in the water; of the pear, orange, and grapefruit; and of being an ox or horse. If, in Guo Xiang's shortened edition, the duplications between the Inner and Outer and Miscellaneous chapters remained so numerous, one can imagine how many there were in the original edition of fifty-two chapters. They cannot rely on comments like Ji Zang's to decide that a certain chapter should or should not appear in a certain place.

(3) Wang Shumin quotes the *Xunzi*, chapter 18, "Zhenglun," which relates, "Someone said that you can't discuss the joy of the Eastern Seas with a frog who lives in a well." Wang says,

> This story quotes a passage from "Qiushui" in the *Zhuangzi*. Since Xunzi lived not much later than Zhuangzi, then although "Qiushui" is in the Outer chapters of the modern edition, it is self-evident that this was written by Zhuangzi.[32]

This kind of argumentation is not "self-evident"; indeed, it is very dubious. What Xunzi quoted is not all that similar to the text in "Qiushui," and the phrase about the frog in the well could have been a metaphor in common use at that time. Stepping back a moment, even assuming that Xunzi's allusion is to "Qiushui," it only proves that "Qiushui" appeared before Xunzi had written "Zhenglun." It certainly does not prove that "Qiushui" was written by Zhuangzi. According to the historical record as examined by modern scholars, Xunzi (325?–238) may have been about forty years younger than Zhuangzi (369?–286?). Thus it is entirely possible that "Qiushui" was written during this period.

We have already mentioned our reasons for contending that "Qiushui" was composed by Zhuangzi's later students. Let us again briefly explain our reasons for holding that it is impossible for "Qiushui" to have been written by Zhuangzi himself. First, Zhuangzi's thought and literary style are extravagant and unrestrained, while "Qiushui" is well reasoned at every level and minutely precise. Moreover, it brings the idea of "not being burned and not being drowned" right back to "distinguishing between safety and danger" and "being circumspect coming and going." There is not the slightest hint of an expansive style, of free and easy wandering. Their two styles are different. Next, "Qiushui" records that "Those who defied the times and denied common custom were called usurpers; those who accorded to the times and conformed to common custom were called followers of righteousness." This is tainted by a hint of a Legalist dictum to follow the times and accord with the customs. It does not evince the Daoist ideal of transcending the world and leaving the commonplace. The contents as well as the styles of the two are different. In addition, "Qiushui" employs such concepts as *li* 禮 (principle, reason), *quan* 權 (power), and *shishi* 時勢 (situation of the time). These are rarely seen in the rest of the book and do not form a single, coordinated body of thought. Finally, "Qiushui" mentions a conversation between Wei Mou (360?–280 B.C.) and Gongsun Long (320?–250? B.C.), who was thirty to fifty years later than Zhuangzi. In addition, it mentions that "Kuai abdicated in favor of Zhi and Zhi was destroyed," using "those of old" as a time phrase, for the event occurred around 312 B.C. So, it appears that the date of the text was already late. These explain that Wang Shumin's arguments concerning the "Qiushui" cannot be accepted on either a logical or factual basis.

We have said that the Inner chapters were essentially written by Zhuangzi, acknowledging that undeniably there will be places where words, sentences, or sections in the Inner, Outer, and Miscellaneous chapters are incongruous. However, to ascertain which places have been corrupted and the extent to which the entire book has been corrupted requires a reliable basis. We cannot make a decision simply on the basis of single words or phrases. Wang Shumin says, "The arrangement of the Inner, Outer and Miscellaneous chapters of the Guo Xiang edition took place through casually moving chapters up into the Inner chapters or down into the Outer and Miscellaneous chapters according to his own ideas of inclusion and exclusion." Wang's exaggerated view of the degree of corruption of the text extends to asserting that there is not the slightest reason for any distinction between the Inner, Outer, and Miscellaneous chapters. Thus, he sharply rejected the traditional opinion that the Inner chapters were for the most part written by Zhuangzi.

Lu Deming (550?–630) says, "The Inner chapters in the various editions all agree." By this he means there is not much difference among the various editions. We can infer that those areas in which there are differences between the Inner chapters and Outer and Miscellaneous chapters are not substantial. Our analysis has verified this point. Some explain Lu's statement as simply meaning that the number of chapters is the same.

This is an inadequate explanation. The original text of Lu Deming's *Jingdian shiwen xulu* reads:

> *Hanshu,* "Yiwen Zhi" [Bibliography in Han history], *Zhuangzi* in fifty-two chapters. This is the volume annotated by Sima Biao and by Mr. Meng. It speaks of the strange and curious. Sometimes it is like the *Shanhaijing,* sometimes like a book of divining dreams. So, annotators rely on their ideas to delete or select. The Inner chapters of the various editions all agree. Apart from these, some editions have Outer but no Miscellaneous chapters. Guo Xiang's commentary is particularly in harmony with the ideas of Zhuangzi and is something the world will treasure.[33]

Obviously, Lu Deming is not discussing here the number of chapters in the Inner, Outer, or Miscellaneous divisions. His remark that "Annotators follow their own ideas to delete or select" merely indicates the text's diverse contents, sometimes like the *Shanhaijing (Classic of Mountains and Seas,* a collection of myths), sometimes like a book on divining dreams. Dispensing with these vague places in no way affects the fundamental appearance of the Inner chapters. Hence, Lu Deming merely says that the Inner chapters of the various editions all agree. Obviously this is not merely spoken with regard to the number of chapters but refers to the contents.

Worth noting is that Lu Deming especially confirmed the value of the Guo Xiang edition, describing it as "particularly in harmony with the ideas of Zhuangzi" and "something the world will treasure." Lu Deming had seen Sima Biao's and Cui Zhuan's annotations and many other kinds of texts. He was both a commentator and philologist. So it is very difficult to imagine that he would not select for study an edition reasonably free of problems. In addition, both Xu Miao (c. 397) and Li Gui (c. 335), who preceded him, are also reputed to have relied on the Guo Xiang text. There must have been a reason for this. Clearly, the results of comparative study by Lu Deming and the others are more reliable evidence than the single words and phrases that appear in the Buddhist canon. It is simply incorrect to dismiss the differences between the Inner chapters and the Outer and Miscellaneous chapters of the Guo Xiang edition.

Here it is convenient to discuss for a moment the question of chapter headings. Those of the seven Inner chapters of the *Zhuangzi* are all three-character combinations, which is comparatively rare in pre-Qin classical texts. Accordingly, some scholars have concluded that the seven Inner chapters were composed during the Han dynasty,[34] and others hold that while they were, for the most part, composed by Zhuangzi, the chapter headings were added later by Liu An (179–122 B.C.) and his followers. For example, Zhang Hengshou is of the opinion that "the pre-Qin philosophers basically used two characters as chapter names." He holds that chapters 52, "Beichengmen" (Preparing walls and gates), and 53, "Beigaolin" (Preparing high vantage points), in the *Mozi* and chapters 68, "Chenchengma" (Minister on horseback), and 74, "Shanguogui" (The rules of a mountainous state), in the *Guanzi* are for the most part not pre-Qin works. Moreover, he holds that "three-character chapter titles are a particular tendency of the opening years of the Western Han."[35]

In point of fact, the use of three relatively uncommon characters as chapter headings must have had a historical beginning. It is not unreasonable to suggest that this was begun in the *Zhuangzi*. Indeed the peculiar characteristic of the book Zhuangzi authored is its unrestrained and unconventional nature. So it is understandable that it would be he who would create such a precedent.[36] We have yet to speak of the essays in the *Mozi* and *Guanzi* which use three-character chapter headings. Judging from the recently unearthed silk books and bamboo slips, three-character chapter headings were often seen in pre-Qin classical texts. For example, in the *Sun Bin bingfa* (Sun Bin's Art of war) there are "Qin Pang Juan" (Capturing Pang Juan) and "Weiwang wen" (King of Wei's questions), while in the *Shiliu jing* (Sixteen classics) there is "Cixiong jie" (Tally of feminity and masculinity). These demonstrate that the three-character chapter heading certainly was not peculiar to the early years of the Western Han. The argument that the chapter headings in the Inner chapters of the *Zhuangzi* were added during the Han is incomplete.

To sum up, the differences between the Inner chapters and the Outer and Miscellaneous chapters in the *Zhuangzi* are reflections of different historical periods. Our opinion that the Inner chapters are earlier than the Outer and Miscellaneous chapters enjoys multi-faceted, objective support.

We can generally be sure that the Inner chapters were produced by Zhuang-zi, while the Outer and Miscellaneous chapters were produced by Zhuangzi's later followers. Thus, when studying Zhuangzi's thought, we should use the Inner chapters as our foundation, though the thought they contain is inconsistent to a certain extent. While there may be some confusion surrounding the Inner and the Outer and Miscellaneous chapters, this does not prevent us from using the Inner chapters as the basis for a study of Zhuangzi's philosophy.

2

Dating the Outer and Miscellaneous Chapters

Background of the Problem

When did the distinction between the Inner and Outer chapters arise, and who separated the Outer and Miscellaneous chapters? These are questions we now have no way of answering. Hence, we are only able to take the Inner chapters as one large block distinguished from the Outer and Miscellaneous chapters as another block and proceed with our study. In the preceding chapter, we examined the dating of the Inner chapters. This chapter, then, will discuss solely the dating of the Outer and Miscellaneous chapters. In the previous chapter we affirmed that the Inner chapters predate the remainder of the *Zhuangzi*, from which it follows that the Outer and Miscellaneous chapters cannot be dated any earlier than the mid–Warring States period. Hence, the problem is essentially one of determining the later limit. Concretely speaking, the question is, Were the Outer and

Miscellaneous chapters of the *Zhuangzi* completed before the latter years of the Warring States period or in the opening years of the Han?

The *Zhuangzi* is a pre-Qin philosophical text, completed prior to Qin Shi Huang's unification of China. This is not problematic. During the Han dynasty, before the disputations concerning the Inner chapters and the Outer and Miscellaneous chapters had begun, Sima Qian (145–86? B.C.), Liu Xiang (77?–6 B.C.), Ban Gu, and others actually held that the entire *Zhuangzi*, of over 100,000 characters, was written by Zhuangzi himself. This caused them to assume that the Outer and Miscellaneous chapters of the text were products of the Warring States period. This belief continued for several centuries through Sima Biao, Guo Xiang, Lu Deming, and others, none of whom raised a single question concerning the origin of these chapters. The first to do so was the Song dynasty scholar Su Shi (1036–1101). In his *Zhuangzi citangji,* he questioned whether "Rangwang," "Shuojian," "Yufu," and "Daozhi" were actually written by Zhuangzi.[1] However, he expressed no doubts as to whether these four chapters were pre-Qin. Some scholars held that the phrase "possessed the state of Qi for twelve generations" in "Quqie" was "from the end of the Qin or early Han."[2] At the beginning of the Qing dynasty, Wang Fuzhi already doubted the date of composition of "Tiandao." He held that it "was written between the Qin and the Han by someone who had studied the methods of Huang-Lao Daoism to oppose what the rulers of the day were doing."[3] Other relatively early figures who suspected that certain essays in the Outer and Miscellaneous chapters were products of the Han include Yao Nai (1731–1815), in his *Zhuangzi zhangyi,* and Wu Rulun (1840–1903), in his *Diankan Zhuangzi duben.* Yao Nai argued that the section concerning Confucius traveling west to deposit his works with the royal house of Zhou was written in the language of the Han, and that *shangxian* 上仙 (super immortals) is also a phrase of the post-Qin.[4] Wu Rulun remarked that "plucking the strings and singing mournfully in hopes of attaining worldly reputation" and similar phrases found in "Tiandi" were not characteristic of the language of the men of Zhou or Qin.[5] In fact, both Yao and Wu considered "Tiandao" and "Tianyun" to be products of the Han.

In modern China, Ye Guoqing's *Zhuangzi yanjiu* dated "Zaiyou," "Tiandi," "Tiandao," and "Tianyun" to the early Han, and "Keyi," "Shanxing," and others as products of the period between the Qin and the Han.[6] Luo Genze also takes "Tiandi," "Tiandao," and "Tianyun" to be products of the Han and "Keyi" and "Shanxing" as works from between the Qin and Han.[7] This view has directly influenced Guan Feng, who states that "Tiandi," "Tiandao" and "Tianyun" "are products of the early Han, at the earliest they appeared after the establishment of a unified Qin empire." He holds that "Keyi" and "Shanxing" "are possibly works from between the Qin and Han."[8] In fact, these points of view are all versions of the theory that the book *Zhuangzi* was completed during the early years of the Han. As soon as we admit that the Inner chapters are earlier than the Outer or Miscellaneous chapters, the theory that the *Zhuangzi* became a book in the early Han then becomes a theory that the Outer and Miscellaneous chapters were completed then. Here, the later limit of the date that the *Zhuangzi* was completed is one and the same thing as the later limit of the date the Outer and Miscellaneous chapters were completed. We can take these two questions as one.

The points of view described above do not hold that the entire body of the Outer and Miscellaneous chapters was written at the beginning of the Han. However, they do affirm that portions of those chapters were produced then. This sets the latest date for completion of the *Zhuangzi* in the early Han. For short, we will call this the "early Han theory." Presently, the early Han theory enjoys relative superiority in the world of learning. Fung Yu-lan says, "The book *Zhuangzi* is a collection written by Daoists from the Warring States to the early Han, especially by the Zhuangzi school."[9] Zhang Hengshou has conducted a detailed examination and analysis of the *Zhuangzi*. His conclusion also echoes this theory: "We can say that the present book *Zhuangzi* encompasses material from various schools of Daoism drawn from a long period from the Warring States to the early Han."[10]

However, how much factual basis is there, ultimately, for the theory that the Outer and Miscellaneous chapters took form during the early years of the Han, or, more specifically, that "Tiandi," "Tiandao," and "Tianyun" and other chapters were composed then? According to our examination, evidence for the early Han theory does not pass careful consideration. Below we will analyze this question in several steps. First, from passages quoted in the *Hanfeizi* and *Lüshi chunqiu,* we will establish the period in which the *Zhuangzi* took shape. Then, from allusions in Jia Yi's (201–169 B.C.) *fu* 賦, or rhyme-prose, we will supplement and explain this conclusion. Then, from the original texts of the "Tianxia," "Tiandao," "Tiandi," "Tianyun," and other chapters, we shall infer when they were written. Finally, we will discuss several important tenets of the early Han theory.

Dating from the *Lüshi Chunqiu* and Other Books

First, to help determine when the Outer and Miscellaneous chapters were written, we will examine those instances where the *Lüshi chunqiu* and *Hanfeizi* quote the *Zhuangzi.*

There are many passages that appear in both the *Lüshi chunqiu* and the *Zhuangzi.* Who was copying whom? Generally speaking, it is possible only that the *Lüshi chunqiu* copied the *Zhuangzi* and impossible that the *Zhuangzi* copied the *Lüshi chunqiu.* There are three reasons for saying this.

First, in the *Lüshi chunqiu,* the editors' objective was to collect what others had said so that it became an all-encompassing system. In the *Shiji,* "Lü Buwei liezhuan" (Biography of Lü Buwei) says,

> Lü Buwei ordered his retainers to record what they had learned. The collected treatise comprised eight Views (*lan* 覽), six Arguments (*lun* 論), and twelve Records (*ji* 紀) in over 200,000 characters. Proclaiming that it embraced Heaven and Earth, the myriad things and all events old and new, he called it *Lüshi chunqiu.* (*S* 2510)[11]

The thought and style of Zhuangzi and his later followers is precisely contrary. They were acknowledged as "brilliant and unrestrained in their pursuit to amuse themselves" (*S* 2144). One cannot create this special literary style from copying other books.

Second, the format of the *Lüshi chunqiu* is that each chapter quotes several historical incidents, anecdotes, or parables, adding a short introduction and conclusion. Often, after a section of a story, several words of an instructive nature are also added to indicate the theme of the entire chapter. Its method is to borrow the words of others to establish its own position. This format guarantees that the *Lüshi chunqiu* must substantially quote from other books. The *Zhuangzi* lacks this requirement. It can freely arrange stories, tell parables, make criticisms, and express thoughts. Hence, to suppose the editors of the *Lüshi chunqiu* quoted a parable from the *Zhuangzi* and then added their own remarks to indicate the main aim of the whole chapter is reasonable and accords with fact. On the other hand, it makes no sense to suppose the *Zhuangzi* dispensed with the instructive remarks from the *Lüshi chunqiu* and simply plagiarized the parable to express its own position.

Third, the chapter of the *Zhuangzi* entitled "Dasheng" says,

> Confucius said, "A good swimmer will be able to row a boat after but a few attempts." You shoot skillfully when you bet on clay tiles in an archery contest. You tremble when you wager for belt buckles. And you become confused when you wager for gold. In all these cases, your skill remains the same—but because one prize means more, external considerations bear down on you. Whenever the external becomes weighty, one gets stupid on the inside. (642)

In the *Lüshi chunqiu,* "Quyou," this passage appears as a quotation from the *Zhuangzi:*

> Zhuangzi said, "You shoot effortlessly in an archery contest when betting on clay tiles. You contend when betting for belt buckles and become dangerously agitated when betting for gold. The fortunes are the same for all three cases. And yet, because one becomes agitated, it must be on account of an external element being more important. Whoever places more importance on the external dissipates his strength and becomes internally confused." The men of Lu could be criticized for emphasizing externals. (*L* 366)

This example is clear evidence that the retainers of Lü Buwei plagiarized the *Zhuangzi.* On the other hand, we are unable to find evidence that the followers of Zhuangzi plagiarized the *Lüshi chunqiu.*

There are also passages in the *Hanfeizi* that were borrowed from the *Zhuangzi.* For example, "Gengsangchu" in the *Zhuangzi* contains the following:

> If a sparrow came within Archer Yi's range, he would certainly shoot it down—an awesome display. But if he had made the whole world into a cage, then the sparrow would have had nowhere to escape. (814)

This appears in the *Hanfeizi,* "Nan san," as

> Therefore *a man from Song said,* "If a sparrow went past archer Yi, he
> would certainly shoot it down—he was a wizard. Had he made the
> whole world into a net, then not a single sparrow would have escaped."
> Now to understand the villainous is also like a large net from which no
> one escapes. (*H* 750–51)

Zhuangzi was from the state of Song, hence Han Feizi's phrase "a man of
Song said. . . ." This is a clear example of borrowing from the *Zhuangzi.*

Table 2.1 lists passages from the *Zhuangzi* quoted in the *Lüshi
chunqiu* and *Hanfeizi.* The table illustrates that at the end of the Warring
States period, there were at least 14 chapters from the *Zhuangzi* which had
been quoted by the *Lüshi chunqiu* and *Hanfeizi.* These 14 chapters are
equivalent to approximately 42 percent of the present 33-chapter edition of
the *Zhuangzi.* This proportion is fairly high. A phenomenon such as this
would have been impossible if the *Zhuangzi* of that time had not been
formed into a widely circulated book. Among the essays quoted in the
Lüshi chunqiu and *Hanfeizi,* there are 3 from the Inner chapters, 6 from the
Outer chapters, and 5 from the Miscellaneous chapters. These proportions
are fairly close to the distribution of chapters in the modern edition of
Zhuangzi, which has 7 Inner, 15 Outer, and 11 Miscellaneous chapters.
This indicates that at that time the three divisions of the *Zhuangzi* had fixed
dimensions. Although it cannot confirm that there were distinctions established among them, it indicates that the content of those three sections had
fundamentally taken shape at that time. This then is to say that the Outer
and Miscellaneous chapters, for the most part, had been completed by the
end of the Warring States period.

It remains to mention correspondences that do not appear in the table.
For example, in the *Zhuangzi,* "Qiushui" reads, "So, if men continue to
describe this way without stop, they *must either be fools or deceivers"* (*fei
yu zi wu* 非愚則誣, 580). In the *Hanfeizi,* "Xianxue" reads, "Hence, it is
clear that those who claim to follow the ancient kings and to have settled
once and for all the ways of Yao and Shun *must either be fools or
deceivers"* (*H* 785). It is possible that the phrase "they must either be fools
or deceivers" was commonly used during the pre-Qin era; but it is also

Table 2.1. *Zhuangzi* Passages in the *Lüshi chunqiu* and *Han Feizi*

Zhuangzi Chapter	Passage	*LQ/HF* Chapter
Inner		
"Xiaoyaoyou" (1)	Yao sought to cede the empire to Xu You	*LQ* Arg. 2: "Qiuren"
"Yangshengzhu" (3)	Cook Ding carves an ox	*LQ* Rec. 9: "Jingtong"
"Dazongshi" (6)	Big Dipper, Sun, and Moon attain the Way	*HF* "Jielao"
Outer		
"Ququie" (10)	Thieves and brigands also have a Way	*LQ* Rec. 11: "Dangwu"
"Tiandi" (12)	Yao ruled the empire	*LQ* View 8: "Changli"
"Dasheng" (19)	Shang Bao nourished what was internal	*LQ* View 2: "Biji"
"	Archery contest for clay tiles or gold	*LQ* View 1: "Quyou"
"	Dongye demonstrates his charioteering	*LQ* View 7: "Shiwei"
"Shanmu" (20)	Zhuangzi spies a large tree	*LQ* View 2: "Biji"
"	People love fox and leopard	*HF* "Yulao"
"	Yangzi was on his way to Song	*HF* "Shuolin A"
"Tianzifang" (21)	Confucius visited Wenbo Xuezi	*LQ* View 6: "Jingyu"
"Zhibeiyou" (22)	Perfect speech loses speech	"
"Gengsangchu" (23)	The world as one's basket; sparrows cannot flee	*HF* "Nansan"
"Xuwugui" (24)	Guan Zhong became ill	*LQ* Rec.1: "Guigong"
"Waiwu" (26)	External things are unreliable	*LQ* View 2: "Biji"

Table 2.1. *cont.*

Zhuangzi Chapter	Passage	*LQ/HF* Chapter
Miscellaneous		
"Rangwang" (28)	Shun wants to cede to the Farmer of Shihu	*LQ* View 7: "Lisu"
"	Shun wants to cede to Wuze	"
"	Tang was about to attack Jie	"
"	Yao wanted to cede to Zizhou Zhifu	*LQ* Rec. 1: "Guisheng"
"	Men of Yue wanted Prince Sou as lord	"
"	Govern oneself with the truth of the Way	"
"	Great King Danfu lives at Bin	*LQ* Arg. 1: "Shenwei"
"	Territorial dispute between Han and Wei	"
"	Prince Mou of Zhongshan said to Zhanzi . . .	"
"	Liezi was living in poverty	*LQ* View 4: "Guanshi"
"	When the Zhou first ascended to power	*LQ* Rec. 12: "Chenglian"
"Daozhi" (29)	Yao was cruel; Shun was not filial	*LQ* Rec. 11: "Dangwu"
"	Man's longevity may extend to 100 years	*LQ* Rec. 10: "Ansi"
Totals		
14 *Zhuangzi* chapters	30 passages	*LQ*: 16 chapters *HF*: 4 chapters

possible that the *Hanfeizi* was influenced by the *Zhuangzi*. In addition, the term *xingming* appears in "Zhibeiyou" and "Shanxing," and the special phrase *xingming zhi qing* 性命之情 (the essence of nature and fate) is employed in "Mati" and "Zaiyou." In the *Lüshi chunqiu* the six chapters "Chongji," "Jinting," "Guanshi," "Wugong," "Zhidu," and "Youdu" all employ the term *xingming zhiqing*. It is possible that the phrase had already come into common use. However, it is also very possible that the authors of the *Lüshi chunqiu* were directly influenced by the *Zhuangzi*, since the term does not appear in the *Xunzi* or *Hanfeizi*. All of this illustrates that the examples of pre-Qin quotation from the *Zhuangzi* in table 2.1 are not exhaustive.

Another point that requires explanation here is that the original text of the *Zhuangzi* had 52 chapters, while the modern text has only 33 chapters, a discrepancy of 19 chapters. It is inconceivable that the *Lüshi chunqiu* and *Hanfeizi* only quoted from the extant 33 chapters and not from the 19 lost chapters. For example, the *Chunqiu Guliangzhuan shu*, (Duke Ai, 2nd year), by Yang Shixun of the Tang, quotes this story from the *Zhuangzi:*

> There was a man of Chu who sold spears and shields. When he met someone who wanted to buy a spear, he told him "There is nothing this spear can't pierce." When he saw someone who wanted to buy a shield, he then said, "What could possibly pierce this shield?" His customer should have asked, "Well then, what would happen if your spear stabbed your shield?"[12]

This parable does not appear in the modern edition of the *Zhuangzi*; so it seems to come from among the 19 lost chapters. The parable of the spear and the shield is mentioned in "Nanyi" in the modern *Hanfeizi*, so it was very possibly derived from the original edition of the *Zhuangzi*. "Nanyi" reads,

> There was a man of Chu who sold shields and spears. He would hold them aloft saying, "My shields are so tough nothing can pierce them." He would also hold up his spears and say, "My spears are so sharp, there is nothing they can't pierce." Someone asked him, "What happens if I stab one of your shields with one of your spears?" and he was unable to answer. (*H* 738)

This is not completely the same as the sentences of the lost text of the *Zhuangzi* quoted above, but the basic plot of the story and its structure are the same. So it is very possible that the *Hanfeizi* relied on the original edition of the *Zhuangzi*.

Another example is in the *Taiping Yulan*, chapter 767, which quotes the *Zhuangzi*:

> The Music Master Kuang performed *Qingjue* for Duke Ping of Jin. The first time he played it, the clouds rose up from the northwest and, as he continued to play, a great wind and rain followed. The window curtains were torn out; the feasting vessels were broken, and the tiles on the roofs were smashed to smithereens. Duke Ping was terrified and hid in his chambers.[13]

This passage was placed in the section on "Miscellaneous Topics," indicating that the compilers of the *Taiping Yulan* did not regard this story very highly. In all probability it is abridged. In section ten, "Shiguo," of the *Hanfeizi*, this story appears as,

> As he played the first section of the music, dark clouds rose up from the northwest. As he continued to play, a great wind came forth, and a violent rain followed, tearing the curtains and hangings, overturning the cups and bowls, and smashing the tiles from the roof. Those who had been sitting scattered in all directions, while the duke was paralyzed with fear and huddled in a corner of the gallery. (*H* 624)

It is very possible that this too was quoted from the 52-chapter text of the *Zhuangzi*. To summarize, it is entirely possible that the *Lüshi chunqiu*, *Hanfeizi* and other texts quote stories from the lost 19 chapters of the *Zhuangzi*.

From the fact that 14 of 33 chapters had been quoted before the Qin dynasty, we may suppose that 7 or 8 of the lost chapters might have been quoted and should be added to the 14 chapters in table 2.1. According to this, the original text of the lost text of the *Zhuangzi* already quoted by the pre-Qin should be 21 or 22 chapters. If this number represents 42 percent of the entire *Zhuangzi*, then the text of the *Zhuangzi* at that time was about 50 odd chapters and generally matches with the 52 chapters described by the *Hanshu*, "Yiwenzhi." Should this argument basically be established, then it shows that it is entirely possible that the *Zhuangzi* became a book during the final years of the Warring States period.

Here, we should discuss for a moment the relationship between chapter 28, "Rangwang," and the *Lüshi chunqiu*. Luo Genze and others have concluded that "Rangwang" was plagiarized from the *Lüshi chunqiu*.[14] Zhang Hengshou, in his *Zhuangzi xintan*, has refined the argument on this point.[15] But according to our investigations, even though the relations between "Rangwang" and the *Lüshi chunqiu* are sometimes extraordinary, they are still insufficient evidence to conclude that the chapter was plagiarized from the *Lüshi chunqiu*. The first section of "Rangwang," for example, is composed of four passages in which phrases appear to be arranged in order and are connected together. The first passage begins with, "Yao wanted to cede the empire to Xu You, but Xu You refused to accept it. Then he tried to give it to Zizhou Zhifu." The second passage begins with, "Shun wanted to cede the empire to Zizhou Zhibo." The third passage begins with, "Shun tried to cede the empire to Shan Juan." The fourth passage begins with, "Shun wanted to cede the empire to his friend, the farmer of Stone Door." The first passage is found in the *Lüshi chunqiu* chapter "Guisheng." The fourth is the same as in the "Lisu" chapter of the *Lüshi chunqiu*. It is not difficult to conjecture that the authors of the "Guisheng" and "Lisu" selected passages from "Rangwang" to support their own main themes. However, if we turn it around and propose that the author of "Rangwang" chose the two passages from "Guisheng" and "Lisu" to serve as the section's first and fourth passages, and then independently created the second and third passages, the reasoning behind it becomes inexplicable. If this was done to supplement or exaggerate the story, then why not use as well the final, thirteenth section, "Shun ceded the empire to his friend from the north, Wu Ze." (This also appears in "Lisu.") Since the authors of "Rangwang" were able to create the second and third passages, why were they unable to create the first and the fourth passages? In fact, the structure of these four passages is complete, their perspectives are mutually comprehensible, and they have a definite connection to Zhuangzi's school. It is very difficult to say they were compiled from unrelated fragments of the *Lüshi chunqiu*. "Only he who has no use for the empire is fit to be trusted with it" in the first passage corresponds to

"I have no use for the rulership of the world!" in the first chapter of the *Zhuangzi*, "Xiaoyaoyou." The second passage's "This is how the possessor of the Way is different from the vulgar man" is also a Daoist phrase. In the third passage, "I wander free and easy between Heaven and earth and feel happy and content in my mind. What would I do with the empire?" is really a special feature of Zhuangzi's school. The fourth passage's "recognizing that Shun's virtue was not yet complete" is consistent with Zhuangzi's thought. Given the close relationship among these four chapters, how could they be formed from unrelated compilations from the *Lüshi chunqiu*?

In addition to this, we can find proof that the *Lüshi chunqiu* quoted from "Rangwang" by looking at the circumstances surrounding the changes in several phrases and sentences. For example, the first section of "Rangwang" puts forward that Yao ceded the empire to Xu You, that Xu You did not accept it, and that Yao then ceded it to his son Zizhou Zhifu. At the end we find, "He who has no use for the empire is fit to be trusted with it," an understandable and totally natural phrasing. But in the "Guisheng" chapter of the *Lüshi chunqiu*, this sentence was changed to "Only those who would not harm the life of all under Heaven can be trusted with all under Heaven." The sudden emphasis on "harming life" is obviously for the purpose of forcing thematic correspondence to the main topic of the chapter, "honoring life" ("Guisheng"). Another example is the fifth section of "Rangwang": "Men like Yan He truly despise wealth and honor." In the "Guisheng" chapter of the *Lüshi chunqiu*, this sentence is changed to "As for men like Yan He, it is not that they simply dislike wealth and honor; it is because they regard life as important that they dislike those things." Again the alteration is obviously made for the purpose of coinciding with the chapter theme of "Guisheng." There remain quite a few other examples showing that the *Lüshi chunqiu* borrowed from "Rangwang," not the other way around.

The next item worth noting is the two passages of the first section of "Rangwang," the second, third, fourth, fifth and sixth sections and the eleventh, twelfth, thirteenth, fourteenth, and fifteenth sections of this chapter. Note that in the *Lüshi chunqiu* these passages appear, respectively, in the second, nineteenth, twenty-first, second, twenty-first, second, sixteenth, twenty-first, fourteenth, nineteenth, nineteenth and twelfth chapters. There is not the slightest apparent order. Why is it this way? It cannot be held that the authors of "Rangwang" did this consciously to confuse others, because after the *Lüshi chunqiu* was completed, "It was announced that a thousand pieces in gold would be hung above Xianyang City Gate and awarded to the lord, itinerant warrior, retainer, whoever could add or subtract one word from the *Lüshi chunqiu*" (*S* 2510). This demonstrates that the contents of the *Lüshi chunqiu* were common knowledge. Under conditions such as these, attempting to plagiarize and deceive others is no different than deceiving oneself. It is illogical to suppose that the author of "Rangwang" plagiarized the *Lüshi chunqiu*.

On the other hand, should we suppose that the compilers of the *Lüshi chunqiu* plagiarized "Rangwang," we do not encounter that sort of contradiction. For example, we begin by noting the first passage of the first section of "Rangwang," "Yao wanted to cede the empire to Zizhou Zhifu"; the third section, "The men of Yue looked for Prince Sou to make him their ruler"; and the fifth section, "The ruler of Lu heard that Yan He had attained the Way." Sections in the "Guisheng" chapter of the *Lüshi chunqiu* coincidentally follow this sequence and are similarly arranged one after the other. Or let us note for a moment the fourth passage of the first section of "Rangwang," "Shun wanted to cede the empire to the farmer of Stone Door"; the thirteenth section, "Shun wanted to cede the empire to the Northerner Wu Ze"; and the fourteenth section, "when Tang was about to attack Jie." Sections in the "Lisu" chapter of the *Lüshi chunqiu* coincidentally follow this sequence and are similarly arranged one after the other. And again another sequence to note is the second section of "Rangwang," "The Great King Danfu lived in Bin"; the fourth section, concerning the territorial disputes between the states of Han and Wei; and the eleventh section, concerning Prince Mou who lived in Zhongshan and asked a question of Zhanzi. In the "Shenwei" chapter of the *Lüshi chunqiu*, these are again sequentially arranged, linked together one after the other. Why this correspondence? There is only one explanation: that the authors of the "Guisheng," "Lisu," and "Shenwei" chapters in the *Lüshi chunqiu* selected for their own use stories from "Rangwang" in the order in which they appeared, following their sequence as they incorporated them into their own essays. Following this pattern of writing saved time; moreover, it did not contradict the demands of the book's editor. Hence, the authors felt no compulsion to adjust the sequence of these stories. It is far more logical that the *Lüshi chunqiu* plagiarized "Rangwang" than that "Rangwang" plagiarized the *Lüshi chunqiu.*

The seventh section of "Rangwang" ("When King Zhao of Chu had lost his state"), the eighth section ("Yuan Xian lived in the state of Lu"), the ninth section ("Zengzi lived in Wei"), the tenth section ("Confucius said to Yan Hui"), and the second and third passages of the first section ("Shun wanted to cede the empire to Zizhou Zhibo" and "Shun ceded the empire to Shan Juan") are not found in the *Lüshi chunqiu.* Anyone contending that "Rangwang" plagiarized the *Lüshi chunqiu* must exclude these sections. Zhang Hengshou holds that the two stories concerning King Zhao of Chu losing his state and Yuan Xian living in Lu were derived from the *Xinxu* (New preface), and the *Hanshi waizhuan.*[16] However, this explanation contradicts Zhang's own position that the chapters of the *Zhuangzi* were fixed during the time of Liu An (179–122 B.C.), the Prince of Huainan. Since Liu Xiang's *Xinxu* could only have been written during the final years of the Western Han, after Emperor Cheng of Han had claimed the throne, it could not have been written prior to the time at which Liu An, the Prince of Huainan, lived. In fact, the only possibilty is that the *Xinxu* followed the *Zhuangzi,* and thus the *Zhuangzi* could not have borrowed from it. An example is the story of Duke She's fondness for dragons, quoted by Li Shan's (630–89) *Wen xuan zhu* (Commentary on Wen Xuan). Li Shan claimed that the story was derived from the *Zhuangzi* instead of the *Xinxu.*[17] This fact suggests that the story in the *Xinxu* concerning Duke She's fondness for dragons had its source in the original text of the *Zhuangzi.* It is simply baseless to say that the *Zhuangzi* took material from the *Xinxu.*

To sum up, it is certainly possible that the *Lüshi chunqiu* copied the *Zhuangzi,* while the grounds for asserting that "Rangwang" "for the most part borrowed from the *Lüshi chunqiu*" or that "the entire chapter is composed of a variety of selections of old stories"[18] are insufficient. However, this issue is certainly not critical to our argument. These conclusions concerning "Rangwang" can even be set aside without fundamentally influencing the methods and conclusions of our analysis above. In sum, from our inference that the *Hanfeizi* and *Lüshi chunqiu* quoted the *Zhuangzi*, it is entirely plausible that the Outer and Miscellaneous chapters of the *Zhuangzi* were completed prior to the end of the Warring States period.

Evidence from Jia Yi's *Fu*

Jia Yi was born in 200 B.C., not much more than two years after Liu Bang (256–195 B.C.) claimed the throne of China. Jia was famous for his writings, including the two *fu* "Diao Qu Yuan fu" (Lament for Qu Yuan) and the "Funiao fu" (Rhyme-prose on the owl). Popular during the Han dynasty, *fu* resembled long poems. As can be seen in Jia Yi's *fu*, he had read the *Zhuangzi* intently and was influenced by it. From this we can deduce that the *Zhuangzi* had become a book by the end of the Warring States period. This is to say that the Outer and Miscellaneous chapters of the *Zhuangzi* were essentially completed during the pre-Qin period.

We will first look at the "Diao Qu Yuan fu" (Lament for Qu Yuan) (the text is based on *Shiji*: "Qu Yuan Jia Sheng liezhuan").

1) The idea for Jia Yi's remark, "The world calls Bo Yi avaricious while saying Robber Zhi is honorable" (*S* 2493), originated in *Zhuangzi*, "Pianmu": "Why must Bo Yi be correct and Robber Zhi be wrong?" (323).

2) Jia Yi's sentence,

> The Spirit Dragons of the Nine Depths hide in the measureless abyss to be all the more rare (*S* 2494)

is drawn from *Zhuangzi, "Lieyukou"*:

> Now a pearl worth a thousand pieces of gold must have been found in the Ninefold Depths under the chin of a black dragon. (1062)

3) Jia Yi's

> How is it that our ordinary ditches and drains are able to contain a fish that swallows boats? So a whale capable of traversing rivers and lakes is eaten by crickets and ants (*S* 2495)

is derived from *Zhuangzi,* "Gengsangchu":

> Now in ditches of ordinary depth, there is no place a great fish can turn its body. . . . As for a fish that could swallow a boat, if left high and dry on shore, the ants would be able to mistreat it. (772–73)

4) "The spirit Virtue of the sage must retreat from this evil age and hide itself away" (*S* 2494). This is found in *Zhuangzi,* "Zeyang": "As for servants of the sage, they bury themselves among the people and hide themselves away" (895).

Next, we will examine the "Funiao fu" (Rhyme-prose on the owl).

5) "Heaven and earth are the furnace, the creator is the smith" (*S* 2499). The allusion for this is found in "Dazongshi," "Now, I take Heaven and earth as a great furnace and the creator as the smith. Where could these changes take me that would not be suitable?" (262).

6) "Combining, scattering, dissipating, and accumulating, where is there a constant rule?" (*S* 2499) This idea is derived from "Zhibeiyou": "Man's life is an accumulation of breath. When it comes together there is life; when it disperses there is death. How can we know its regulations?" (733).

7) "A thousand changes, ten thousand transformations; there has never begun to be an end" (*S* 2500). The phrasing is the same as a passage in "Dazongshi": "The human form undergoes a myriad changes whose end has yet to begin" (244).

8) "Suddenly one becomes a man, but is this enough to give a second thought?" (*S* 2500) The idea here is the same as in "Dazongshi": "Now, having already benighted human form once, if I were to shout and say, 'I'll be a man, only a man!' the creator would certainly take me as an inauspicious sort of fellow" (262).

9) "These transformations will make you into something different, how can this cause you grief?" (*S* 2500). The idea here is the same as is found in "Dazongshi":

> Now why should I hate this? Perhaps my left arm gradually will be transformed into a rooster, and I will have him keep watch 'til dawn. Perhaps my right arm gradually will become a crossbow bolt, and I will

use it for roast owl at dinner. . . . It has long been known that things cannot overcome Heaven. So why should I hate this? (260)

10) "Men of lesser knowledge, full of self and partial, belittle others while vaunting their own" (*S* 2500). The idea is the same as in "Qiushui": "Seen from the point of view of things, each vaunts his own and belittles others" (577).

11) "The man of comprehension takes the larger view; he sees that everything is acceptable" (*S* 2500). This is similar to a passage in "Qiushui": "Things all have that which is so and things all have that which is acceptable. Nothing is not so; nothing is not acceptable" (69). This statement also appears in "Yuyan."

12) "The Perfect Man abandons the things of the world; alone, he unites with the Way" (*S* 2500). In "Tianzifang" we find, "It seems you have abandoned the things of the world, left mankind, and established yourself in the solitary" (711). In "Shanmu" we find, "You wander alone with the Way in the land of vast expansiveness" (674–75).

13) "The True Man is quiet and unmoved, he rests alone with the Way" (*S* 2500). In "Shanxing" we find the men of old were "one with the times and were quiet and unmoved therein" (550). The idea of "resting alone with the Way" is also found in "Shanmu." There, one "wanders alone with the Way in the land of vast expansiveness" (674). The "True Man" is also a phrase commonly found in the *Zhuangzi*.

14) "Let go of knowledge, abandon form; thus ascendant, the self is laid to rest" (*S* 2500). This idea is drawn from "Dazongshi": "Dispense with form, cast off knowledge, unite with that Great Thoroughfare" (284). And in "Qiwulun" we find, "Now, I have laid myself to rest" (45).

15) "Solitary, remote, yet sudden and swift, he soars and roams with the Way" (*S* 2500). The idea is the same as in "Shanmu": "He mounts the Way and its Virtue to float and wander on" (668).

16) "His life resembles floating, his death resembles rest" (*S* 2500). Identical phrasing is found in "Keyi" (539).

17) "Tranquil as stillness found in the depths of the abyss, drifting as an unmoored boat" (*S* 2500). The latter phrase is derived from "Lieyukou": "He eats until full and wanders leisurely along, drifting as an unmoored boat" (1040).

18) "He does not take his life as a pretext to value self; he nourishes emptiness and floats away" (*S* 2500). Citing Fu Qian (c. 184–89), Yan Shigu (581–645) says in the commentary to the *Hanshu:* "The Daoist nourishes the empty, the void, as if one were a floating boat."[19] This then is the parable of the empty boat from *Zhuangzi,* "Shanmu":

> Assume that a boat crossing a river is bumped by an empty boat that happens along. No matter how pugnacious the occupant of the first boat may be, he will not become angered. . . . So, if a man is able to empty himself and float through this world, who could harm him? (675)

The idea of "nourishing emptiness and floating away" is the same as emptying oneself to float in this world." The idea behind it, that he "does not take his life as a pretext to value self," is expressed in "Qiushui": "He is born, yet it is not for rejoicing; he dies, yet it is not a calamity" (568).

19) "The man of Virtue is unencumbered; he knows what is fated and does not grieve" (*S* 2500). The idea of being "unencumbered" appears in "Zaiyou": "He is established in Virtue and is unencumbered" (348). An idea similar to "he knows what is fated and does not grieve" is found in "Yangshengzhu": "If you rest in the times and reside in following along, grief and joy cannot enter" (128). The "man of Virtue" is found in "Tiandi": "The man of Virtue rests without thought and moves without consideration" (441).

20) "The greedy man seeks his gain; the hero risks death for his fame" (*S* 2500). The idea for this derives from "Pianmu": "The petty man will risk death for profit; the knight will risk it for the sake of fame" (323). The lost text of the *Zhuangzi* also contains the statement "The knights pursue fame and the greedy men rush after gain."[20]

21) "The great man is not one-sided, to him a million changes even out to be the same" (*S* 2500). The idea is the same as in "Qiwulun": "Heaven and earth are one attribute, the ten thousand things are a single horse" (66).

Jia Yi's "Diao Qu Yuan fu" and "Funiao fu" together total no more than 800 characters. Among them, there are over 20 places in which ideas from the *Zhuangzi* have been borrowed or developed from about 14 of the Inner, Outer, and Miscellaneous chapters. Three are from the Inner chapters, 8 are from the Outer chapters, and 3 are from the Miscellaneous chapters. On the one hand, this indicates that Jia Yi was deeply influenced by *Zhuangzi*. On the other, this also shows that the *Zhuangzi* had a set form at that time and had a relatively wide influence.

Jia Yi was about twenty-three when he composed the "Diao Qu Yuan fu," and about twenty-six when he wrote the "Funiao fu." The histories say, "When he was eighteen, he could recite poetry and compose books and was well known in his prefecture . . . he was rather well versed in the books of the hundred schools of philosophers" (*S* 2491). These books include, of course, the *Zhuangzi*. From this we know that Jia Yi read the *Zhuangzi* in his teens, not much more than ten or so years before Liu Bang claimed the throne. If the *Zhuangzi* that was circulating at that time was only partial, then after the other had been completed there would be two versions of the *Zhuangzi* in circulation. If this were the case, then Sima Qian, who lived during this time, and Liu Xiang, Liu Xin (?–23), and Ban Gu, who lived somewhat later, would certainly have written about it. Hence, the text of the *Zhuangzi* that Jia Yi read must have been the completed volume.

When, then, was the complete edition finished? First, it would not be after Liu Bang had assumed the throne, because during his reign the Qin laws concerning the proscription of books were still in effect. This remained so until the fourth year of Hui Di's reign (191 B.C.), when he began "dispensing with the laws proscribing books." So during this time it is not likely that work on the *Zhuangzi* was underway. In that age of hand-copied silk and bamboo slips, it would have been very difficult for a book of several hundred thousand characters to be completely compiled and widely circulated in the twenty or so years between Liu Bang's assumption of the throne and Jia Yi's reading of the text. Second, it would not have been while Chu and Han were fighting or during the unceasing war and disorder between the Qin and Han. Third, it would not be during the Qin, when private holdings of the "Poetry, History and Philosophers" were strictly forbidden. From this we deduce that the *Zhuangzi* was probably formed into a book before the First Emperor of Qin united the six states.

Generally speaking, a book written during a certain era should reflect that era. For example, the *Lüshi chunqiu,* "Guanshi," says,

> And now the house of Zhou has been extinguished; the Son of Heaven has been discarded. There is no disorder greater than there being no Son of Heaven. When there is no Son of Heaven, the strong vanquish the weak, the many do violence to the few. Destroying one another with weapons, ceaselessly proceeding to our own destruction, this is what our world is. (*L* 400)

This shows that the *Lüshi chunqiu* was probably written after the house of Zhou was destroyed and before the First Emperor of Qin unified the empire. Another example is Lu Jia's (c. 200 B.C.) *Xinyu* (New words), which says, "Duke Huan of Qi esteemed virtue and became the Hegemon. The Qin esteemed punishments for two generations and perished,"[21] and "The dynasty of Wen and Wu enjoyed many who were good and worthy, while in the court of the Qin there were many who were ignoble."[22] These lines show that the *Xinyu* was written after the demise of the Qin. Jia Yi's *Xinshu* (New books) reads, "Now the Han have been in ascendance for thirty years, but the empire is even more destitute. Food is extremely scarce."[23] This clearly shows that the *Xinshu* was written during the early years of the Han. In the *Huainanzi* it is written,

> When objects abound the desires are reduced. When pursuits are placid, then wrangling is stopped. During the reign of the King of Qin some people would murder their newborn children because their provisions were insufficient. When the house of Liu took over the government, single fathers adopted orphans because there was a surplus of wealth.[24]

This clearly reflects the era in which the *Huainanzi* was written. However, we do not find in the *Zhuangzi* evidence clearly showing that the Outer and Miscellaneous chapters were written during the Qin or the early years of the Han.

If we suppose that certain among the Outer and Miscellaneous chapters of the *Zhuangzi* were completed during the Han dynasty, then we have no way of explaining why important events, such as the first Qin emperor's destruction of the six states and unification of the empire and Liu Bang's extermination of the various heroes and pacification of all the land within the four seas, do not find the slightest reflection in these chapters. Why do we find stories about King Hui of Liang, King Wei of Chu, and King Yan of Song and yet find no trace of the first Qin emperor or the first emperor of the Han? Why are the characters in the parables of the *Zhuangzi* all figures from before the Warring States period? Why is there not a single general of Qin or minister of Han? If we admit that these essays are a reflection of social reality, there is only one answer to this question.

To sum up, the theory that the *Zhuangzi* took form as a book during the early years of the Han is insufficiently grounded. It remains entirely possible that the Outer and Miscellaneous chapters are works composed prior to the closing years of the Warring States period.

Dating from the Text of the *Zhuangzi*

Our main task above was to use other books as supplemental proof of our inference concerning when the *Zhuangzi* became a book. Here we will examine for a moment the dating of the Outer and Miscellaneous chapters of the *Zhuangzi* itself. The crux of our argument is that these chapters were written prior to the Qin. Hence, we shall discuss only chapters that most scholars consider works of the early Han, such as "Tianxia," "Tiandi," "Tiandao," and "Tianyun." If we eliminate the questions concerning these chapters, then the questions concerning our contention as a whole will be resolved.

We will first consider the era in which "Tianxia" was written. "Tianxia" occupies an important position in the history of ancient Chinese learning. The theories concerning when it was written are many and various. Some scholars support the pre-Qin theory; some prefer an early Han theory. An examination of the heading of each chapter in the *Zhuangzi*, reveals that "Tianxia" is earlier than "Zhile," affirming the pre-Qin theory.

There is a regularity to the chapter names in the *Zhuangzi*. All of the Inner chapters have meaningful three-character headings. With the exception of "Rangwang," "Daozhi," "Shuojian," and "Yufu," the Outer and Miscellaneous chapters basically take their names from the first two or three characters in each chapter. Table 2.2 presents a detailed view of this situation.

It is easy to see from the table that the principle governing chapter titles in the Outer and Miscellaneous chapters is that they are derived from the first two or three characters of the chapter text. Sometimes these two or three characters are a personal name such as Ze Yang or Xu Wugui. Sometimes the title is a two-character notional word such as *Waiwu* or *Qiushui*. At other times, it is a three-character word group such as *Zhibeiyou* (Knowledge wandered north), the meaning of which is relatively complete and which does not include a function word. There are two exceptional cases. The first is if the opening two or three characters in the chapter contain a function word or a single-character word; then, the full phrase after it is used. For example, "Quqie" does not use the empty characters *jiang* 將 or *wei* 為. "Zaiyou" does not use the single-character word *wen* 聞. The second exception is when the personal name at the beginning of the chapter is Laozi or Zhuangzi; then, the next full phrase after it is selected to avoid a chapter title duplicating the book titles *Laozi* or *Zhuangzi*. Examples are "Gengsangchu" and "Shanmu." (This is exactly like the first chapter in *Mencius* which begins "Mencius had an audience with King Hui of Liang." "King Hui of Liang" was chosen as the chapter title, not "Mencius.") How these exceptional situations were dealt with only confirms that the principle governing chapter names was that the first few characters of the chapter form the name. Since the first sentence of the chapter entitled "Zhile" reads: "Is there such a thing as perfect happiness in the world?" (*Tianxia you zhile wu you zai* 天下有至樂無有哉), *tianxia* 天下 should have been chosen as the chapter title. Why wasn't it? There is only one possibility: chapter 33, "Tianxia" (The world 天下), had already taken those two characters as its title. Hence, the next full two-character phrase was selected. It is difficult to find any other reasonable explanation. Accordingly, we can conclude that "Tianxia" was written earlier than "Zhile." And since there is no reason to doubt that "Zhile" was written prior to the Qin, we should not doubt that "Tianxia" was too.

Table 2.2. Derivation of the Titles of the Outer and Miscellaneous Chapters

Title	First Line	Position of Title Characters
Outer Chapters		
"Pianmu" (8)	*Webbed toes* or a sixth finger issue from a man's nature	1st & 2nd
"Mati" (9)	The *horse* has *hooves* to tread in frost and snow	1st & 2nd
"Ququie" (10)	If you intend to take precautions against those who *rifle trunks*	3rd & 4th (omits particles)
"Zaiyou" (11)	I have heard of *leaving* the world *be*	2nd & 3rd (omits "I have heard")
"Tiandi" (12)	*Heaven and earth,* though great, are alike	1st & 2nd
"Tiandao" (13)	The *Way of Heaven* turns and allows no accumulation	1st & 2nd
"Tianyun" (14)	Does *Heaven turn?*	1st & 3rd (omits particles)
"Keyi" (15)	To be *constrained in will,* lofty in action, apart from the world	1st & 2nd
"Shanxing" (16)	*Mending the nature* through the commonplace	1st & 2nd
"Qiushui" (17)	The season of *autumn floods* arrived and all the streams poured	1st & 2nd
"Zhile" (18)	Does the world possess such a thing as *perfect happiness?*	4th & 5th (omits *tian dao* & "possess")
"Dasheng" (19)	He who has *mastered* the essentials of *life*	1st & 2nd
"Shanmu" (20)	Zhuangzi was walking in the *mountains* when he saw a great *tree*	5th & 9th (omits *Zhuangzi* & particles)
"Tianzifang" (21)	*Tian Zifang* sat in attendance beside the Marquis Wen of Wei	1st, 2nd, & 3rd
"Zhibeiyou" (22)	*Knowledge wandered north* across . . .	1st, 2nd, & 3rd
"Gengsangchu" (23)	Among the followers of Lao Dan was *Gengsang Chu*	6th, 7th, & 8th (omits *Lao Dan* & particles)

Table 2.2, *cont.*

Title	First Line	Position of Title Characters
Miscellaneous Chapters		
"Xuwugui" (24)	*Xu Wugui,* through the introduction of Nü Shang, had an audience with . . .	1st, 2nd, & 3rd
"Zeyang" (25)	When *Ze Yang* traveled to Chu	1st & 2nd
"Waiwu" (26)	*External things* cannot be relied upon	1st & 2nd
"Yuyan" (27)	*Imputed words* are nine-tenths of it	1st & 2nd
"Lieyukou" (32)	*Lie Yukou* was on his way to Qi	1st & 2nd
"Tianxia" (33)	There are many *in the world* who practice some strategy or art	1st & 2nd

One might ask when the chapter names were added to the *Zhuangzi.* If they were added all at once by someone who arranged the text after the Qin or Han, then our statements above will have lost their basis. However, according to our investigation, there is practically no possibility of this. First, in the ancient texts of the Warring States period, it was already fairly common to assign a name following the writing of the chapter. For example, the bamboo slips of the *Sun Bin bingfa* from the Han tomb at Yinque shan, the silk books *Jingfa, Shiliu jing* from the Han tomb at Ma Wang dui, and other old texts all have chapter names. These recently excavated texts were transcribed during the early Han but are works composed during the Warring States period.[25] Since a copyist is not one who compiles or arranges material, the majority of the chapter headings in these old texts should be original. Basing our inference on this class of material, it is entirely possible that each chapter of the *Zhuangzi* had its own heading by the Warring States period.

There are three different kinds of chapter titles in the *Zhuangzi:* first, the regular three-character headings of the Inner chapters; second, those exemplified in table 2.2, with titles taken from the first two or three characters of the chapter; and third, titles such as "Rangwang," "Daozhi," "Shuojian," and "Yufu," in which two characters summarize the contents of the chapter. This further indicates that the entire *Zhuangzi* was not strung together by some later editor adding topic headings, but was gradually assigned topic headings as the chapters were written. Hence, our conclusions on the method of assigning topic headings remain tenable.

Next we will prove the date of "Tianxia" from its text. "Tianxia" opens by delineating its content: "There are many in the world who practice strategies or arts, and they all see their own methods as complete." The intention clearly is to comment on the circumstances of the world at that time, and not to pursue historical events. Later on, follows,

> The world is greatly disordered, worthies and sages lack clear vision, the Way and its Virtue are not one, so many in the world take only a single aspect of it, only that single aspect is examined and taken as good for itself . . . of the men of the world, each takes what he desires of it and makes it his own strategy. How sad. The hundred schools going off on their own tangents and not returning, never to reunite. (1069)

What is described here is certainly the Warring States period, with the swarming surge of the various philosophers and the hundred schools contending with one another. The last exclamation emphasizes that the hundred philosophic schools had just come forth. So the author had yet to see the Qin and the Han, when the whole world was unified and the world of learning had returned to a single thread.

In addition to this, "Tianxia" says the ancient arts of the Way "are scattered throughout the world and are implemented in the Central Kingdom. The scholars of the hundred schools often make reference to it or speak of it" (*baijia zhi xue shi huo cheng er dao zhi* 百家之學時或稱而道之). In other words they often (*shi* 時) speak about the ancient learning. In this context the character *shi* is an adverb, "often," modifying "speak," rather than a noun meaning "time" or "age." If this were someone from a later era recalling the scholars of the hundred schools, and *shi* were being used as a noun, then he would have said *Baijia zhi xue zhi shi* 百家之學之時. The character *zhi* 之 (of) in front of *shi* cannot be omitted. Similarly the characters *jin* 今 (now) in "Now only Mozi advocates no singing in life and no mourning for death" and in "until now it has not ended" and *jiang* 將 (will) in "This will in the future cause the Moists of later ages" show that "Tianxia" was written when the Moist school was not yet extinct. Hence, it is impossible that it was completed after the Qin or Han.

Concerning "Tiandi," "Tiandao," and "Tianyun," scholars have historically expressed many doubts. Yet according to our investigation, while the essays from these three chapters may be later than "Tianxia," they are still products of the pre-Qin.

In "Tiandi," there is a conversation between Yao and the border guard of the state of Hua. In it, Yao says "Many sons mean many fears. Riches mean many troubles. Long life means much shame" (420). This certainly reflects the boundless anxiety of the Warring States period, when sons killed their fathers and ministers murdered their lords. In addition, the "Changli" chapter in the *Lüshi chunqiu* quotes the parable from "Tiandi" concerning Bocheng Zigao's resignation as a feudal lord when Yao ruled the empire. This, too, proves that "Tiandi" was a product of the pre-Qin.

The date of "Tiandao" should be later than Mencius but earlier than the Qin. In it we find parables such as the following:

> Lao Dan said "May I ask about humanity and righteousness; are they part of human nature?" Confucius said, "Of course. If the gentleman is not humane, he is incomplete; if he is not righteous, he cannot live. Humanity and righteousness are the nature of the true man. Aside from these two, what else could human nature be?" (478)

Considering humanity and righteousness as the fonts of human nature is typical of Mencius' theory. This section of the essay is clearly influenced by Mencius. We also find in "Tiandao," "Now, as for universal love, isn't that impractical? By not being selfish one is then selfish" (479). This is an argument against the Moist tenets of universal love and mutual benefit and shows that when "Tiandao" was written the Moists were still influential. Hence, "Tiandao" cannot have been written after the Qin. And again, another passage in the chapter reads:

Quietude, emptiness, to be solitary and unmoving, these are the roots of the myriad things. . . . Retiring with these to live in leisure and roam among the rivers and seas, one will be served by the recluses of the mountains and forests. Advancing with them to conduct the events of the age, one will attain great works and bright fame and will unify the world. (457–58)

The author of the chapter repeatedly advocates the principles of "emptiness and non-action" and holds that "advancing with them" one can "conduct the events of the age" and then "unify the world." This shows that the Daoists of that time had yet to occupy the positions of rulers and the world had yet to be peacefully unified. Hence, "Tiandao" would not be a work from after the Qin.

"Tianyun" says,

And thus the ritual and regulations of the Three August Ones and the Five Emperors were not revered because of their similarity but because of their power to bring order. Hence the rituals and regulations of the Three August Ones and the Five Emperors may be compared to the cherry-apple, pear, orange, and citron. Their flavors are different but they all please the palate. Hence, ritual and regulations are things that change according to the times. Dress a monkey in the clothes of the Duke of Zhou, and he will not rest until he has torn them to shreds. A single glance shows the differences between past and present are the same as those between a monkey and the Duke of Zhou. (514)

Arguments for changing the laws to accord with the times are characteristic of Warring States thought and consistent with several sources from that time. In the *Hanfeizi*, "Wudu" says, "As the ages differ, so do their events. As events differ, then how they are put in order is changed," and "Do not practice the ways of antiquity nor follow its constant norm" (*H* 779, 778). In the *Lüshi chunqiu*, "Chajin" says, "When the ages change and the times move on, changing the regulations is fitting" (*L* 397). The question of whether one should follow the times and change regulations was decided following the unification of China by the First Emperor of the Qin. Hence, "Tianyun" would not be a work of the Qin or Han.

Concerning the chapter entitled "Keyi," Yao Nai once said, "This chapter belongs to the same category as Sima Tan's discourse on the essential points of the six schools; this is literature of the Han."[26] Many modern scholars also hold that this chapter is a work of the Qin or Han. However, "Keyi" discusses separately the Confucians, who "discuss humanity, righteousness, loyalty, and truthfulness, respect, temperance, and humility," and the Legalists, who discuss "great accomplishments, establishing great fame, defining ritual relations between lord and minister, and correcting the relations of superior and inferior." At the same time, its discussions extend to the "gentlemen of the mountains and ravines, who criticize this world," "the gentlemen of the rivers and seas, who avoid this world," and "the man who practices breathing exercises and nourishes his body." Essentially, this is a description of an era in which the hundred schools had yet to undergo unification. It is not at all similar to the conditions after the Qin, when one school alone was honored. The author of "Keyi" also describes one who

> does not constrain his will, yet he raises himself up; he has no benevolence or righteousness, yet he is cultivated; he is without accomplishments and fame, yet he brings good order; he is not near rivers and seas, yet he is leisurely; he does not do calisthenics, yet he lives a long life; he has forgotten everything, and yet possesses everything; he is at ease in the illimitable, and yet this host of good things follows him—this is the Way of Heaven and earth, the Virtue of the sage. (537)

He has criticism for each kind of person mentioned above, such as Confucians, Legalists, those who criticize the world, and those who avoid the world. In addition, he also raises his own tenet of being "at ease in the illimitable." This differs from Sima Tan's discourse on the essential points of the six schools in Han China, which is an objective and general summary of the Confucian, Moist, Daoist, and Legalist schools. In addition, "Keyi" contains expressions such as "revere the sovereign and strengthen the state" and "render meritorious service and annex other states." These patterns of speech are surely pre-Qin. After the Qin and Han, annexation and battles had ceased, and there would be no reason to write of "strengthening the state" or "annexing other states."

People have also raised doubts about "Zaiyou"; however, the chapter states,

> In the present day and age, those condemned to death are tethered back-to-back, those in cangues and stocks are fastened arm-in-arm, and those who are mutilated are never out of sight. And so come the Confucians and Moists, rolling up their sleeves as they walk amid the bound and manacled. (377)

The "present day and age" is clearly an era when Confucianism and Moism were prominent branches of learning. This is certainly not a post-Qin product.

We have demonstrated that it is possible that all of the essays of uncertain date in the Outer and Miscellaneous chapters of the *Zhuangzi* were written during the pre-Qin. What, then, is the basis for the Early Han theory?

Shortcomings of the Early Han Theory

The fundamental reason for holding that "Tianxia" and other chapters are products of the Han is the appearance in these chapters of such terms as "the six classics," "the twelve classics," "the Three August Ones and the Five Emperors" (*san huang wu di* 三皇五帝), and the "Uncrowned King" (*suwang* 素王).

Liu Jie has pointed out that the *Yi* (易 Book of Changes, also known as *Yijing* or *Zhouyi*) was not originally grouped with the classics and only gradually became the first of the six classics (*Liu jing*).[27] Based on this hint, our examination of the arguments concerning the six classics resulted in an evolutionary history.

Xunzi was the first to raise the concept of the "classic" (*jing* 經). In the chapter entitled "Quanxue," he asks, "Where does learning begin and where does it end? I say that as to the program, learning begins with recitation of the classics and ends with the reading of the ritual texts" (*X* 122). This is the beginning of calling Confucian texts "classics." After this statement, Xunzi continues to praise the *Li* (Ritual), *Yue* (Music), *Shi* (Poetry), *Shu* (History), and *Chunqiu* (Spring and Autumn) as classics. In the "Ruxiao" chapter, Xunzi states, "The *Shi* speaks of one's intentions, the *Shu* speaks of deeds, the *Li* speaks of conduct, the *Yue* speaks of harmony, and the *Chunqiu* speaks of intricacies." At this time, the *Yi* had yet to enter the canon.

Early Han texts that mention the six classics include Jia Yi's *Xinshu* and *Huainanzi*. In the *Xinshu*, the order of the six classics is *Shi, Shu, Yi, Chunqiu, Li,* and *Yue*.[28] In the *Huainanzi*, "Taizu" chapter, there are two forms of arrangement. The first is *Shi, Shu, Yi, Li, Yue, Chunqiu*. The other is *Yi, Yue, Shi, Shu, Li, Chunqiu*.[29] Here, the *Yi* has jumped into the first position. The *Yi* also appears first in Sima Qian's preface to *Shiji*, where the order is *Yi, Li, Shu, Shi, Yue, Chunqiu*. At this time it had still not been settled that the *Yi* would take the first position among the six classics. Liu Jie holds that it was the *Hanshu*, "Yiwenzhi," that finally established the position of the *Yi* as first among the six classics. Hence, the "progressive" arrangement of *Yi, Shu, Shi, Li, Yue, Chunqiu* was settled. If the *Yi* were placed in the third position during the opening years of the Han and then very quickly moved into the first position, at what point had the *Yi* just entered the corpus in the last position?

Worth noting is that Lu Jia's *Xinyu* already has a description of the *five* classics: "Checking and correcting the five classics from beginning to end."[30] According to Gu Jiegang's study, the idea of five classics appeared after the six classics, as a result of the Han recognizing that the *Yue* had scores but no text and deleting it from the list.[31] Hence, the *Yi* must have become part of the six classics prior to Lu Jia's *Xinyu*. The *Xinyu* was written when Liu Bang had not been on the throne for long, and it is impossible that the Qin dynasty produced and circulated the term "six classics." The term must have been produced in pre-Qin classical texts.

Now let us look at two lists of the six classics in the *Zhuangzi*. In "Tianyun," we find, "Confucius said to Lao Dan, 'I have been studying the six classics—the *Shi, Shu, Li, Yue, Yi,* and *Chunqiu*—for what I would call a long time . . .'" (531). "Tianxia" says, "Use the *Shi* to describe intention, use the *Shu* to describe deeds, use *Li* to describe behavior, use *Yue* to describe harmony, use the *Yi* to describe brilliance, and use the *Chunqiu* to describe distinctions" (1067). In both places, the *Yi* appears as the last single-character classic. It is very possible that this is the earliest reference to the *Yi* as one of the classics. Appending the *Yi* after the paired-character *Chunqiu* would break the rhythm of the language; hence, at the outset, the *Yi* was placed before the *Chunqiu*. It is possible that this is why texts from the early years of the Han contain no list of the six classics in which the *Yi* is at the end. It follows from this that the six classics theory may well have arisen in the pre-Qin period. The references in the *Zhuangzi* to the six classics are admittedly early but do not in themselves justify pushing the date of the text up into the early Han.

Strangely, in "Tiandao" the term "twelve classics" appears (477). Lu Deming offered three explanations of this, but none is satisfactory. Recently, it has been suggested that "twelve" is a corruption of the character for "six," which was split into two characters and then, through interpolations, became twelve.[32] This is very reasonable. In fact, the canon of twelve classics was formed only in the middle of the Tang dynasty, and the Han dynasty had no such concept. Since not even pushing the date of "Tiandao" to the Han dynasty can explain the source of the phrase "twelve classics," the phrase cannot be used in dating the chapter.

Nor are allusions to the "Three August Ones" *(san huang* 三皇*)* or the "Five Emperors" *(wu di* 五帝*)* unique to the Han. *Xunzi*, "Dalüe," says, "Remonstrations do not reach to the Five Emperors, and vows and pledges do not reach to the Three Kings" (*X* 293). *Hanfeizi,* "Wudu," says, "He who would surpass the Five Emperors of antiquity and rival the Three Kings must proceed by this method" (*H* 783). The Three August Ones and Five Emperors are referred to together in the *Lüshi chunqiu*. For example, the "Guigong" chapter says, "The myriad things are all benefited by them and receive their favors, and yet none know their beginning; this is the Virtue of the Three August Ones and the Five Emperors" (*L* 248). In the chapter entitled "Yongzhong" we find, "Now if we seek it in the masses, this is why the Three August Ones and Five Emperors have established a reputation for great achievements" (*L* 307). In "Xiaoxing" it says, "Now filial piety is the fundamental task of the Three August Ones and the Five Emperors and the regulations of all deeds" (*L* 371). In his *Shuowen Jiangyi,* Wang Guowei notes, "the appellation 'Three August Ones and Five Emperors' is somewhat late, an idea that arose sometime during the Warring States period."[33] This is completely accurate. Even though Luo

Genze admits this point, he goes on to say, "Applying the term 'August Ones' (*huang* 皇) to heads of state and separating by politics August Ones, emperors (*di* 帝), hegemons (*ba* 霸), and kings (*wang* 王) is something that was popular in the Western Han."[34]

This explanation is unclear at best. Luo selected several examples from Han dynasty books of charms and omens appended to the classics. Only a few among them discuss the Three August Ones and Five Emperors. For instance, the "Yuanshen qi" appendix to the *Xiaojing* says, "The Three August Ones are without pattern, the Five Emperors drew the forms (of the hexagrams), and the Three Kings used corporeal punishment." In the "Gouming jue" appendix to the *Xiaojing* it says, "The Three August Ones would stride pace by pace, the Five Emperors hastened, the Three Kings were relaxed, while the Five Hegemons were alarmed." It also says "The Three August Ones spoke and the people did not disobey. The Five Emperors drew the patterns of the hexagrams, and deeds accorded with their patterns. The Three Kings practiced corporeal punishments and calculations gradually increased. Complying to the times, the shrewd and false increased."[35] If this is typical of "separating by politics August Ones, emperors, hegemons, and kings," then what is said in "Tianyun" is clearly different. Below are all the sentences in "Tianyun" that make reference to the Three August Ones and Five Emperors.

> 1) Now the Three Kings and the Five Emperors governed the empire differently, but the reputations of their lineages are one. (526)

> 2) Oh young one, come closer and I will tell you how the Three August Ones and Five Emperors ruled the empire. (527)

> 3) When the Three August Ones and Five Emperors ruled the empire, they called it ruling, but it was in fact plunging the world into terrible disorder. (527)

> 4) And thus, the rituals and regulations of the Three August Ones and Five Emperors were revered not because of their similarity but because of their power to bring order. Hence, the rituals and regulations of the Three August Ones and Five Emperors are compared to the cherry-apple, pear, orange, and citron. (514)

What similarity is there between these statements and those from the appended texts on omens? Can these be considered "separating by politics August Ones, emperors, hegemons, and kings"? And if they can be considered as such, then what do we do with the *Lüshi chunqiu,* "Xianji" chapter, where "The Five Emperors placed the Way first and Virtue came after. The Three Kings placed teaching first and punishments came after." Is this not closer to the texts quoted by Luo Genze, an even clearer example of separating by politics August Ones, emperors, hegemons, and kings?

Of "Tianyun," Luo Genze asserts: "The chapter not only mentions the Three August Ones and the Five Emperors, it also mentions the government of the Three August Ones and Five Emperors, which is also proof that it was written in the Western Han."[36] These statements seem careless. If the pre-Qin were able to speak of the Three August Ones and Five Emperors, why would they be unable to speak of their government? Further, "Tianyun" does not mention "the governing of the Three August Ones and Five Emperors," it merely mentions that they "ruled the empire." One need only glance at the examples listed above to understand this point.

The phrase *suwang* 素王, "the Uncrowned King," is also an important element in the early Han theory. Yao Nai says "The 'Uncrowned King' is a Han phrase."[37] Zhang Hengshou says,

> Examining the phrase "Uncrowned King," we find it is a term of praise used in the Gongyang commentary on the *Chunqiu* and contains the idea that Confucius should be an emperor. . . . No matter what it means, all of our considerations demonstrate that this appellation did not appear until the early Han.[38]

What is emphasized here is that since "Tiandao" mentions the Uncrowned King, it must have been written in the Han. In fact, "Uncrowned King" in "Tiandao" is a general term. The Way of the Uncrowned King is "empty, still, quiescent, silent, and without action" and has no relation to Confucius. The *Shiji,* "Yinbenji," records of Yi Yin that "only after refusing five times did he consent to go to submit to Tang, and talk about the matter of the Uncrowned King and Nine Lords" (*S* 94). The source of these terms has never been clear. The excavation of the silk books at the Mawangdui Han tomb has proven there were pre-Qin writings attributed to

Yi Yin which discussed the meaning of the "Nine Lords." Hence, what Sima Qian recorded really was based in fact, and the phrase "Uncrowned King" was not joined to Yi Yin's name on a whim. And it is possible that there were pre-Qin texts attributed to Yi Yin that used the phrase "Uncrowned King." The *Hanshu,* "Yiwen zhi," records that among the texts of the Daoists, there was a *Yi Yin* in 50 chapters. And in the section on "Xiaoshuojia," there was *Yi Yin shuo* in 27 chapters. In addition to this, in *Heguanzi,* the "Wang Fu" chapter contains the phrase the "Uncrowned August One": "Therefore, his grandeur is established and is not reckless. It circulates afar and is not dissipated. This is the method of the Uncrowned August One, the Internal Emperor."[39] The ideas of the Uncrowned August One and the Uncrowned King are similar. The *Heguanzi* "Wang Fu" chapter should be a product of the pre-Qin.[40] The presence of the phrase "Uncrowned August One" shows that the use of such terms as the "Uncrowned King" did not originate in the Confucians' transmitted appellations for Confucius. The phrase "Uncrowned King" also appears in the early Han text *Huainanzi,* in the "Zhushu" chapter: "Those who were not known for their bravery and strength and concentrated their activities to teaching the Way to become an Uncrowned King were rare indeed."[41] Dong Zhongshu's *Tianren sance* began canonizing Confucius as an Uncrowned King: "Confucius wrote the *Chunqiu* first to correct the kings and to order the myriad deeds and to affect the patterns of an Uncrowned King therein."[42] According to the *Hanshu,* "Wudi ji," *Tianren sance* was written after the first year of the Yuanguang reign period (134 B.C.). Hence, it was later than the *Huainanzi,* which was presented to the emperor Wu in 139 B.C.

Summarizing what we have discussed above, the phrase "Uncrowned King" originally was used by pre-Qin Daoists and had no connection to Confucius. Praise of Confucius as an Uncrowned King occurred after the rise of the Han Confucians. Hence, when "Tiandao" speaks of the "Uncrowned King," the term does not refer to Confucius and is indeed a special feature of pre-Qin Daoism.

In fact, many of the reasons given for considering "Tianxia," "Tiandao," and "Tianyun" as products of the Han are doubtful conjecture or speculation that do not stand up under careful scrutiny. For example, Yao

Nai says that the section relating how "Confucius went to deposit books with the royal house of Zhou" in "Tiandao" is a Han dynasty story. "Depositing books indicates that he was a sage since he knew the Qin would burn books and prepared for it by preserving them in advance."[43] In fact, this section is simply a parable. It serves as a vehicle for Lao Dan's critical remarks concerning Confucius and simply gives no hint at all about Confucius' reasons for depositing books. Moreover, book burning was not confined to that single event during the Qin. The *Hanfeizi*, "He shi," records,

> Lord Shang taught Duke Xiao of Qin how to organize the people into groups of five and ten families that would spy on each other and be corporately responsible for crimes committed by their members; he advised him to burn the *Shi* and *Shu* and elucidate the laws and regulations, to reject the private requests of powerful families and concentrate upon completing public works. (*H* 636)

This proves that the burning the *Shi* and *Shu* also occurred prior to the Qin. It cannot be proven that "Tiandao" is a product of the Han on the basis of this story about Confucius depositing books.

Another example comes from Lin Xiyi, who cites the use, in "Daozhi" of the term *zaixiang* (prime minister): "During the Warring States period there were no officials called *zaixiang*. It is quite clear this is something privately composed by someone at a later date."[44] However, in the *Hanfeizi*, "Xianxue," there appears: "In the bureaucracy of an enlightened ruler, the prime minister *[zaixiang]* has come up from the post of district manager, and the renowned generals have risen from the ranks" (*H* 786). Hence, Lin Xiyi's basis for discussion is insubstantial.

There are quite a few similar examples of groundless speculation that does not bear careful examination. For example, Yao Nai says that *shangxian* (super immortals) is a phrase which was current after the Qin;[45] Wu Rulun says "*Baiyun* [white clouds] and *dixiang* [the native place of an emperor] also are not well turned phrases; the Zhou and Qin did not use them";[46] and so forth. Mere speculation cannot replace evidential research; and doubt is not equivalent to fact. Those who propound the idea that the *Zhuangzi*'s Outer and Miscellaneous chapters are products of the Qin and Han in fact have no compelling proof. When the date of these chapters is viewed in the light of the quotations from them in *Hanfeizi, Lüshi chunqiu,* and Jia Yi's rhyme-prose and in the light of the historical background reflected in them our observations all confirm that the Outer and Miscellaneous chapters were written no later than the last years of the Warring States period. Generally speaking, the Inner, Outer, and Miscellaneous chapters of the *Zhuangzi* could all have absorbed several decades of phrases; however, this "corruption" was not that serious. The *Zhuangzi* is still a relatively reliable pre-Qin text.

3

Classification of the Outer and Miscellaneous Chapters

History and Present State of the Problem

In the preceding chapter we examined the question of the dates of the Outer and Miscellaneous chapters of the *Zhuangzi*. However, merely examining their dates is insufficient. Because the Outer and Miscellaneous chapters did not derive from the hand of a single author, the differences among their points of view require careful examination. In their attitude toward the virtues *ren* 仁 (benevolence) and *yi* 義 (righteousness) for example, some passages heatedly attack them, some absorb and amalgamate them, others view them lightly or disparage them. Without analyzing these varying points of view, one cannot clearly perceive the thought of these later followers of Zhuangzi or depict its evolution. At the same time, it would be impossible to accurately select reference material for the study of Zhuangzi's thought. Hence, we must proceed with an orderly classification of the Outer and Miscellaneous chapters.

During the Ming and Qing dynasties, some people made classificatory schema of these chapters. However, their classifications were modelled upon a Confucian commentary explaining a classical text. Taking the seven Inner chapters as the classical text, the Outer and Miscellaneous chapters became the explanatory commentary. Occasionally, chapters or parts of chapters from the Outer and Miscellaneous sections were separated out and appended to the seven Inner chapters. For example, the *Nanhua zhenjing benyi,* by the Ming dynasty author Chen Zhi'an (c. 1632) supposes "Dasheng" explains "Xiaoyaoyou"; "Yuyan" explains "Qiwulun"; "Waiwu" explains "Yangshengzhu"; etc.[1] In his *Nanhua jing zhuanshi,* the Qing dynasty scholar Zhou Jinran (c. 1722) used "Qiushui," "Mati," and "Shanmu" to explain "Xiaoyaoyou" and "Xuwugui," "Zeyang" and "Waiwu" to explain "Qiwulun," etc.[2] This method is not without value; however, viewing it from a larger perspective, it is completely forced and is not sufficiently instructive.

Several modern scholars have also proceeded with classification of the Outer and Miscellaneous chapters of the *Zhuangzi.* For example, Ye Guoqing's *Zhuangzi yanjiu* takes the five chapters "Pianmu," "Mati," "Quqie," "Keyi," and "Shanxing" as one group and holds that they are works from between the Qin and Han. He takes the four chapters "Zaiyou," "Tiandi," "Tiandao," and "Tianyun" as one group and holds that they are works of the Han dynasty.[3] Ye Guoqing's classification is relatively early and his examination is somewhat simple. Luo Genze's examination is rather detailed. In his "Zhuangzi waizapian tanyuan," he takes "Pianmu," "Mati," "Quqie," and "Zaiyou" as one group and holds that they are the work of a radical Daoist at the end of the Warring States period. He takes "Qiushui," "Dasheng," "Shanmu," "Tianzifang," and "Yuyan" as a group and holds that they are the work of the Zhuangzi school. He also takes "Zhile," "Zhibeiyou," and "Gengsangchu" as a group and holds that this group is the work of the Laozi school.[4] Luo's influence in the field of Zhuangzi research is quite extensive. In addition, the Japanese scholar Takeuchi Yoshio has also made a classification of the Outer and Miscellaneous chapters. He holds that the seven chapters "Zhile," "Dasheng," "Shanmu," "Tianzifang," "Zhibeiyou," "Lieyukou," and "Yuyan" form a group and are the work of Zhuangzi's students. He takes the four chapters

"Gengsangchu," "Xuwugui," "Zeyang," and "Waiwu" as forming a group that is the product of writers somewhat later than Zhuangzi. This classification has also had some influence.[5]

Since 1949, Guan Feng has worked on a classification of the Outer and Miscellaneous chapters. In his "Zhuangzi waizapian chutan," he took "Pianmu," "Mati," "Quqie," and "Zaiyou" as one group and labeled them as the work of the radical later followers of the *Laozi*. He perceives "Tiandi," "Tiandao," and "Tianyun" as another group and holds that they are the work of the later followers of Song Xing and Yin Wen. He takes "Qiushui," "Zhile," "Dasheng," "Shanmu," "Tianzifang," "Zhibeiyou," and "Gengsangchu" as a group and holds they are somewhat complete compositions of the later followers of Zhuangzi.[6] Guan Feng selected several points of view from Luo Genze; however, his attitude is somewhat dogmatic. Zhang Hengshou's examination of the *Zhuangzi* in his *Zhuangzi xintan* is the most detailed. He takes "Pianmu," "Mati," "Quqie," and the first two essays of "Zaiyou" as the work of the radical element of the Daoist school prior to Qin unification. He takes "Tiandi," "Tiandao," "Tianyun," "Keyi," "Shanxing," and other chapters as the work of the "rightist school." He takes the six chapters "Qiushui," "Zhile," "Dasheng," "Shanmu," "Tianzifang," and "Zhibeiyou" as the work of the direct lineal branch of Zhuangzi. He takes "Gengsangchu," "Xuwugui," "Zeyang," "Waiwu," "Yuyan," and "Lieyukou" as products of the pre-Qin period. He also takes "Rangwang," "Daozhi," and "Yufu" as having some relations to Daoist thought. And he holds that "Tianxia" is the work of scholars who lay between Confucianism and Daoism.[7] Zhang Hengshou's classifications are the results of important research on the Outer and Miscellaneous chapters in the 1980s.

Since several classifications have been done by previous scholars, why must we undertake it anew? What differences are there between the classification that follows and earlier ones? First, none of the studies mentioned above were strictly classificatory. Their classifications were part of an effort to determine when the chapters were written. Since the basis for a study of dates differs from the basis for a classification of thought, they should be conducted separately. We have already examined the dates of the Outer and Miscellaneous chapters in the essay above. In this essay then, we can focus on conducting the work of classification. Second, the classifications of the authors above lack a clearly unifying standard. It seems that sometimes classification is based on the date of the work, sometimes on the thought content or the literary style. We will attempt to use the point of view of thought, and especially its relationship to the Inner chapters, as the unifying standard. Third, these differences of both intent and method have caused differences in the results of classification. I suspect this incoherent approach is the reason why the majority of classifications have been comparatively fragmented. For example, Luo Genze separated the chapters into twelve groups; Guan Feng divided them into eight. We will try to describe the sequence of the transformation of thought among Zhuangzi's followers and separate the Outer and Miscellaneous chapters into three groups.

There are essentially two different attitudes toward the Outer and Miscellaneous chapters of the *Zhuangzi*. The first emphasizes their "disorder" and "miscellaneousness" and fails to take into account a certain sort of consistency among them. It separates them as the work of the schools of Laozi, Song Xing and Yin Wen, Yang Zhu, the Recluses, the Immortals and all the others. The other view does not recognize dissimilar thoughts and points of view in the Outer and Miscellaneous chapters and uncritically uses material from them all to study Zhuangzi's thought. In sum, the former perceives only miscellaneousness and disorder and does not see the consistency among the chapters. The latter perceives their consistency and fails to see their miscellaneousness and disorder. We, however, advocate that we should both perceive the miscellaneousness of these chapters and also take note of their unity. (When we say Outer and Miscellaneous chapters, generally, we are excluding "Shuojian.") Fundamentally, they are the work of Zhuangzi's later followers, although their thought is quite divergent on certain topics.

For the most part, previous classificatory methods work from samples of the text, which they use to establish the differences or similarities between one chapter and another. Using this methodology, different people can take different examples and obtain different conclusions concerning the same question. Even though some conclusions are reasonably reliable, they may still be perceived as personal and subjective views. To avoid circumstances such as these we shall select two points concerning our method of argumentation for general examination in this chapter. First, we will select the original texts that for the most part clearly display similarity and difference and make an item-by-item comparison. If at all possible, we will rely upon the original texts themselves to explain our conclusions and will not rely on our explanation of texts. Second, we will attempt to list complete original text materials that clearly reveal their similarity and difference. Moreover, we will proceed with statistical comparisons of examples of these original texts. Hence, we will explain the mutual relations and differences among the various kinds of essays in the Outer and Miscellaneous chapters and even between the Inner chapters and the various essays in the Outer and Miscellaneous chapters. This method still cannot attain the level of natural science's statistical analysis. However, it can improve the objectivity of our argumentation and prevent complete bias. This form of argumentation can be called "complete comparison." Of course, this is essentially a method of argumentation. It concerns fundamental principles governing the classification of the Outer and Miscellaneous chapters; still, it reveals relations of similarity and difference in the realm of thought. For convenience of explication, we will first present the results of our classification in table 3.1, then proceed, step-by-step, to discuss them.

The salient feature of the first group of essays in the table is that they explain or develop thought from the Inner chapters and do not raise important points of their own or points clearly different from those of the Inner chapters. In the wrangling of the hundred schools, these writings essentially fought to transcend the conflicts between Confucians and Moists.

The important characteristic of the second group of essays is that they do not discriminate among the lessons of the hundred schools. Instead, they assimilate and accommodate several Confucian and Legalist points of view. They emphasize the arts of the ruler occupying the throne and expound the principle that the lord should be inactive while his ministers are active.

The distinctive characteristic of the third group of essays is that they directly assail reality; they seek the release of the nature of man. They

Table 3.1. Classification of the Outer and Miscellaneous Chapters

Group I	Relation to Inner Chapters
Outer Chapters	Similarities greater than differences
17 "Qiushui"	(Transcend Confucianism and Moism)
18 "Zhile"	
19 "Dasheng"	
20 "Shanmu"	
21 "Tianzifang"	
22 "Zhibeiyou"	
Miscellaneous Chapters	
23 "Gengsangchu"	
24 "Xuwugui"	
25 "Zeyang"	
26 "Waiwu"	
27 "Yuyan"	
32 "Lieyukou"	

Group II	Relation to Inner Chapters
Outer Chapters	Balance of similarities and differences
11B "Zaiyou B"*	(Fusion of Confucianism and Legalism)
12 "Tiandi"	
13 "Tiandao"	
14 "Tianyun"	
15 "Keyi"	
16 "Shanxing"	
33 "Tianxia"	

Group III	Relation to Inner Chapters
Outer Chapters	Differences greater than similarities
8 "Pianmu"	(Attack Yang Zhu and Mozi)
9 "Mati"	
10 "Quqie"	
11A "Zaiyou A"*	
Miscellaneous Chapters	
28 "Rangwang"	
29 "Daozhi"	
31 "Yufu"	

* "Zaiyou A" refers to the first section of the chapter, "Zaiyou B" to the remaining sections. See page 122.

imagine that in the society of highest virtue, there is no distinction of ruler and subjects, and no class pressure.

Below, we will compare and quantify those clearly consistent materials regarding thought and language to examine and prove the results of classification in the chart above.

Group I: Explaining and Expanding upon the Inner Chapters

The first group includes six of the Outer chapters: chapters 17–22, namely "Qiushui," "Zhile," "Dasheng," "Shanmu," "Tianzifang," and "Zhibeiyou" and six of the Miscellaneous chapters: chapters 23–28, 32, namely "Gengsangchu," "Xuwugui," "Zeyang," "Waiwu," "Yuyan," and "Lieyukou." The essays in these twelve chapters are mutually consistent, and there are many places where they are related. Moreover, each chapter has a fairly direct relation with the Inner chapters. We will first examine the relationships within this group, then examine the relationships between this group and the Inner chapters. Then, we will examine the differences between this group and the Inner chapters and the question of how they received their names.

In the first group there are about 29 places in the original text where the forms of linguistic expression and intellectual points of view are consistent. These are listed below.

1) In "Zhile" we find the story, "Once a sea bird stopped in the suburbs of Lu" (621). This is also seen in "Dasheng," where "Once a bird stopped in the suburbs of Lu" (665).

2) In "Zhile" we find several notable ideas expressed in a story concerning Zhuangzi's wife:

> Amid the jumble and confusion, there was a change and she had breath (*qi* 氣). With another change of breath, she had a body. With another change of her body, she had life. (615)

This is similar in idea to a passage in "Zhibeiyou" where it says,

> Man's life is the accumulation of breath (*qi*). When it accumulates, there is life; when it disperses, there is death. (733)

3) In "Zhile" we find that "Life and death are day and night" (616). This is the same as a passage in "Tianzifang," where "Life and death, beginning and end will be day and night" (714).

4) In "Dasheng" the form of expression "The arrival of life cannot be postponed; its departure cannot be stopped" (630) is similar to a passage from "Tianzifang." There we find, "I take its arrival as unavoidable, its departure as inevitable" (726). This is also similar to a passage in "Zhibeiyou," where we find, "We are unable to prevent the arrival of happiness or sadness, nor can we prevent their going" (765).[8]

5) In "Dasheng" a passage describing how "life and death, alarm and terror do not enter a drunken man's breast" (636) is roughly the same as a passage in "Tianzifang," where it states, "Joy, anger, grief, and happiness will not enter your breast" (714).[9]

6) In "Dasheng" we find the passage

> Now you display your wisdom to confound the ignorant, cultivate your conduct to dazzle the contemptible, gleaming as if you were the traveling companion of the sun and moon. (664)

The same passage is found in "Shanmu":

> Your intent is to display your wisdom to confound the ignorant, cultivate your conduct to dazzle the contemptible, gleaming as if you were the traveling companion of the sun and moon. That's why you can't escape. (680)

7) According to Zhang Hengshou, in "Shanmu" the interrogative phrasing in the passage "Treat things as things and do not let them treat you as a thing. So, how could you ever get into trouble?" (668) is similar to a passage in "Zhibeiyou": "Between Heaven and earth all in movement is *qi* [material and life force]. So how could you ever gain possession of them?" (739).

8) In "Zhibeiyou" we find,

> Though eighty years old, the Grand Marshal's buckle-maker had lost none of his proficiency. The Grand Marshal said, "What art is this! Is

there a special way to it?" The reply was "Your servant has something he preserves." (760)

In "Dasheng" we find,

> When Confucius was traveling to Chu, he passed through a forest where he saw a hunchback catching cicadas with a sticky pole as easily as picking them up with his hand. Confucius said, "What art is this! Is there a special way to it?" The reply was, "I possess the Way." (639)

9) In "Qiushui" we find the story of a sacred tortoise that would have preferred to remain alive, dragging its tail in the mud, to being sacrificed and worshipped on an altar (604). The idea is similar to another story found in "Dasheng," where the Invocator of the Ancestors plans a sacrifice and looks at his plans for fattened sacrifices from the point of view of the pigs; "It would be better to eat chaff and bran and remain in the pen" (648). Moreover, this is similar to a parable in "Lieyukou," where a sacrificial ox might wish he were a lonely calf once again (1062).

10) In "Zeyang" we find the phrasing,

> You may cut and analyze until you have reduced it to something so fine that it is immeasurable or is so large it cannot be taken in. (916)

This is similar to a passage in "Qiushui":

> The finest thing has no form and the largest thing cannot be encircled. (572)

11) The passage in "Lieyukou,"

> A man such as this will become lost and confused in time and space; his body entangled, he will never know the Great Beginning (1047),

is similar to a passage in "Zhibeiyou" that states,

> Those such as this will never perceive the universe beyond them or understand the Great Beginning that is within them. (758)

12) In "Zeyang" we find,

> "Qu Boyu has gone on for sixty years and has changed sixty times. . . . Who can say whether what he now calls right is not what he called

wrong for the past fifty-nine years. . . . Leave it alone! Leave it alone! There is no place you can escape it." (905)

A nearly identical passage concerning Confucius is found in "Yuyan":

"Confucius has gone on for sixty years and has changed sixty times. . . . So who is to say whether what he now calls right is not what he called wrong for the past fifty-nine years. . . . 'Leave it alone! Leave it alone! I will never attain to that.'" (952)

13) In "Lieyukou" we find, "Lieyukou was going to Qi . . . by chance he met Bohun Wuren" (1036). The names of these two men also appear in "Tianzifang," where Lieyukou was demonstrating his archery to Bohun Wuren (724).

14) In "Xuwugui" we find, "Ziqi of South Wall sat leaning on an arm rest gazing up at the heavens and sighing. Yan Chengzi entered to see him" (848). These two names also appear in "Yuyan": "Yan Chengzi said to Ziqi of the East Wall. . . ." (956).

15) In "Gengsangchu" the phrasing "Knowledge that rests in what it cannot know is finest" (792) is similar to what is found in "Xuwugui": "Words that rest where knowledge does not know are finest" (852).

16 "Heaven the Leveller" is found in "Gengsangchu": "If you do not attain this goal, Heaven the Leveller will destroy you" (792). It also appears in "Yuyan,"

Beginning and end are part of a single ring; no one understands this principle. This is called Heaven the Leveller, which is the same as the Heavenly Balance. (950)

17) In "Lieyukou" we find,

He who masters life's true form is a giant; he who masters knowledge is petty. He who masters the Great Fate follows it; he who masters the little fates accepts them. (1059)

This is roughly similar to a passage in "Dasheng":

He who masters life's true nature does not labor over what life cannot do. He who masters fate's true form does not labor over what cannot be avoided in fate. (630)

18) In "Lieyukou" we find,

> When the petty man encounters external punishments, metal and wood crush him; when he encounters internal punishment, the *yin* and *yang* devour him. (1053)

This is similar to a passage in "Dasheng," where we find,

> Shan Bao looks after what is inside him, while a tiger devours what is outside, and Zhang Yi looks after what is outside, while sickness attacks his insides. (646)

19) A passage in "Gengsangchu" states, "Being cannot create being out of being; it must come from non-being" (800). There is a similarity in ideas between this and a passage in "Zhibeiyou": "That which treats things as things is not a thing. Things that come forth cannot but precede other things" (763).

20) In "Zeyang" there is a story concerning the creatures that live on the body of the snail, "On its left horn is the kingdom of the Chu clan; on its right horn is the kingdom of the Man clan" (891). This resembles a story in "Xuwugui," where lice on a pig "pick out places among the bristles to be their sprawling mansions and vast park" (863). This illustration of the relativity of perspective through stories concerning small creatures is similar to a parable in "Qiushui" where a frog in the well comes out and hops around the railing (598).

21) In "Xuwugui" we find,

> The foot strikes a very small area on the ground; though the area is small, the foot can rely on the support of the untrod ground around it; only then can the foot go forward. (871)

The idea of this passage is similar to another in "Waiwu":

> To be sure, heaven and earth are vast, though a man uses only the area he puts his feet on. But, if you dug away from around his feet until you reached the Yellow Springs, would he still be able to make use of it? (936)

22) In "Xuwugui" we find,

Man's knowledge is insignificant. Though insignificant, only after relying on what it does not know can it know what is meant by Heaven. (871)

This is similar to a passage in "Zeyang," which states,

Men all pay homage to what knowledge knows, but no one knows enough to rely upon what knowledge does not know and so arrive at knowledge. Can we call this anything but great perplexity? (905)

23) In "Zhile" we find, "Lack-limb Shu and Hobble Shu were sight-seeing at Dark Lord Hills" (615). The name "Lack-limb" is similar to a passage in "Lieyukou," where we find, "Zhu Pingman studied the art of butchering dragons under Lack-limb Yi" (1046).

24) In "Yuyan" we find, "If darkness and light move, then I move with them" (960). The special phrase *qiang yang* 強陽 (move, movement) also appears in "Zhibeiyou": "Between Heaven and earth all in movement is *qi*" (739).

25) In "Shanmu" we find, "If a man could empty himself to wander through the world, then who could do him harm?" (675). This is similar to a passage in "Lieyukou," where a man is empty and idly wanders about (1040). The phrase wandering through the world *(youshi)* is also found in "Waiwu": "Only the Perfect Man can wander through the world without taking sides" (938).

26) In "Dasheng" the line "wander to the end and beginning of the myriad things" (634) resembles "drifting and wandering with the ancestor of the myriad things" in "Shanmu" (668) and "letting my mind wander in the beginning of things" from "Tianzifang" (712).

27) The phrase "to wander in the field of nobody" from "Shanmu" (671) shares the same idea as the phrase "to wander in the palace of nothing at all" from "Zhibeiyou" (752).

28) According to Zhang Hengshou, the sentence "The Perfect Man wants no fame; why do you delight in it so?" from "Shanmu" (680) is similar to a sentence in "Qiushui," where we find, "The Man of the Way enjoys no fame; the highest virtue acquires no gain" (574).

29) The phrase "He who changes along with things is identical with him who does not change" in "Zhibeiyou" (765) is the same as a passage from "Zeyang," where we find, "And because he changed daily with things, he was one with the man who never changes" (885).

The material above demonstrates that there are very close relations between the essays in the twelve Group I chapters. These relations are diagrammed in figure 3.1. The dotted lines represent relations between essays. The numbers on the dotted lines correspond to the list above. By following the numbers you can trace the evidentiary basis of each line. The diagram explains in a more directly perceivable manner that there is a solid basis for holding that these twelve chapters form a group.

Now we will examine the relations between this group and the Inner chapters. Arranged below are lists of material from each of the Group I chapters that corresponds with material from the Inner chapters.

"Qiushui" and the Inner Chapters

1) In "Qiushui" it is said that

One is not pleased having acquired something nor worried if it is lost. . . . Great Wisdom does not look on life with great joy nor look on death with great sorrow. (568)

The idea is similar to "Dazongshi," where we find,

The true man of ancient times did not know to love life and did not know to hate death. He emerged without delight and returned without a fuss. (229)

2) In "Qiushui" it says, "When the myriad things are one and equal, then where is short and long?" (584). A similar idea is found in "Qiwulun": "Heaven and earth are a single attribute; the myriad things are a single horse" (66).

3) "Qiushui" says,

A summer insect can't discuss ice, he's limited to a single season. (563)
The same idea is found in "Xiaoyaoyou":

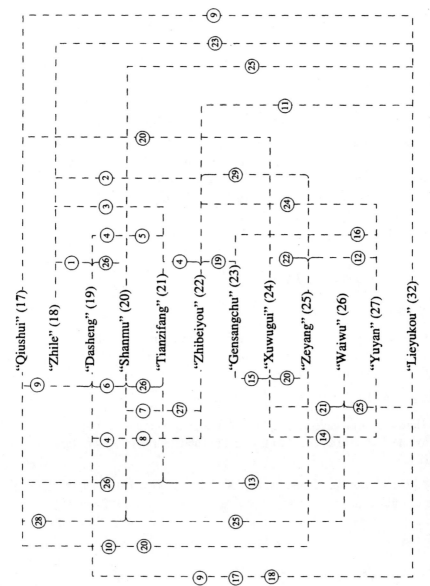

Figure 3.1. Connections among the Group I Chapters in Terms of Syntactic Similarities

How do I know this is so? The morning mushroom is ignorant of dusk and dawn; the summer cicada knows nothing of a year. (11)

4) "Qiushui" relates:

Yet man takes the smallest things and tries to exhaust the largest. Hence he is muddled and confused and you can never get anywhere. (568)

This is similar to a passage in "Yangshengzhu," which reads,

Your life has a limit but knowledge has none. Using what is limited to pursue what is limitless is dangerous. (115)

5) In "Qiushui" we find,

From the point of view of the Way, things are not noble or base. From the point of view of things, each regards itself as noble and others as base. (577)

A similar idea is found in "Dechongfu," where we read,

Seen from the point of view of their differences, then the closeness between liver and gall bladder is like the distance from the state of Chu to the state of Yue. But from the point of view of their sameness, the myriad things are all one. (190)

6) In "Qiushui," the phrasing "He begins in Dark Obscurity and returns to the Great Thoroughfare" (601) is also found in "Dazongshi":

I destroy my limbs and body, dispense with perception and intellect, cast away form, throw off understanding, and become identical with the Great Thoroughfare. (284)

7) In "Qiushui" we find,

Horses and oxen have four feet. This is what is meant by the Heavenly. Draping a halter on a horse's head, piercing an ox's nose, this is what is meant by the human. (590)

The ideas of the Heavenly and human are similar to a passage in "Yangshengzhu":

What is heavenly is not human. What springs forth from Heaven is unique. By this we know it is from Heaven and is not human. (124)

8) "Qiushui" says,

> If we regard a thing as right because there is a certain right to it, then nothing among the myriad things is not right. If we regard a thing as wrong because there is a certain wrong to it, then nothing among the myriad things is not wrong. (578)

This is similar to a passage in "Qiwulun," where we find,

> What makes things so? Making them so makes them so. What makes them not so? Making them not so makes them not so. (69)

9) "Qiushui" describes a man of perfect virtue as one whom "fire cannot burn, water cannot drown" (588). The same idea is found in a description of the True Man in "Dazongshi."

> A man like this could climb the high places and not be frightened, could enter water and not get wet, could enter fire and not get burned. (226)

In "Xiaoyaoyou" we find,

> If a great flood reached to the heavens he would not drown. If a great drought scorched the land and mountains, melting stone and metal, he would not become hot. (30)

This is also similar to "Qiwulun," where we find,

> The perfect man is spirit like. If the oceans boiled off, he would not feel hot. If the Milky Way froze, he would not feel cold. (96)

In addition, "Qiushui" records four parables concerning Gongsun Long's listening to Zhuangzi, the King of Chu's invitation to Zhuangzi, the story of Huizi searching for Zhuangzi, and Zhuangzi and Huizi viewing fish from the Hao river bridge. These also demonstrate the close connection between "Qiushui" and Zhuangzi's thought.

The Ming scholar Chen Zhi'an observed that "'Qiushui' resembles 'Xiaoyaoyou.'"[10] The Qing scholar Wang Fuzhi says, "'Qiushui' followed and expanded upon 'Xiaoyaoyou' and 'Qiwulun.'"[11] Lin Yunming (c. 1663) says the major themes of this chapter were picked up from "Xiaoyaoyou."[12] The modern scholar Liu Xianxin says, "Qiushui" has taken ideas from both "Xiaoyaoyou" and "Qiwulun."[13] Luo Genze says,

"'Qiushui' advances and further develops Zhuangzi's epistemology."[14] The Taiwan-based scholar Zhang Chengqiu says, "Generally speaking, the position that this chapter resembles 'Qiwulun' is incontestable."[15] Zhang Hengshou says, "Viewing this from an intellectual perspective, it ['Qiushui'] synthesizes the theories of 'Xiaoyaoyou' and 'Qiwulun.'"[16] The position of every author indicates the close relationship between the Inner chapters and "Qiushui."

"Zhile" and the Inner Chapters

1) "Zhile" contains a parable concerning "Uncle Lack-limb" and "Uncle Hobble" (615). Uncle Lack-limb also appears in "Renjianshi" (180).

2) In "Zhile" a conversation takes place between these two "Uncles":

> "Do you resent it?" said Uncle Lack-limb.
> "What have I to resent?" said Uncle Hobble. . . . "Why would I have anything to resent?" (616)

The phrasing is similar to a conversation in "Dazongshi":

> "Do you resent it?" asked Master Si.
> "Why no, what would I resent?" said Master Yu. . . . "What would I have to resent?" (260)

3) In "Zhile" the idea contained in the parable concerning Yan Hui traveling east to Qi and the worried look in Confucius' face (620) is similar to a story from "Renjianshi," where Yan Hui was going to the state of Wei whereupon Confucius exclaimed, "So now you will probably go and get yourself executed" (131–34).

4) In "Zhile" we find,

> Is goodness really complete goodness or isn't it?. . . In the end, is there really complete happiness or isn't there? (609, 661)

The phrasing is similar to a statement from "Qiwulun":

> So, in fact, is there a this and a that; or, in fact, is there no longer a this and a that. . . . But do completion and injury really exist, or do they not? (66, 74)

In addition, "Zhile" records Zhuangzi's beating on a tub and singing after his wife's death and the fable of his seeing a human skeleton when traveling to Chu. These and similar stories demonstrate a close intellectual relationship to Zhuangzi.

Chen Zhi'an holds that "'Zhile' is also a commentary on 'Dazong-shi.'"[17] Lin Yunming also says,

> There has never been anything like this chapter with its penetrating understanding in four sections, namely the beating on a tub, Uncle Lack-limb, the empty skeleton, and the hundred years skeleton [614, 615, 617, 623]. You can almost compare it to the three sections in "Dazongshi," namely "Zisi," "Zisanghu," and "Mengsuncai" [258, 264, 274]. However its arguments are somewhat inferior.[18]

Hu Yuanjun says, "'Zhile' and 'Dazongshi' have similar main themes but 'Zhile's' phrasing is more idiosyncratic."[19] Zhang Hengshou says, "Except for the first and fifth essays of 'Zhile,' the remaining essays are all similar to the contents of 'Qiwulun' and 'Dazongshi.' This is, in fact, thought from the orthodox school of Zhuangzi's thought."[20] All of these commentators hold valid opinions.

"Dasheng" and the Inner Chapters

1) In "Dasheng" we find a description of the perfect man that says,

> He forgets liver and gall and leaves behind his eyes and ears. Inarticulate and aimless, he wanders beyond the dirt and dust; free and easy, his career is to tend to nothing. (663)

A nearly identical description is found in "Dazongshi":

> They forget liver and gall, leave behind ears and eyes. Circling and revolving, ending and beginning again, they do not know if they are starting or finishing. Roaming idly beyond the dust and dirt, they wander free and easy, their careers devoted to inaction. (268)

2) In "Dasheng" we find the following passage:

> The perfect man can walk under water and not choke, tread on fire and not be burned, and travel above the myriad things without fear. (636)

This description is consistent with descriptions of the perfect man as not being drowned, burned or frightened in "Dazongshi," "Qiwulun," and "Xiaoyaoyou" (226, 96, 30).

3) In "Dasheng" we find the phrase "life and death, alarm and terror do not enter his breast" (636). This is similar to phrasing in "Dazongshi" and "Yangshengzhu," where "grief and joy are unable to enter" (260, 128).

4) There is a description of the perfect man in "Dasheng" which states,

> He may rest within the bounds that know no limit, hide within the borders that know no source, wander where the myriad things end and begin." (634)

This is similar to "Dazongshi," where we find,

> They have joined with the creator to wander in the single breath of Heaven and Earth. (268)

5) In "Dasheng" we find, "With your body complete and your vitality returned, you may become one with Heaven" (632). This is consistent with "Dazongshi," where we find, "In being one, he was acting as the companion of Heaven" (234).

Gui Youguang (1506–71) says, "'Dasheng' and 'Yangshengzhu' elucidate each other."[21] Lin Yunming says, "The major points in this chapter expound what had not been covered in 'Yangshengzhu' in the Inner chapters."[22] Zhou Jinran and Hu Yuanjun also use "Dasheng" to explain "Yangshengzhu."[23] Wang Fuzhi says,

> Among all the Outer chapters, "Dasheng" is most deep. It alone can capture the key points expounded in "Yangshengzhu" and "Dazongshi" in the Inner chapters. . . . Its literary language is deep and expansive, and it completely reaches the fine points. Though it may not be a product of Zhuangzi's hand, it was done by someone who has attained Zhuangzi's real ideas.[24]

Luo Genze says, "'Dasheng' has extended and employed Zhuangzi's arts of caring for life."[25] Zhang Hengshou also holds that "Dasheng" is a fairly early product of Zhuangzi's school.[26]

"Shanmu" and the Inner Chapters

1) "Shanmu" says, "This tree uses its worthlessness to live out the years Heaven gave it" (667). This idea is similar to a passage from "Renjianshi," where we find, "It's not a source of timber. It's good for nothing. That's how it got to be so old" (171).

2) In "Shanmu" we find, "Cleanse your mind, dispose of desire, and wander in the empty fields" and "Wander alone with the Way in the land of Great Silence" (671, 674–75). This idea is similar to an idea from "Xiaoyaoyou" and "Qiwulun" where we find, "Wander beyond the four seas" and "wander beyond the borders of the dust and dirt" (28, 96–97).

3) The passage in "Shanmu,"

> If a man could empty himself to wander through the world, then who could do him harm? (675),

expresses a sentiment similar to a passage from "Renjianshi," where we find,

> Just go along with things to roam with your mind. Accept what cannot be avoided and nourish what is within you. This is best. (160)

4) In "Shanmu" there is a dialogue in which Confucius questions a Master Sanghu (684). This same name appears in "Dazongshi," where it says that "Master Sanghu, Mengzi Fan, and Master Qinzhang were good friends" (264).

5) Zhang Hengshou says that the passage

> It is best to let the body go along with things. It is best to let the emotions follow where they will. (686)

is similar to a passage from "Renjianshi":

> It is best to let the body follow along with him; it is best to let the mind harmonize with him. (165)[27]

6) In "Shanmu" we find,

> Whoever serves as a minister does not dare abandon his lord. And if he upholds the way of a true minister, how much more would it be if he were to serve Heaven. (691)

According to Zhang Hengshou, this expresses an idea similar to a passage found in "Renjianshi":

> That a minister should serve his ruler is duty. There is no place he can go and be without his ruler, no place he can escape to between Heaven and earth. (155)[28]

The chapter also records stories concerning Zhuangzi's travels: a trip into the mountains to view a large tree, his visit to the king of Wei while wearing a coat of coarse cloth, and his seeing a strange type of magpie while wandering in the park at Diaoling. These stories indicate that the author shared similar ideas with Zhuangzi.

Wang Fuzhi has said that "Shanmu" quotes the teachings of "Renjianshi" and draws from a miscellany of other sources to illustrate them.[29] Yao Nai says, "The teachings of this chapter are the same as 'Renjianshi.'"[30] Lin Yunming says, "This chapter explains and develops the reasons behind keeping oneself intact and distancing oneself from harm. It can supplement what has not been expressed in 'Renjianshi' from the Inner chapters."[31] Lu Shuzhi (c. 1796) says, "This chapter discusses the way of living in the world. It develops these themes along with 'Renjianshi' from the Inner chapters."[32] Wang Xianqian (1842–1917) quotes Su Yu, who says, "This is also what was recorded by Zhuangzi's students. Its lessons are the same arts of living in a corrupt world and avoiding harm as 'Renjianshi.'"[33] Zhang Chengqiu says, "The majority of this chapter was completed by the hands of Zhuangzi's followers; also, it mostly quotes the teachings of 'Renjianshi.' It does not stray far from the teachings of Zhuangzi and is sufficient to act as a reference for us."[34]

"Tianzifang" and the Inner Chapters

1) In "Tianzifang," we find the passage

> Having received this fixed form, I will hold onto it, unchanging, waiting for the end. I move modelling other things, day and night, ceaselessly, but I do not know what the end will be. (707)

This is similar to a passage in "Qiwulun":

Once a man receives his fixed form, he does not forget it as he waits for the end. Sometimes clashing with things, sometimes turning away from them, he runs his course like a blind charger and nothing can stop him. (65)

2) In "Tianzifang" we find,

Carry out the minor changes; do not lose the constant. So, joy and anger, grief and happiness can never enter your breast. (714)

This is similar to passages from "Dazongshi" and "Yangshengzhu," where we find,

If you rest in the times and can follow along, then grief and joy will be unable to enter it. (128, 260)

3) In "Tianzifang" we find,

Mild, genial my bodily form takes shape. I understand my fate but I cannot determine what preceded it. (707)

This is similar to a passage in "Dechongfu":

Day and night alternate before us and wisdom cannot determine their source. (212)

4) In "Tianzifang" we find,

In this world, the myriad things are one, and if you can find that one and become one with it, then your four limbs and hundred joints will become dust and dirt. (714)

This is the same as the passage from "Dechongfu," where we find,

If you view them from their sameness, then the myriad things are all one. . . . As for things, he sees them as one and does not see their loss. He regards the loss of a foot as a lump of earth thrown away. (190–91)

5) In "Tianzifang" there is the passage

There is no greater grief than the death of the mind. The death of the body is secondary to it. (707)

This is similar to a passage from "Qiwulun":

I have yet to perish! he says, but what good is that? His body is transformed, his mind follows. Is this not a great sorrow? (56)

6) "Tianzifang" contains the phrasing "But the old man of Zang looked blank and did not respond. He mumbled and excused himself" (723). In "Dechongfu" we find, "He was blank, yet responded. He mumbled and excused himself" (206).

7) Lao Dan's statement "I was letting my mind wander in the beginnings of things" (712) is similar to a passage from "Dechongfu": "A man such as this does not know the proper functions of his ears or eyes. He lets his mind play in the harmony of virtue" (191).

8) In "Tianzifang" we find,

> Since the myriad transformations continue and their end has yet to begin, how could that warrant an anxious mind? (714)

In "Dechongfu" we find,

> You have assumed human form and you are delighted. But the human form undergoes a myriad changes whose end has yet to begin. Can your happiness be fully measured? (244)

9) In "Tianzifang" we find a story of Lie Yukou demonstrating archery to Bohun Wuren (724). The name Bohun Wuren is also found in "Dechongfu" (196).

10) In this chapter we find the passage "I stand before you and see you are calm and unconcerned. Do you have some unique way of using your mind?" (726). Zhang Hengshou says this is similar to a passage in "Dechongfu": "A man such as that, does he have a unique way of using his mind?" (188).[35]

11) We also find the passage

> Indeed, life and death are great affairs; yet they are no change to him. So, how much less to him are things like rank and wealth. (727)

This is the same as one of Confucius' statements from "Dechongfu":

> Indeed, life and death are great affairs, yet they are no change to him. (189)

The story of Zhuangzi's audience with Duke Ai of Lu also appears in "Tianzifang" (717). Though this event may not have occurred, it still shows that the author had some intellectual connection to Zhuangzi.

Lu Xixing (c. 1578) says that "Tianzifang" should be read along with "Dazongshi,"[36] while Chen Zhi'an says that "'Tianzifang' emphasizes virtue within and leaves form on the outside. These are the work of 'Dechongfu.'"[37] Wang Fuzhi says, "The central teaching of 'Tianzifang' is to forget language; this is, in its essentials, like that of 'Qiwulun,' that is, to see all in the light of Heaven."[38] Zhang Chengqiu says, "Generally speaking, the essays and sentences in this chapter are similar to the 'Qiwulun,' 'Yangshengzhu,' and 'Dechongfu,' and its contents more often than not expound the words of Zhuangzi."[39] Zhang Hengshou says, "It is beyond doubt that 'Tianzifang' is a reasonably good product done by the later Zhuangzi school."[40]

"Zhibeiyou" and the Inner Chapters

1) In "Zhibeiyou" it says,

> Since life and death are companions, what have we to dread? Hence, the myriad things are one. . . . (733)

This is similar to a passage in "Dechongfu," which says,

> If you view them from their sameness, the myriad things are one. (190)

2) The sense of this passage in "Zhibeiyou":

> Thus it is said, one must only comprehend the single breath that is the world. The sage values oneness (733),

is similar to that of a passage from "Qiwulun":

> Only the man of far-reaching vision knows how comprehensiveness makes them one. (70)

3) In "Zhibeiyou" we read: "He is really good, because he says he doesn't know" (734). The esteem given to not knowing is similar to that found in "Yingdiwang," where Nie Que questions Wang Ni:

> He asked a question four times and four times Wang Ni said he didn't know. Nie Que then hopped around in great amusement (287).

4) The phrase "Body like a withered corpse, mind like dead ashes" (738) is similar to a passage from "Qiwulun." There we find, "Can you really make your body like a withered tree and mind like dead ashes?" (43).

5) The idea expressed in "[Your body] is a form lent to you by Heaven and earth. You do not possess your life; it is a harmony lent to you by Heaven and earth" (739) is similar to a passage from "Dechongfu," where we find, "The Way gave him a face; Heaven gave him form" (221).

6) The idea expressed in "Look and it has no form; listen and it has no voice" (757) is similar to passages from "Dazongshi" and "Qiwulun" (246, 83).

7) The idea expressed in "What makes it enough to decide that Yao is good and Jie is bad?" (744) is similar to a passage found in "Dazongshi," where we find, "Rather than praising Yao and condemning Jie, it would be better to forget both and transform yourself with the Way" (242).

8) "Why not wander with me to the Palace of Nothing at all" (752) is similar to "I'll ride out beyond the six directions, wandering in the village of Nothing at all and live in the vast borderless fields," in "Yingdiwang" (293).

9) In "Zhibeiyou" we find that one "should pursue nothing and welcome nothing" (765). In "Yingdiwang" we find, "The Perfect Man . . . pursues nothing, welcomes nothing; he responds, but does not lay aside" (307).

10) In "Zhibeiyou" we find, "Nie Que asked Beiyi about the Way" (735). The names of these two men also appear in "Yingdiwang" (287).

In addition, this chapter records a conversation between Zhuangzi and Dong Guozi, in which they discuss the Way. This indicates that the author was certainly intellectually connected to Zhuangzi.

Wang Fuzhi's explanation of "Zhibeiyou" is that "This chapter amplifies the teachings on spontaneity; its theories are derived from 'Dazongshi.' It develops and explains what is found in the Inner chapters; these then are their illustrations."[41] Zhang Hengshou observes that "In all, there are fifteen sections to the entire chapter. . . . Generally speaking, all are fairly explanatory of or develop the thought of the Inner chapters."[42]

"Gengsangchu" and the Inner Chapters

1) In "Gengsangchu" we find,

> The eyes are part of the body. I don't know how they could be different from it. Yet a blind man cannot see for himself. The ears are part of the body. I don't know how they could be different from it. Yet a deaf man cannot hear for himself. The mind is part of the body. I do not know how it could be different from it. Yet a madman cannot comprehend for himself. (778)

This idea is similar to "Xiaoyaoyou," where we find,

> The blind man does not have the wherewithal to appreciate beautiful patterns. The deaf man does not have the wherewithal to listen to bells and drums. Are blindness and deafness part of the body alone? Knowledge also has them. (30)

2) The sense of "The body is like a branch of a withered tree, the mind like dead ashes" (790) is similar to a passage from "Qiwulun": "Can you really make your body like a withered tree and mind like dead ashes?" (43).

3) In "Gengsangchu" we find, "Knowledge that rests in what it does not know is finest" (792). An identical passage is found in "Qiwulun" (83).

4) "If you do not attain this goal, then Heaven the Leveller will destroy you" (792). This sentence in "Gengsangchu" is echoed by a sentence in "Qiwulun." There, we find, "So the sage harmonizes with right and wrong and rests in Heaven the Leveller" (70).

5) "Gengsangchu" says, "If you act thus and yet are visited by a myriad evils, they are all the work of Heaven, not the work of man. They cannot destroy your composure; they cannot enter the Spirit Tower" (793). In "Dechongfu" we find that the workings of fate "should not destroy your harmony; they should not enter the Spirit Storehouse" (212).

6) "There are no enemies greater than the *yin* and *yang,* for there is nowhere between Heaven and earth to escape from them" (795). A passage from "Renjianshi" has Confucius saying, "there is no place a man can go without his lord, no place he can escape to between Heaven and earth" (155).

7) "Gengsangchu" says,

> The Way comprehends all things. Their separateness is their completeness; their completeness is their dissolution. (798)

An identical passage appears in "Qiwulun":

> The Way makes all things into one. Their separateness is their completeness, their completeness is their dissolution. (10)

8) In "Gengsangchu" we find,

> The knowledge of the men of ancient times extended a long way. How far did it go? There were some who believed that things never existed. They went far to the end, where nothing can be added. Next were those who thought that things exist. They looked upon life as a loss. . . . (802)

This is practically identical to a passage from "Qiwulun":

> The knowledge of the men of ancient times extended a long way. How far did it go? There were some who believed that things never existed. They went far to the end, where nothing can be added. Next were those who thought that things exist, but recognized no boundaries between them. (74)

9) "Gengsangchu" says,

> In the beginning there was non-being. Later there was life, and then suddenly, there was death. Non-being is the head, life is the body, death is the rump. Whoever knows that being and non-being, life and death are a single way, I will be his friend. (802)

In "Dazongshi" we find,

> Who can look upon non-being as his head, life as his back, and death as his rump? Whoever knows that life and death, existence and annihilation, are a single body, I will be his friend. (258)

10) In "Gengsangchu" we find, "Men today are like the cicada and little dove who agreed because of what they share" (807). A similar metaphor appears in "Xiaoyaoyou": "The cicada was laughing at the little dove and said . . ." (9).

11) "Whoever acts and wishes to do so correctly must accord with what is inevitable. Those things that are inevitable are the Way of the sage" (815). The important phrase "those things that are inevitable" is also found in "Dazongshi" and "Renjianshi" (148, 238).

Wang Fuzhi says,

> The main theme of this chapter is to encompass the infinitely great. In "Qiwulun," what is called "Heavenly Leveller" is used to embody it . . . it is Zhuangzi's main theme. In this chapter he expends every effort to expose it and show it to us. It is what he calls forgetting the distinction between great and small; it is seeing things in the light of Heaven; it is achieving long life and unifying with complete purity; it is what issues from similarity. It is not seeing an entire ox; it is knowing what Heaven has wrought; and knowing our Ancestor existed before there was a beginning.[43]

Hu Yuanjun says, "This chapter and 'Xiaoyaoyou' elucidate each other."[44] Zhang Hengshou says, "The chapter called 'Gengsangchu' is not a product of the Laozi school; rather, it is a product of Zhuangzi's school; it is a rather early chapter."[45]

"Xuwugui" and the Inner Chapters

1) In "Xuwugui" we find,

> Ziqi of South Wall[46] sat leaning on his armrest, staring up at the sky and breathing. Yan Chengzi entered and said. . . . (848)

In "Qiwulun" we find,

> Ziqi of South Wall sat leaning on an armrest, staring up at the sky and breathing. He was empty and distant as though he had lost his companion. Yancheng Ziyou stood in attendance before him. (43)

2) A passage in "Xuwugui,"

> Those men followed what is called the Way that is not a way, and this
> dialogue is what is called disputation that is not spoken (852)

expresses an idea similar to a passage from "Qiwulun":

> Therefore knowledge that rests in what it does not know is finest. Who
> can understand disputation that is not spoken, the Way that is not a
> way? (83)

3) In "Xuwugui" we find, "When my sons and I wander, we wander
through Heaven and earth" (857–58). This is somewhat similar to a passage in "Dazongshi," where we find, "They have joined with the Creator to
wander in the single breath of Heaven and earth" (268).

4) The passage

> He and I sit astride the sincerity of Heaven and earth and do not oppose
> it because of things . . . (858),

is similar to a passage from "Xiaoyaoyou":

> If he had mounted on the truth of heaven and earth, ridden the changes
> of the six breaths. . . . (17)

5) The passage "When I was young I used to wander beyond the Six
Realms. . . ." (832) is similar to a passage from "Xiaoyaoyou," where one
"wanders beyond the Four Seas" (28).

6) In "Xuwugui" we find, "Nie Que happened to meet Xu You" (860). The
name Nie Que also appears in "Qiwulun" and "Yingdiwang" (91, 87).

7) In "Xuwugui" we find, "When virtue is resolved in the unity of the Way,
and words come to rest where knowledge does not know, we have perfection" (852). This is similar to a passage in "Qiwulun": "Knowledge that
rests in what it does not know is finest" (83).

8) In "Xuwugui" we find,

> What I call the self-satisfied are those who have learned the words of
> a single master. They look so satisfied and privately pleased, thinking

what they have is quite enough, not knowing that they haven't begun to get anything at all. (863)

In "Qiwulun" we find a similar phrase, in which some men believed

there was a time at which there had not begun to be anything at all. (74)

In addition, this chapter records Zhuangzi's discussion of an archer who hits his target without first taking aim and Zhuangzi's remarks on passing Huizi's grave. This shows that the author of this chapter retained a fairly close intellectual relationship to Zhuangzi.

Zhang Chengqiu says,

This chapter is certainly a product of Zhuangzi's disciples or later followers. It is entirely an expression of Daoist theory. Some of its contents are close to Laozi, others to Zhuangzi, and still others approach the disputation of Legalist intrigues.[47]

In discussing "Xuwugui," Zhang Hengshou says,

When we carefully examine its contents, we find numerous places that are precious historical material or penetrating theoretical discussions which have value similar to "Xiaoyaoyou" and "Qiwulun" in the Inner chapters. They are not far separated from one another.[48]

"Zeyang" and the Inner Chapters

1) In "Zeyang" we find,

The sage penetrates confusion and complication, rounding all into a single body. But he does not know it is so. This is his inborn nature. (880)

This is similar to a passage in "Qiwulun":

He relies on this alone, relies on it and does not know it is so. This is called the Way. (70)

2) In "Zeyang" we find, "He returns to fate and acts accordingly, taking Heaven as his teacher. . . ." (880). In "Dazongshi" we find that man can act as the "companion of Heaven" (234).

3) In "Zeyang" we find, "Mr. Renxiang held on to the empty socket and followed it to completion" (885). In "Qiwulun" we find, "When the hinge is fitted into the socket, it responds without end" (66).

4) In "Zeyang" we find, "Do you know that when the mind wanders in the boundless and returns to the lands we traverse, they seem so small they may not even exist" (892). The phrase "to wander in the boundless" appears in "Xiaoyaoyou" (17), while the phrase "the mind wanders in the harmony of virtue" appears in "Dechongfu" (191).

5) In "Zeyang" we find,

> They turn away from the Heavenly, distance themselves from the inborn nature, destroy the true form, and shatter the spirit. . . . (899)

This is similar to a passage from "Yangshengzhu," where we find,

> This is to turn away from Heaven, turn your back on your true form, and forget your endowment at birth. The ancients called this the crime of turning away from Heaven. (128)

6) In "Zeyang" we find, "Leave it alone. Leave it alone. There is no place you can escape it" (903). This is also found in a passage from "Renjianshi" (183).

7) In "Zeyang" we find the passage,

> Men all revere what knowledge knows, but no one knows to rely upon what knowledge does not know and so arrive at knowledge. (905)

In "Dazongshi" we find,

> Knowing what Heaven does, he lives with Heaven. Knowing what man does, he uses the knowledge of what he knows to support the knowledge of what he doesn't know. (234)

8) In "Zeyang" we find,

> The man who looks to the Way does not try to follow what has disappeared, does not try to uncover the source of what springs up. This is where debate comes to an end. (914)

In "Qiwulun" we find,

> The sage admits that something exists beyond the Six Realms, but does not speculate. He speculates about what exists within the Six Realms, but does not debate. (63)

In addition, "Zeyang" records Zhuangzi's criticism of Changwu Fengren, which further indicates its intellectual connection with Zhuangzi.

Lu Xixing says, "This chapter contains a good deal of sharp, carefully crafted words. There is no difference between it and the Inner chapters."[49] Wang Fuzhi says, "The essential themes in 'Zeyang' are all compatible with what appears in the Inner chapters."[50] Hu Yuanjun says, "This chapter develops alongside of 'Qiwulun.'"[51] Zhang Hengshou says,

> Among the Miscellaneous chapters, "Zeyang" is relatively well arranged, and its philosophical thought and disputation are extremely well defined, sharp, and well crafted. The various sections in the chapter have places which reinforce the seven Inner chapters and other chapters, including "Qiushui."[52]

"Waiwu" and the Inner Chapters

1) In "Waiwu" we find,

> Rather than praising Yao and condemning Jie, it would be better to forget both and put a stop to what is praised. (930)

In "Dazongshi" we find,

> Rather than praising Yao and condemning Jie, it would be better to forget both and transform yourself with the Way. (242)

2) "Waiwu" records a conversation in which Huizi says to Zhuangzi, "Your words are useless" (936). A similar conversation appears in "Xiaoyaoyou," where Huizi says "Your words are big and useless, and so everyone turns away from them" (39).

3) In "Waiwu" we find,

> Whatever possesses the Way does not wish to be obstructed. If there is obstruction, there is choking. When choking does not cease, there is disorder. . . . (939)

"Renjianshi" contains a passage that reads,

> The Way does not wish things mixed with it. When it becomes a mixture, it becomes many. With multiplicity, there is confusion. And where there is confusion, there is trouble. (134)

4) In "Waiwu" we have

> Only the Perfect Man can wander in the world without bias, and accord with others without losing himself. (938)

A passage from "Renjianshi" reads,

> Now sit astride things to let your mind wander. Resign yourself to what is inevitable and nourish what is within you. This is best. (160)

5) "The breast is a many-storied vault; the mind has its Heavenly wanderings" (939). "The mind has its Heavenly wanderings" is similar to "the wandering mind" in "Renjianshi," Dechongfu," and "Yingdiwang" (160, 190, 294).

6) In "Waiwu" we find the statement,

> Virtue in excess results in a concern for reputation, and concern for reputation in excess results in a love of notoriety. Schemes lead to crisis; knowledge leads to contention. . . . (942)

An identical sentiment appears in "Renjianshi":

> Virtue is destroyed by reputation, and knowledge arises from contention. (135)

In addition, the chapter contains three stories concerning Zhuangzi's activities, including his attempt to borrow grain from the Marquis Jianhe, his discourse on the utility of uselessness, and his discussion of man's ability to wander. This also indicates that "Waiwu" enjoys a certain relation to Zhuangzi's thought.

Wang Fuzhi says, "'Waiwu' accords with all of the major themes of the Inner chapters."[53] Zhang Hengshou characterizes sections of "Waiwu" by saying,

> Though the characteristics of their content are different and their phraseology varies, they are entirely capable of expressing a certain

aspect of Zhuangzi's thought. The chapter should be considered a pre-Qin legacy of the Zhuangzi school.[54]

"Yuyan" and the Inner Chapters

1) In "Yuyan" we find,

> These goblet words emerge daily, let them become uniform through Heaven the Leveller, let them accord to their endless changes, and so live out your years. (949)

Similar sentiments are found in "Qiwulun":

> Let them become uniform through Heaven the Leveller, let them accord to their endless changes, and so live out your years. (108)

2) A passage from "Yuyan" asks,

> What makes things so? Making them so makes them so. What makes things not so? Making them not so makes them not so. What makes them acceptable? Making them acceptable makes them acceptable. What makes them not acceptable? Making them not acceptable makes them not acceptable. All things must have that which is so and that which is acceptable. (949–50)

In "Qiwulun" we find,

> What makes things so? Making them so makes them so. What makes things not so? Making them not so makes them not so. All things must have that which is so and that which is acceptable. (69)

3) "Yuyan" contains the statement, "Beginning and end are like a circuit; no one can grasp its principle. This is called the Heavenly Leveller" (950). In "Qiwulun" we find, "The sage harmonizes with right and wrong and rests in the Heavenly Leveller" (70).

4) In "Yuyan" we find, "Leave it alone. Leave it alone. Can we hope to catch up to this?" (953). Similar phrasing appears in "Renjianshi" (183).

5) The two names Yancheng Ziyou and Ziqi of East Wall appear in "Yuyan" (956). The same or similar names are found in "Qiwulun": "Ziqi

of South Wall was sitting at a table. . . . Yancheng Ziyou was standing before him and waiting for instruction" (43).

6) In "Yuyan" there is the parable,

> The penumbra said to the shadow, "A while ago you were looking down; now you're looking up. A while ago your hair was bound up; now it's loose. A while ago you were sitting; now you're standing; you were walking and now you're still. What is the reason for this?" (959)

In "Qiwulun" we find,

> The penumbra said to the shadow, "A while ago you were walking; now you're standing still. A while ago you were sitting; now you're standing up. What is the reason behind this lack of purpose?" (110)

Lu Shuzhi says, "This chapter is comparable to the ideas in 'Qiwulun' that there should be no right *(shi* 是*)* or wrong *(fei* 非*),* nor should there be any verbalization."[55] Zhuang Wanshou says,

> Everything prior to Zhuangzi's conversation with Huizi in "Yuyan" can be attributed to later followers of Zhuangzi who have extended the phrasing found in "Tianxia." Everything after that develops Zhuangzi's thought.[56]

Zhang Hengshou says, "This chapter is a continuation and expansion of the orthodox school of Zhuangzi's thought."[57]

"Lieyukou" and the Inner Chapters

1) In "Lieyukou" we find the story of Lie Yukou going to Qi and encountering Bohun Wuren (1036). The name Bohun Wuren (same pronunciation, one different character) also appears in "Dechongfu" (196).

2) "The clever man has to work hard; the wise man has many worries. But the man of no ability pursues nothing" (1040). This idea finds similar expression in "Renjianshi": "Because of their ability, their life is miserable" (172).

3) In "Lieyukou" we read,

He eats his fill and wanders about in comfort. Drifting like an unmoored boat, vacant and effortless, he wanders along. (1040)

Similar ideas are found in "Dechongfu":

A man such as this does not know the proper functions of his ears or
eyes. He lets his mind play in the harmony of virtue. (190)

4) In "Lieyukou" we find,

In ancient times this was called the crime of turning away from Heaven.
(1043)

This is very similar to a passage in "Yangshengzhu," where it is said,

This is to turn away from Heaven, turn you back on your true form, and
forget your endowment at birth. The ancients called this the crime of
turning away from Heaven. (128)

5) The ideas expressed in the passage, "The ancients emphasized the
Heavenly, not the human" (1045), are similar to a passage in "Dazongshi,"
where we find, "they do not employ men to assist Heaven" (229).

6) In "Lieyukou" we find,

The perfect man returns his spirit to the beginningless and lies down to
sweet slumber in the Village of Nothing at All. (1047)

This is similar to a pronouncement in "Yingdiwang," where a nameless
man says,

I'll ride out beyond the six directions, wandering in the Village of
Nothing at All to live in the boundless fields. (293)

In addition, this chapter records five anecdotes about Zhuangzi,
including his ridicule of Cao Shang, comparing him to someone who
would lick a king's piles; his description of the King of Song as a black
dragon; his refusal of an invitation to service; the events surrounding his
impending death; and his discussion of Heaven. These indicate that
"Lieyukou" enjoys a reasonably close connection to Zhuangzi's thought.

Wang Fuzhi says,

As for the main themes of this chapter, they generally take internal
release as their principal point, containing one's light within and not

displaying it on the outside as its substance, to dispel fame and nurture the spirit as its essence; it is, then, an introduction to Zhuangzi. Though what is quoted is varied, there being differences of coarse and fine, its essentials can be communicated.[58]

Hu Yuanjun says, "This chapter develops alongside 'Yangsheng-zhu.'"[59] Zhang Hengshou holds that "Lieyukou" is "a mixed compilation formed from fragments of discussions by Zhuangzi and his students."[60]

Summarizing what we have discussed above, there are about 90 places where the twelve chapters in Group I are identical with or correspond to the Inner chapters; that is, approximately 7.5 places per chapter. At the same time, within this category, with the exception of "Dasheng" and "Gengsangchu," each of the chapters contains passages that directly record Zhuangzi's activities. The chapter "Waiwu" contains as many as five sections. In all there are 25 records of Zhuangzi's activities in the Outer and Miscellaneous chapters. Of these, 23 are found in Group I. These facts, in conjunction with the conclusions of earlier scholars, all indicate that there is a relatively close relationship between the 12 chapters of Group I and the Inner chapters. This advances our argument that the authors of these 12 chapters probably belonged to a single school.

Now we will examine the differences between the Group I essays and the Inner chapters and determine on a descriptive name for the writings in this group. To be sure, there are differences between Group I essays and the Inner chapters. We will only take phrases or terms as examples. Among these 12 chapters, there are 7 that use the term *xing*, nature ("Qiushui," once; "Dasheng," 4 times; "Shanmu," once; "Gengsangchu," twice; "Xuwugui," once; "Zeyang," 7 times; and "Lieyukou," once, for a total of 17 times). Two essays use *daode* ("Shanmu," 3 times, and "Gengsangchu," once). Two chapters use *xingming* ("Xuwugui," once, and "Zhibeiyou," once). Two chapters use the compound *jingshen* ("Zhibeiyou," twice, and "Lieyukou," once). The Inner chapters do not contain *xing, daode, xingming,* or *jingshen.* In addition, the Inner chapters very rarely use *li* 理, principle, or *cheng* 誠, sincerity, while "Qiushui," "Zhibeiyou," and "Zeyang" discuss *li* several times. Though we find the relationship between the Inner chapters and these 12 chapters relatively close, we are still unable to view them as identical.

Still, while there are also differences between them, the essential aspect is their similarity and close relationship. First, even though they employ some new terms, fundamentally they do not raise any important new thought. For example, "Shanmu" says, "It would not be so, if I were to sit astride the Way and its Virtue and wander aimlessly without praise or blame, now a dragon, now a snake, changing with the changing times, unwilling to focus my actions. . . ." Although the phrase *daode* is used here, still the passage expands and completes the fundamental main theme of the Inner chapters. "Idly they roam beyond the dust and dirt; they wander free and easy in their careers of inaction" ("Dechongfu"). "Xuwugui" says, "If my lord attempts to satisfy all your tastes and desires and indulge your pleasures and dislikes, you injure the essentials of your inborn nature." Though the phrase *xingming* is used here, the passage is still an explanation and extension of the basic thought of the Inner chapters: "Let your mind wander in simplicity" ("Yingdiwang").

Second, a somewhat interesting new point of view will occasionally emerge from these essays and yet will find no response in other essays. For example, "Qiushui" says, "Emperors and kings have ceded the throne in different ways; the Three Dynasties succeeded one another under different customs. Those who were at odds with the times and opposed custom were called usurpers; those who struck the temper of the times and followed custom were called companions of righteousness." To advocate "striking the temper of the times and following custom" and to oppose "being at odds with the times and opposing custom," is a point of view missing from the Inner chapters. However, it does not occupy an essential position in "Qiushui" and finds no response in other chapters.

Third, though some points of view in this group of essays do not completely resemble those of the Inner chapters, ultimately their essence still shares the same foundation. For example, "Qiushui" uses the phrases "distinguishing between safety and danger" and "being careful in one's comings and goings" to explain how fire cannot burn nor water down the man of perfect virtue. There is not the slightest trace of the charming prose of the Inner chapters describing casting off the common shroud of the everyday world. But in the final analysis, the author does nothing but intentionally explain the point of view of the Inner chapters. "Dasheng" tells the parables of the hunchback catching cicadas and the extraordinary swimmer. They still do not compare to the transcendence and boundless quality of the Inner chapters. However, there are still places that are mutually consistent with Zhuangzi's basic advocacy of peaceful spirituality and relying on one's spontaneous nature.

In general, the Group I chapters are fairly closely related to the Inner chapters. Almost every essay is intended to explain or expand the thought of the Inner chapters or to record Zhuangzi's activities. Not one raises a new point of view. The authors of these chapters are, in relation to Zhuangzi's thought, "transmitters, not creators." Hence, we will call these the essays of the "Transmitter" school 述莊派. This school is the legitimate branch of Zhuangzi's later followers. Their works are primary reference material for the study of Zhuangzi's thought.

Group II: Incorporating Confucianism and Legalism

The second group includes a total of 7 chapters. From the Outer chapters, there are "Zaiyou B," "Tiandi," "Tiandao," "Tianyun," "Keyi," and "Shanxing," and from the Miscellaneous chapters, "Tianxia" (i.e., chapters 11b–16, 33).

We divide "Zaiyou" into two sections. "Zaiyou A" begins with the first section ("I have heard of letting the world be" to "what leisure have I now to govern the world"). The sections following this belong to "Zaiyou B." We take "Zaiyou A" as part of a group of chapters that includes "Pianmu," "Mati," and "Quqie." This grouping is based on three points: First, these chapters display a similar style; they are all political treatises that directly express their ideas. They are quite different from the chapters that use parables or stories to express ideas in an indirect or roundabout style. They all emphasize disputation. They all use propositions, counter-propositions, and comparative sentences, and their criticisms are sharp and decisive. Second, they share similar thought. They all directly face reality and oppose all human activity and all methods of control. They seek release in the nature of the spontaneous and do not discuss insubstantial philosophic principles. Third, they share a common terminology. They all particularly emphasize "human nature," and discuss it in conjunction with "virtue." They habitually discuss "the essentials of inborn nature" *xing-ming zhi qing*. Within the context of the entire book, these chapters are relatively singular and clearly form a unified whole.

The division of Zaiyou into two parts is based on the following considerations. While the first section of "Zaiyou" contains only about 560 characters, the chapters it closely resembles, "Pianmu," "Mati," and "Qu-qie," are the shortest chapters in the entire book. ("Mati" is only about 640 characters long.) The latter sections of "Zaiyou," that is, "Zaiyou B," contain over 2,000 characters, and easily stand as an independent chapter. The latter sections of "Zaiyou" are not the same as the first section. They belong with the chapters that follow: "Tiandi," "Tiandao," and "Tianyun." These chapters employ a style that uses parable and emphasizes the arts of governing. They advocate that the ruler practice non-action, while his ministers are active. They often play up insubstantial philosophic principles. They hold that the Way is conditioned by Heaven, emphasize the relation between Heaven and Virtue, etc. From these differences we can see that it is very possible that "Zaiyou" was originally two chapters. Because of the relatively few characters in the first section, during the process of transmission and compilation it was mistakenly joined with the material that followed it into a single chapter. Hence, we designate the first section "Zaiyou A" and the latter sections "Zaiyou B." By separating them and returning them to two groups we can reveal their clear distinctions.

The classification of the "Zaiyou" chapter has been somewhat difficult. Ye Guoqing classified "Zaiyou" as a member of a group that included "Tiandi," "Tiandao," and "Tianyun,"[61] while Luo Genze and Guan Feng classified it with "Pianmu" and others.[62] These contradictions arose from the fact that there are similarities between the first section of this chapter and "Pianmu" and other chapters preceding it, while at the same time there are sections consistent with chapters following it, such as "Tiandi." The Qing scholar Yao Nai, the Japanese scholar Takeuchi Yoshio, and others had already seen this problem and took the first two sections to be discussed together with such chapters as "Pianmu."[63] Zhang Hengshou also supports this approach.[64] We have not completely accepted it, placing only the first section of "Zaiyou" with the "Pianmu" group of chapters. This is because the second section of "Zaiyou" uses a literary style composed of parable and conversation. Though the content of Lao Dan's conversation in this section is generally consistent with chapters such as "Pianmu," those chapters discuss only the Yangists and Moists, whereas this section discusses only the Confucians and Moists. Hence, it is not necessary to group the second section of "Zaiyou" with the "Pianmu" chapters. That "Pianmu," "Mati," and "Quqie" originally were all essentially texts of short discussions is quite remarkable within the context of the entire book. The addition of "Zaiyou A" preserves the special features of this group of essays. We have taken the second section and returned it to the group of chapters that includes "Tiandi," "Tiandao," and "Tianyun." This group is somewhat heterogeneous anyway; an additional section will do no harm.

The separation of "Zaiyou" into two parts resolves a clear contradiction, yet we have not resolved the entire dilemma. For example, in "Tiandi," there is the passage, "In an age of perfect Virtue, the worthy are not honored nor are the able employed; rulers are like the lofty branches of a tree, the people become like deer grazing the fields" (445). In "Mati" we find a passage similar in every way in its style of thought: "In an age of perfect Virtue men dwell together like birds and beasts; clustered beside the myriad things, who would know of lord or petty men" (336). Or again, the last section of "Tiandi" discusses "A hundred-year-old tree [that] is carved up to make sacrificial goblets . . ." (453). This is completely consistent with the expression in "Mati": "If the plain, unwrought substance had not been shattered, how would there be any sacrificial goblets?" (336). Moreover, the last section of "Tiandi" discusses Zeng and Shi and Yangzi and Mozi and clearly belongs with the group of essays "Pianmu," "Mati," and "Quqie." However, if we wish to move these disparate fragments together, it would be necessary to re-order the chapters of the entire book. This is neither necessary nor meaningful. There are a good many chapters of the book *Zhuangzi* that show some traces of being jumbled, but this certainly doesn't affect our general classification of the Outer and Miscellaneous chapters.

Now we will examine the basis for arguing that "Zaiyou B," "Tiandi," "Tiandao," "Tianyun," "Keyi," "Shanxing," and "Tianxia" form a group of their own.

1) "Zaiyou B" says,

> To be inactive and command reverence is the Way of Heaven. To be active and become enmeshed in it is the Way of man. The ruler is the Way of Heaven; his ministers are the Way of man. (401)

This clearly discusses the ruler's non-action and the ministers' action and is the same as a passage from "Tiandao":

> Superiors must be inactive and employ the world; inferiors must be active and serve in the employ of the world. This is the unchanging way. (465)

2) "Zaiyou B" says,

> What is the Way? There is the Way of Heaven and the Way of man. . . . The Way of Heaven and the way of man are far apart. (401)

This resembles a passage from "Tiandao," where we find,

> The Way of Heaven is to revolve and not accumulate. Hence, the myriad things come to completion. The Way of the emperor is to revolve and not accumulate. Hence, the world reverts to his court. (457)

3) "Zaiyou B" says,

> What is already correct and yet must be increased is Virtue. What is one and yet must be altered is the Way. What is spirit-like and yet must be active is Heaven. (398)

This holds that Heaven is higher than the Way and is identical to a passage in "Tiandi":

> Righteousness is completed in Virtue, Virtue in the Way, and the Way in Heaven. (404)

This is also the same as a passage in "Tiandao":

> The Virtue of emperors and kings takes Heaven and earth as its ancestor, the Way and its Virtue as master, having no action as a constant rule. (465)

This is also similar to a passage from "Tianxia":

> Whoever makes Heaven his ancestor, Virtue his root, and the Way his gate . . . is called a sage. (1066)

4) In "Tiandao" we find, "In movement, he is of Heaven; remaining still, he is of earth" (462). The movement of Heaven and the stillness of earth are the same as in the opening line of "Tianyun": "Does Heaven revolve, does the earth remain still?" (493).

5) "Tiandao" says, "These men are rhetoricians, men concerned with one corner of learning" (473). This is the same as in "Tianxia": "None stands alone, none is universal. The scholar concerned with one corner of learning. . . ." (1069).

6) "Tianyun" contains the passage,

> The Perfect Man of ancient times found a borrowed path in benevolence and a sheltering lodge in righteousness. He wandered free and easy in emptiness. . . . (519)

This does not completely reject benevolence and righteousness and coincides with "Zaiyou B":

> He complies with benevolence but does not rely upon it. He embraces righteousness, but does not accumulate it. (398)

This also is similar to "Shanxing":

> When virtue encompasses all, there is benevolence. When the Way directs all, there is righteousness. (548)

This, again, is similar to a passage from "Tianxia," where

> The Sage exercises kindness through benevolence, ritual through righteousness. (1066)

"Tiandao" also says,

> When the ancients made clear the Way and its Virtue, they followed with benevolence and righteousness. (471)

"Keyi" says,

> To discourse on benevolence, righteousness, loyalty, and good faith, to be courteous, temperate, modest, and deferential, became his entire course of cultivation. . . . (535)

7) In "Tiandi" we find,

> Observe words through the Way, then the lord of the world will be correct. Observe distinctions through the Way, then the duties of lord and minister will be clear. (404)

This discusses the social differences between ruler and minister. It is similar to "Tiandao," where it is said, "The court honors nobility. . . . Lords take priority; their ministers follow" (469).

8) In "Tiandi" we find, "The Master said, 'The Way covers and supports the myriad things. So vast are its expanses'" (406). We also find, "So deep the dwelling of the Way, so pure its clearness" (411). This is similar to "Tiandao," where we find,

> The Master said, "The Way does not end at greatness, does not remain at the tiny. Hence, the myriad things are complete in it. Vast and ample, there is nothing it does not encompass. Deep and profound, how can it be measured?" (486)

9) "Tiandi" says,

> When the world has the Way, the sage joins in the chorus with all other things. When the world is without the Way, he cultivates his Virtue and retires in leisure. (421)

This is similar to "Shanxing," which says,

> If the fate of the age allowed them to do great deeds in the world, they returned without a trace. If the fate of the age brought them great hardship in the world, they became firmly fixed and waited reposing in perfection. (555)

10) "Tiandi" has "Whoever is complete in Virtue is complete in body. Complete in body, he is complete in spirit" (436). This spiritual completeness stemming from completeness of Virtue is similar to a passage in "Keyi," "Noxious airs cannot violate him. Hence, his Virtue remains complete, his spirit unimpaired" (538).

11) "Tiandao" has

> Emptiness, stillness, softness, silence, inaction—these are the level of Heaven and earth, the substance of the Way and its Virtue. Therefore, the emperor, king, and sage find rest therein. (457)

It also says, "Emptiness, stillness, softness, silence, inaction are the root of the myriad things" (457). This is the same as "Keyi," where it says,

> Softness, silence, emptiness, inaction—these are the level of Heaven and earth, the substance of the Way and its Virtue. Thus, it is said, when the sage rests, he comes to rest in peaceful ease. (538)

12) "Tiandao" says,

> Birds and beasts remain in their flocks; trees and shrubs remain in their stands. . . . Why present these vain displays of benevolence and righteousness as if you were beating a drum in search of a lost child? (479)

This is the same as a passage from "Tianyun," where we find,

> Why all this huffing and puffing as if carrying a big drum in search of a lost child? The snow goose remains white without a daily bath; the crow remains black without a daily inking. (522)

13) "Tianyun" says,

> When the Heavenly devices are not set in motion, yet the five vital organs are complete, this is called the happiness of Heaven. (507)

This is similar to "Tiandao," where we find,

> Harmonizing with Heaven, this is called happiness of Heaven. . . . He covers and supports Heaven and earth, crafts a multitude of forms but doesn't consider himself skilled. This is what is called happiness of Heaven. (458, 462)

14) "Keyi" says,

> Therefore, it is said, the sage's life is the course of Heaven, his death is the transformation of things. When still, he and the *yin* share a single Virtue. When in motion, he and the *yang* share a single surge. . . . Therefore, he suffers no disaster from Heaven, no entanglement from things, no blame from man, no spirit punishment. . . . His spirit is pure and clear, his soul never depleted. (539)

In "Tiandao" it says,

> Therefore, it is said that whoever knows Heavenly joy, his life is the course of Heaven; his death is the transformation of things. When still,

he and the *yin* share a single Virtue; when in motion, he and the *yang* share a single surge. Thus, whoever knows Heavenly joy suffers no anger from Heaven, no blame from man, no entanglement from things, no spirit punishment . . . the spirits do not afflict him, his soul does not tire. (462)

15) "Shanxing" says,

> The time came when Virtue began to decline and dissolve; then Sui Ren and Fu Xi took control of the world. On account of this there was compliance, but no unity. Virtue continued to decline and dissolve; then Shen Nong and the Yellow Emperor took control of the world. On account of this there was security, but no compliance. Virtue continued to decline and dissolve; then Yao and Shun took control of the world. They began the fashion of transforming through governing. In so doing, they defiled purity and shattered simplicity. They deviated from the Way for the sake of goodness; endangered Virtue for the sake of proper conduct. . . . Afterward, the people became confused and disordered. They were unable to return to the true form of their inborn nature or to return again to the Beginning. (551–52)

In other words, from the time of the ancient emperors to the time of Tang Yao and Yu Shun, the Way and its Virtue declined daily, while the world daily became more disordered. This resembles a passage from "Tianyun," which says,

> In ancient times, when the Yellow Emperor ruled the world, he caused the people's hearts to be one. So, there was no blame attached to someone who did not weep at the death of a parent. When Yao ruled the world, he caused the hearts of people to be affectionate. So, there was no blame attached to someone who varied his conduct according to degrees of kinship. When Shun ruled the world, he caused the hearts of the people to be contentious. So, while wives conceived and gave birth in the usual ten months, their children were not five months old before they were able to talk . . . then they began to die young. When Yu ruled the world, he caused the hearts of the people to change . . . as a result there was great confusion in the world; then the Confucians and Moists arose together. (527)

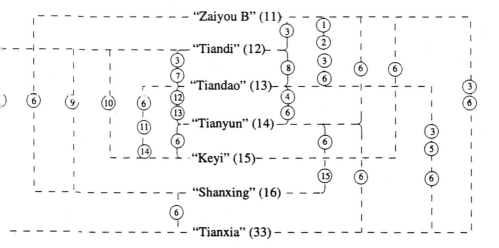

Figure 3.2. Connections among the Group II Chapters in Terms of Syntactic Similarities (Numbers correspond to examples enumerated in the text.)

Based on the fifteen examples above, we can diagram the mutual relations among the chapters of Group II (figure 3.2). From the above materials and diagram, it is easy to see that considering the seven chapters "Zaiyou B," "Tiandi," "Tiandao," "Tianyun," "Keyi," "Shanxing," and "Tianxia" as a single group is completely substantiated.

Now we will consider the similarities and differences between the chapters of this group and the Inner chapters and determine a title for the group. The differences between the Group II chapters and the Inner chapters are obvious. First, "Zaiyou B," "Tiandi," "Tiandao," and "Tianxia" all take Heaven as containing the Way within it or perceive Heaven to be superior to the Way (see number 3 above). This is diametrically opposed to the thought of the Inner chapters, in which the Way gave birth to Heaven and earth. This is also clearly different from the other two groups of essays in the Outer and Miscellaneous chapters. Next, "Zaiyou B," "Tianyun," "Tiandao," "Keyi," "Shanxing," and "Tianxia" all have a clear tendency toward tolerance of benevolence and righteousness. (See number 6 above.)

In addition, "Tiandao" discusses those who could count to five in sequence and pick out "forms and names" or count to nine and discuss "rewards and punishments." "Tianxia" discusses "laws to settle position, names to fix rank, comparisons to establish actualities, examinations to make decisions. . . ." Generally, this group is somewhat lenient with the two schools of Confucianism and Legalism. Moreover, there are portions that have absorbed and approve of those forms of thought. Third, this group seeks to harmonize the superior and inferior relations between lord and minister (see number 7), which is clearly different from the Inner chapters. Fourth, this group distinctly advocates that the ruler perform non-action while the ministers are active, a concept somewhat infrequent in the *Zhuangzi*. The differences between this group and the Inner chapters are important and distinctive.

One of the characteristics this group of seven chapters collectively exhibits is an appreciation of and tolerance for concepts from schools other than Daoism, namely, benevolence and righteousness (Confucianism), ritual and law (Legalism), and universal love (Moism). This is exactly consistent with Sima Tan's description of Daoism: "They selected the good parts of Confucianism and Moism and gathered the essentials of the School of Names and the Legalists" (*S* 3289). What was called Daoism at the beginning of the Han Dynasty is not the Daoism we discuss today, as represented by Laozi and Zhuangzi. Rather, it was composed of what is presently called the arts of the Yellow Emperor and Laozi or Huang-Lao learning. Hence, the authors of the second group can be identified from among the followers of Zhuangzi as members of the Huang-Lao school 黃老派.

The points of similarity between the second group and the Inner chapters are relatively clear.

1) "Zaiyou B" states,

> I will enter the gate of the inexhaustible to wander in the boundless fields. . . . (384)

which is similar to "Yingdiwang":

> out beyond the six directions, wandering in the village of Nothing at All and living in the vast and borderless fields. (293)

2) "Zaiyou B" states,

> Shatter limbs and body, spit out intelligence and understanding, forget you belong with other things, and join in great unity in the depths of the boundless. (390)

This is similar to "Dazongshi," where Yan Hui says,

> I shatter my limbs and body, dispense with intelligence and understanding, cast off form, discard knowledge, and join in unity with the Great Thoroughfare. (284)

3) In "Tiandi" it says,

> The Great Ravine is something you can pour into and it never becomes full; dip from it and it never dries up. (440)

This is almost identical with "Qiwulun," where we find a description of the Way that includes,

> Pour into it and it never becomes full, dip from it and it never dries up, and yet we do not know from whence it arises. (83)

4) "Tiandi" states,

> Should a praying mantis angrily wave its arms to stop an approaching carriage, it will certainly fail to complete its task. (430)

This resembles a passage found in "Renjianshi":

> Do you know about the praying mantis that angrily waved its arms to stop an approaching carriage, not knowing that it would fail to complete its task? (167)

5) In "Tiandi" we find,

> Lao Dan said, "A man like this endures a slave's drudgery and craftsman's bondage, exhausting his body, grieving his mind." (427)

In "Yingdiwang," we find,

> Lao Dan said, "To the sage, this man endures a slave's drudgery and craftsman's bondage, exhausting his body, grieving his mind." (295)

6) In "Tiandi," we find, "Some men seek to control the Way as though subduing an opponent, making the unacceptable acceptable, the not so, so" (427). In "Qiwulun" we have, "Making an affirmative a negative and the so, not so" (108).

7) In "Tiandao" we find,

> Zhuangzi said "My teacher, my teacher. He judges the myriad things but is not severe. His bounty extends to a myriad generations, but he is not benevolent. He is older than the most ancient, but he doesn't think himself long-lived. He covers and supports Heaven and earth, carves and fashions a multitude of forms, but is not skilled. This is called Heavenly Joy." (462)

This is the same as "Dazongshi," where we find,

> Xu You said, "Ah, I'm not quite sure. Let me put it this way. My teacher, my teacher. He judges the myriad things but is not severe. His bounty extends to a myriad generations, but he is not benevolent. He is older than the most ancient, but he doesn't think himself long-lived. He covers and supports Heaven and earth, carves and fashions a multitude of forms, but is not skilled. This is where you should wander." (281)

(This section is also a proof for the contention that "Tiandao" is later than "Dazongshi" and that "Dazongshi" was written by Zhuangzi.)

8) In "Tiandao" we find that the perfect man

> perceives what is without falsehood and is unmoved by gain. He carries to completion the truth of things and can hold to their source. (486)

In "Dechongfu" we find,

> He perceives what is without falsehood and is unmoved by things. He takes the transformation of things as fate, and holds to the ancestor. (189)

9) In "Tiandao" we find, "If you called me an ox, I'd say I was an ox; if you called me a horse, I'd say I was a horse" (482). This is the same as a passage from "Yingdiwang": "Sometimes he thought he was a horse, sometimes a cow" (287).

10) In "Tianyun" we find,

> The ritual and regulations of the Three August Ones and the Five Emperors can be compared to the cherry-apple, pear, orange, and citron. (514)

"Renjianshi" contains a similar passage:

> When the fruit has ripened on the cherry-apple, pear, orange, citron, and other fruit-bearing trees and shrubs, they are torn apart and abused. (172)

11) In "Tianyun" we find,

> When the springs dry up and the fish are stranded on dry land, they spit on each other with moisture and soak each other with foam. Would it not be better if they were able to forget each other in the rivers and lakes. (522)

An identical passage is found in "Dazongshi" (242).

12) In "Tianyun" we find,

> Dumbfounded you stand before the complete emptiness of the Way. You lean against your desk and sigh. (504)

This is similar to a passage from "Dechongfu," where we find,

> You exhaust yourself leaning against a tree and sighing, bent over your desk, dropping off to sleep. (222)

13) In "Keyi" we find that the sage "sleeps without dreaming, rises unworried" (539). In "Dazongshi" we find, "The True Man of antiquity slept without dreaming and rose unworried" (228).

14) In "Shanxing" we find,

> The Way is inherently adverse to petty conduct. Virtue is inherently adverse to petty understanding. Petty understanding harms Virtue; petty conduct harms the Way. (556)

This is similar to a passage in "Qiwulun," where we find,

> When the Way is obscured by petty accomplishments, and words obscured by glorious display, you have the rights and wrongs of the Confucians and Moists. (63)

There are a total of 14 places where there are clear relations between the second group and the Inner chapters. On average, each chapter contains 2 such correspondences. Hence, this second group should be seen as works of Zhuangzi's later followers. The so-called Huang-Lao school then would be the Huang-Lao school from among the ranks of Zhuangzi's later followers. It is also the later followers who were relatively more influenced by Confucianism and Legalism to form a branch of Huang-Lao theory. This was a product of the contention between and merging of the Hundred Schools of philosophy during the Warring States period. The seven chapters in this second group are material for the study of the thought of Zhuangzi's later followers and for the study of pre-Qin Huang-Lao learning.

Group III: Criticizing Confucianism and Moism

The third group takes the four short chapters "Pianmu," "Mati," "Quqie," and "Zaiyou A" as its main frame and core. Because the three chapters "Rangwang," "Yufu," and "Daozhi" enjoy a certain relation to these, they are included in the same group.

We will first examine the basis for placing these seven chapters in a single group. We have already discussed above the relations among "Pianmu," "Mati," "Quqie," and "Zaiyou A." Here we can add some supplemental discussion.

1) These chapters refer to the contrast between Music Master Kuang and Li Zhu and between hearing and sight. For example, "Pianmu" says,

> Whoever subordinates his nature to the five notes, though he may be as intelligent as Music Master Kuang, I would not call this good hearing. Whoever subordinates his nature to the five colors, though he may be as intelligent as Li Zhu, I would not call this good eyesight. (327)

In "Quqie" it says,

> Block off the ears of Music Master Kuang, and the people of the world will begin to exercise the sense of hearing they possess on their

own. . . . Cover up the eyes of Li Zhu, and the people of the world will begin to exercise the eyesight they possess on their own. (353)

And "Zaiyou A" says,

Do men delight in their eyesight? They are seduced by colors. Do they delight in thcir sense of hearing? They are seduced by sound. (367)

2) Group III chapters emphasize the "essentials of inborn nature" *(xing-ming zhi qing)*. "Pianmu" says,

He who holds to complete rightness does not lose the essentials of his inborn nature. . . . Men of no benevolence cut short the essentials of their inborn nature as they lust for rank and wealth. . . . What I call expertness has nothing to do with benevolence or righteousness; it is relying on the essentials of your inborn nature, nothing more. (317, 319, 327)

"Zaiyou A" says,

How could anyone have any leisure to rest in the essentials of his inborn nature. . . . Should the world rest in the essentials of its inborn nature, then these eight delights could exist or pass away with no consequence. When the world does not rest in the essentials of its inborn nature, these eight delights become untrue and unrestrained, bringing confusion to the world. . . . When there is inaction, one may rest in the essentials of his inborn nature. (365, 367, 369)

The phrase "essentials of inborn nature" appears 8 times in the entire *Zhuangzi.* Seven of these occurrences are listed above. The only other example is in "Tianyun."

3) The two figures Zeng and Shi are habitually mentioned, as are the two pairs Zeng and Shi and Yang and Mo. "Pianmu" says,

Growing benevolence like an additional finger—Zeng and Shi did that. Continuing argumentation like webbed toes—Yang and Mo did that. (314)

In "Quqie" it says,

Wipe away Zeng and Shi; gag the mouths of Yang and Mo; wipe out and cast away benevolence and righteousness, and at last the Virtue of the world will reach mysterious leveling. . . . Men like Zeng, Shi, Yang, Mo, the Master Musician Kuang, Artisan Chui, and Li Zhu all made an external display of their virtues and misled and confused the world. (353)

"Zaiyou A" says,

So it began that the world grew restless and ambitious. Soon afterward the ways of Robber Zhi, Zeng and Shi appeared. . . . (365)

4) Group III chapters habitually employ the phrase "from the Three Dynasties on down." In "Pianmu" we find,

From the Three Dynasties on down, why has there been all this fuss in the world?. . . From the Three Dynasties on down, everyone in the world has traded his inborn nature for something or another. (319, 323)

In "Quqie":

So great is the world's disorder that comes from the lust for knowledge. From the Three Dynasties on down, this has been happening. (359)

In "Zaiyou A," we find,

From the Three Dynasties on down, there has been nothing but fuss over this business of rewards and punishments. (365)

5) Another special phrase is "In an age of perfect virtue." In "Mati" we find,

Therefore, in an age of perfect virtue, the gait of men does not falter; their gaze is steady. . . . In this age of perfect virtue, men live with birds and beasts in flocks and herds beside the myriad things. (334, 336)

In "Quqie" we find,

Have you alone not heard of that age of perfect virtue? (357)

In the entire *Zhuangzi,* there are only 4 occurrences of this phrase. The other is in "Tianyun."

6) Another phrase is "Let me try to explain what I mean." In "Pianmu" we find,

Let me try to explain what I mean. From the Three Dynasties on down, everyone in the world has traded his inborn nature for something or another. (323)

In "Quqie" we find,

Hence, let me try to explain what I mean. Is not what the ordinary world calls a man of knowledge merely someone who accumulates things for a great thief? (343)

There we also find,

Let me try to explain what I mean. Is not what the ordinary world calls a man of perfect wisdom merely someone who accumulates things for a great thief? (346)

The material cited above supports our perception of "Pianmu," "Mati," "Quqie," and "Zaiyou A" as a single group of essays. Our remaining question concern "Rangwang," "Daozhi," and "Yufu." These three chapters, along with "Shuojian," were the earliest to be suspected of being forgeries. There would be no objections should we say that these four chapters were not written by Zhuangzi. According to our examination, the chapter "Shuojian" in fact has absolutely no relation to Zhuangzi. When studying Zhuangzi or his philosophy, there is no need whatsoever to consider it. However, "Rangwang," "Daozhi," and "Yufu" are not the same. Though these three chapters are not products of the legitimate branch of Zhuangzi's later followers, they were influenced by Zhuangzi and the Zhuangzi school. There are unmistakable relations among them and between these three chapters and "Pianmu."

7) In "Rangwang" it says,

Our Master was twice driven from Lu. They wiped away his footprints in Wei, chopped down a tree on him in Song, made trouble for him in Shang and Zhou, and have beseiged him at Chen and Cai. (981)

In "Daozhi" we find,

You call yourself a gentleman of talent, a sage? Twice they drove you from Lu; they wiped away your footprints in Wei, made trouble for you in Qi, and beseiged you at Chen and Cai. No place in the empire will accept you. (997)

In "Yufu" we find,

Twice I have been driven from Lu; they wiped away my footprints in Wei, chopped down a tree on me in Song, and besieged me at Chen and Cai. I do not know where I have erred. (1031)

8) In "Rangwang" there is the passage,

Yao wanted to cede the empire to Xu You. . . . The empire is a thing of utmost importance, yet he did not harm his life by accepting the throne. (965)

It also says,

Shun tried to cede the empire to Shan Juan. (966)

In "Daozhi" we find,

Yao and Shun acted as emperors and there was harmony . . . they would not let goodness harm their lives. Shan Juan and Xu You could have acquired the throne but declined . . . they did not let affairs of state harm them. (1011)

9) In "Rangwang" we find, "Only he who has no use for the world can be trusted with it" (965). This phrasing is similar to "Zaiyou A": "If he values his own person more than governing the world, he can be trusted with the world" (369).

10) In "Daozhi" we find,

The people knew their mothers but not their fathers. . . . They plowed for their food, wove for their clothing, and had no thought of harming one another. This was the pinnacle of perfect virtue. (995)

This is similar to "Mati," where we find,

The people have a constant inborn nature. They weave their clothing; they till for their food. . . . So, in an age of perfect virtue. . . . (334)

11) In "Daozhi" we find, "Confucius . . . declined the mat placed before him, stepped back a pace or two, and bowed twice to Robber Zhi" (993). In

"Yufu" we find, "Confucius retreated a pace or two, bowed twice, and stepped forward" (1026).

12) In "Daozhi" we find,

> When the world speaks of loyal ministers, we are told none compare to Prince Bi Gan and Wu Zixu. Wu Zixu drowned in a river and Bi Gan had his heart cut out. The world calls these two men loyal ministers, yet they died as jokes of the empire. (999)

This is similar to a reference in "Quqie," which states, "Bi Gan was disemboweled. . . . Wu Zixu was left to rot. . . ." (346)

13) In "Daozhi" we find, "The petty thief is locked up, while the big thief becomes a lord. . . ." (1003). This is similar to "Quqie," where we find, "Whoever steals a belt buckle is put to death; whoever steals a state becomes a lord. . . ." (350).

14) In "Daozhi" we find,

> The petty man will perish for wealth; the gentleman will perish for reputation. The reasons why they alter their true form and change their inborn nature are different. But in so far as they cast aside what is already theirs and are willing to perish for what is not, they are the same. (1005)

In "Pianmu" we find,

> The petty man will risk death for profit. The knight will risk it for fame . . . they conduct their business in different ways and enjoy different reputations. But they are the same in harming their inborn nature and risking their lives. (323)

Based on the materials above, we can draw a diagram of the relations among the chapters of Group III (figure 3.3).

Now we will examine the differences and similarities between Group III and the Inner chapters, as well as the question of the title of this group.

"Pianmu," "Mati," "Quqie," and "Zaiyou A" are obviously different from the Inner chapters. First, these four chapters are all short, strong

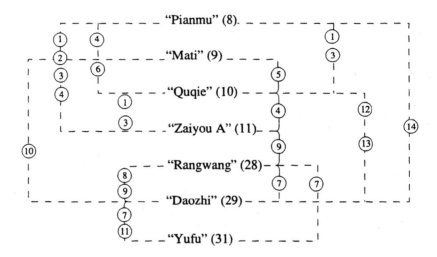

Figure 3.3. Connections among the Group III Chapters in Terms of Syntactic Similarities (Numbers correspond to examples enumerated in the text.)

arguments; there is nothing of the changeable, artful allegories of the Inner chapters. Second, all four chapters directly address the real world. They do not display the transcendental attitude of roaming beyond the four seas found in the Inner chapters. Third, all four take as their highest purpose the liberation of the individual's nature or original nature. This contrasts with the Inner chapters, where the mystical experience of obtaining the Way is held as the highest pursuit. "Rangwang," "Daozhi," and "Yufu" have consistently been seen as forgeries. Their differences from the Inner chapters and the rest of the *Zhuangzi* are clear and obvious. Wang Fuzhi said,

> "Rangwang" mentions that Bian Sui and Wu Guang despised Tang and killed themselves. They perished for their reputations and regarded life lightly; this was Zhuangzi's greatest despair.

> "Yufu" and "Daozhi" are the vulgar noises of jealous women arguing in the market or the wild barking of mad dogs. They are ranked with the mid-level chapters. Like the parables of the praying mantis or wild rose, they do not dispute yet are self-evident.[65]

Wang Fuzhi completely dismissed these three chapters; however, he correctly indicated clear differences between them and other essays.

The thought in this third group closely resembles the anarchism (*wu-jun lun*, theories of no sovereigns) discussed in the "Jie Bao" chapter of the *Baopuzi*. This school emphasized "resting in the essential form of one's original nature and destiny." Anarchists in *Baopuzi* also advocated that "each should return to that in which he rests" and "hold to the soft and hard to follow one's nature."[66] This school opposed morality, benevolence, and righteousness, recompense, rites, and ceremony. Anarchists in *Baopuzi* also opposed the dictum "Separate them with ritual and rank, keep them in order with punishments and penalties."[67] This school is in fact against any form of control; the anarchists also said, "Long ago, there were no lords. This is superior to today's world."[68] This school said,

> Thus, if the plain unwrought block had remained undamaged, how would there be sacrificial goblets? If the white jade had remained unbroken, how would there be any scepters or batons? If the Way and its Virtue had not been discarded, how would there be any pursuit of benevolence and righteousness. ("Mati," 336)

The anarchists in *Baopuzi* also argued,

> Therefore if the white jade had remained unbroken, how would there be any scepters or batons? If the Way and its Virtue had not been discarded, how would there be any pursuit of benevolence and righteousness?[69]

This school admired a simpler time:

> During the time of He Xu, the people lived in their communities and did not know what they did. They travelled without knowing a destination, they ate their morsels and basked in the sun or wandered about drumming on their bellies. ("Mati," 341)

The anarchists also admired the idea that

> Long ago, there were no lords, no ministers . . . the people ate their morsels and basked in the sun or wandered about drumming on their bellies.[70]

We find other traces of anarchist rhetoric in "Rangwang": "At sunrise, they began work, at sunset they rested." In "Mati" we find a description of an age in which "mountains had no paths or trails, lakes no boats or bridges" (334). These same sentiments are found in anarchist remarks in *Baopuzi*. It is evident this school was the harbinger of anarchism in Chinese thought. Hence, we can call these chapters the work of the Anarchist school 無君派, or no-sovereignists, among Zhuangzi's followers.

Though there are important differences between the Group III chapters and the Inner chapters, there are still some faint traces of relations between them.

1) In "Pianmu" we find, "Why then must we say that Bo Yi be right and Robber Zhi wrong?" (323). This strikes a chord similar to a sentence in "Dazongshi": "Rather than praising Yao and condemning Jie, it would be better to forget both and transform yourself with the Way" (242).

2) In "Pianmu" we find,

> If someone is pleased by what pleases other men, but finds no pleasure in what could please himself, then whether he is Robber Zhi or B or Yi, he is equally deluded and depraved. (327)

This is the same as a passage in "Dazongshi," where ancient worthies are described as having

> slaved in the service of others, taken pleasure in pleasing others, but were unable to find pleasure of their own. (232)

3) In "Daozhi" we find, "In the age of Shen Nong, the people slept soundly, arose wide-eyed and blank" (995). This is identical with a phrase from "Yingdiwang," where we find, "The clansman Tai slept soundly and woke wide-eyed and blank" (287).

4) In "Daozhi" we read, "Take this time-bound toy, place it in those endless spaces. . . ." (1000). A similar juxtaposition of "bound" and "unbound" takes place in "Yangshengzhu." There we find "If you use what is limited to pursue what is limitless, you will be in danger" (115).

5) In "Rangwang," we read that

Yao wanted to cede the empire to Xu You, but Xu You refused to accept it. . . . Only he who has no use for the empire can be trusted with it. (965)

This resembles a passage from "Xiaoyaoyou":

Yao wanted to cede the empire to Xu You. . . . Xu You said, . . . "Go home and forget the matter my lord. I have no use for governing the world." (22–24)

6) In "Rangwang" we find,

At sunrise, I wake; at sunset, I rest. I wander free and easy between Heaven and earth, finding all that I could wish for. What use have I for the world? (966)

This is similar to a passage from "Dazongshi" that describes "wandering in the single breath between Heaven and earth" (268), and one from "Xiaoyaoyou": "Why should he wear himself out over the affairs of the world?" (30).

For the most part these six are the clearest examples of relations between the Group III chapters and the Inner chapters. On average, there is one instance per chapter. Among the three groups, the third has the fewest correspondences with the Inner chapters. In spite of this, these seven chapters still are related to the Inner chapters, and we can view them as products of Zhuangzi's later school. The so-called anarchists are, then, anarchists within the ranks of Zhuangzi's school.

Above we have separately examined the relations between the Inner chapters and each of the three groups in the Outer and Miscellaneous chapters. We have also concluded that all are products of Zhuangzi's followers. Now we will examine the relations among these three groups in the Outer and Miscellaneous chapters and will advance another step and explain the consistent nature that exists in these three groups.

There are quite a few correspondences between Group I and Group II. Ten are listed below.

1) In "Zaiyou B" we find,

> Whoever understands that by treating other things as things one is no longer a mere thing, he alone can govern the empire and the hundred clans. (394)

This is similar to a passage from "Zhibeiyou," where we find,

> That which treats things as things is not a thing. Things that issue forth cannot but precede other things. . . . (668)

2) In "Tiandi" we find,

> Some men seek to control the Way as if they were subduing an opponent, making the unacceptable acceptable, the not so, so. The rhetoricians have the saying, "he can separate hard from white as if they were draped over the eaves." (427)

In "Qiushui" we find,

> I reconcile similarity and difference, distinguish hard and white, and prove not so is so, the unacceptable, acceptable. (597)

3) In "Tianyun" we find,

> What issues forth from the center is not received on the outside. . . . What is taken in from the outside is not entertained in the center. . . . (517)

In "Zeyang" it says,

> When things are taken in from the outside, they are entertained but not seized upon. When issuing from the center, they are corrected but not resisted. (909)

4) In "Tianyun" it says, "There is no affection in perfect benevolence" (498). In "Gengsangchu" we find, "There is no affection in perfect benevolence; perfect trust eliminates gold as proof" (804).

5) In "Tianyun" we find,

> Before straw dogs are arranged at the altar, they are kept in bamboo boxes and covered over with fine embroidery, while the impersonator of the dead and the priest fast and abstain prior to using them. But after they have been arranged at the altar. . . . (511)

The sense of this allegory and the pattern of speech "covered over with fine embroidery" are reminiscent of a passage from "Lieyukou" that describes a sacrificial ox

> dressed in fine embroidery, fattened on sweet grasses. But when it comes time to be led off to the great ancestral temple. . . . (1062)

6) In "Tianyun" Confucius' treatment is described thus:

> They chopped down a tree on him in Song, wiped away his footprints in Wei, and made trouble for him in Shang and Zhou. . . . (512)

In "Shanmu" we find,

> "I was twice driven from Lu. The people chopped down a tree on me in Song, wiped away my footprints in Wei, made trouble for me in Shang and Zhou, and beseiged me in Chen and Cai." (684)

7) In "Tiandao" we find, "They are rhetoricians, men cramped in one corner of learning" (473). In "Qiushui" we find, "A cramped scholar can't discuss the Way. . . ." (563).

8) In "Keyi" we find,

> these are favored by scholars of the mountains and valleys, the men who condemn the world, the withered and worn who plunge into the depths. (535)

In "Xuwugui" we find, "Withered and worn scholars reach out for fame" (834).

9) In "Tianxia" we find that the scholar cramped in one corner of learning

> tries to determine the beauty of Heaven and earth, to examine the principles of the myriad things. . . . (1069)

This is similar to phrasing found in "Zhibeiyou," where

> the sage seeks to uncover the beauty of Heaven and earth and comprehend the principles of the myriad things. (735)

10) In "Tianxia" we find that Zhuangzi

> used goblet words to pour out endless changes, weighted words for a ring of truth, and imputed words to give greater breadth. (1098)

This is consistent with the opening line of "Yuyan":

> Imputed words make up nine-tenths of it; weighted words make up seven-tenths of it; goblet words daily issue forth. . . . (947)

There are at least 5 places where Group I corresponds with Group III.

1) In "Mati" the carpenter says,

> I handle wood well. My curves are true to the arc. My straight edges follow the line. (330)

In "Xuwugui" we find,

> When I judge a horse, if he can run straight as a plumb line, cut corners true to the curve. . . . (819)

2) In "Pianmu" we find,

> The duck's legs are short, adding more onto them would make him worry. The crane's legs are long; cutting them down would sadden him. (317)

In "Xuwugui" we find,

> The owl's eyes have their own abilities; the crane's legs are properly jointed. To cut away anything would sadden them. (868)

3) "Ququie" says, "In times past Guan Longfeng was cut in two; Bi Gan was disemboweled. . . ." (346). In "Waiwu" we find the passage, "hence, Longfeng was punished, Bi Gan was executed . . ." (920).

4) In "Rangwang" we find,

> being without wealth is called poverty; being unable to put into practice what one has learned is called wretchedness. I am poor, but I am not wretched. (976).

This is similar to "Shanmu," where we find,

> When a man possesses the Way and its Virtue but is unable to put them into practice, then he is exhausted. When his clothes and shoes are tattered and torn, he is poor, but not exhausted. (688)

5) In "Rangwang," "Daozhi," and "Yufu," we find the story of Confucius twice being driven from Lu (981, 997, 1031). "Shanmu" also contains a story of Confucius being driven from Lu and having a tree chopped down on him by the people of Song (684).

There are 3 places where Group II and Group III correspond.

1) In "Tianyun" we find,

> The wisdom of the Three August Ones was such as to interrupt the brightness of sun and moon above, drain the essence of hills and streams below, and overturn the cycle of the four seasons. (527)

There is an almost identical passage in "Quqie":

> This is how the great confusion emerges to interrupt the brightness of sun and moon above, drain the essence of hills and streams below, overturn the cycle of the four seasons. (359)

2) In "Tianyun" we find the story concerning Confucius and how the people of Song chopped a tree down on him, the people of Wei wiped away his footprints, and people made trouble for him in Shang and Zhou (512). The story also appears in "Rangwang," "Daozhi," and "Yufu" (981, 997, 1031).

3) In "Tianyun" we find, "nothing was allowed to rest in the essentials of its nature. Still, they considered themselves sages" (527). The phrase "essentials of its nature" appears several times in "Pianmu" and "Zaiyou A."

The examples above demonstrate that there are several links among the three groups of Outer and Miscellaneous chapters. We are completely justified in viewing the authors of these three groups as constituting a single large school and the differences among them as differences among its branches. Because there are relations of varying degrees between these three groups and the Inner chapters, they can all be characterized as products of Zhuangzi's later school.

Statistics and Comparisons

In the chapters above we discussed and individually characterized the three groups of Outer and Miscellaneous chapters. We have characterized the first, that with the closest relations to the Inner chapters and exemplified by "Qiushui" and "Gengsangchu," as products of the school succeeding Zhuangzi, the Transmitters. We have characterized the Group II chapters, which synthesize Daoist, Confucian, and Legalist tendencies and are exemplified by "Tiandao," as products of the Huang-Lao school. We have characterized the Group III chapters, which vehemently criticize things as they are and are exemplified by "Pianmu," as products of the Anarchists. Now, we will make some further comparative observations.

1) The similarities among the Outer and Miscellaneous chapters

Among the three groups of Outer and Miscellaneous chapters, there are points of both convergence and divergence. There are about 10 clear points of correspondence between the essays written by the Transmitters, Zhuangzi's immediate successors, and those of the Huang-Lao school. There are about 5 between those of the Transmitters and those of the Anarchists. There are about 3 between the essays of the Huang-Lao school and those of the Anarchists. Hence, we should view the Outer and Miscellaneous chapters of the *Zhuangzi* as an anthology of writings by Zhuangzi's later followers, rather than a disparate collection of materials from various Daoist schools. All three groups of the Outer and Miscellaneous chapters (excluding "Shuojian") are related to a greater or lesser degree to Zhuangzi's thought. These materials were not assembled together by chance. Because their authors had all been influenced by Zhuangzi's thought to one extent or another, and because they all tended to revere Zhuangzi's legacy to different degrees, they appended their works to his. Hence, despite the fact that there are several places in the book that are corrupted and out of order, if viewed from an inclusive perspective, the *Zhuangzi* is still a deliberately assembled collection of works by Zhuangzi and his followers.

2) The internal relations within each of the three groups

Each of the three groups of Outer and Miscellaneous chapters contains quite a few points of convergence and coherence. There are 28 correspondences among the essays of the Transmitter school, about 15 among those of the Huang Lao school, and 14 among those of the Anarchists. On average, there are 2.3 instances per chapter for the Transmitter school, 2.1 instances per chapter for the Huang-Lao school and 2.0 instances per chapter for the Anarchists. These averages are relatively close to one another, indicating that the internal coherence of each group is about the same. The somewhat greater coherence among the Group I materials demonstrates a higher concentration of Zhuangzi's thought. All this suggests that this classification of Outer and Miscellaneous chapters coincides with historical reality.

3) The relations between the three groups and the Inner chapters

There are 90 instances of clear relations between the works of the Transmitter school and the Inner chapters, 14 instances of relations between the products of the Huang-Lao school and the Inner chapters, and 6 instances of relations between the essays of the Anarchists and the Inner chapters. On average there are 7.5 correspondences per chapter in the writings of the Transmitter school, 2.0 per chapter in those of the Huang-Lao school, and 0.9 in those of the Anarchists. The margins of difference are substantial.

The pattern is confirmed by an examination of the use of the two terms *you* 遊 and *xiaoyao* 逍遙, which occur, on average, 4.6 times per chapter in the Inner chapters. In the works of the Transmitter school, *you* and *xiaoyao* are used a total of 40 times; in the works of the Huang-Lao school, they are used 21 times. In Group I they appear 3.3 times per chapter; in Group II, 3.0 times per chapter; and in Group III, 1.1 times per chapter. This reinforces our conclusion that the works of the Transmitter school are closest to Zhuangzi's thought, while the works of the Anarchists are farthest from it.

In addition, there are a total of 25 passages in the Outer and Miscellaneous chapters recording Zhuangzi's activities. Twenty-three of these, or 92%, appear in the writings of the Transmitter school. Two such passages appear in the products of the Huang-Lao school. None appears in the work of the Anarchists. This further corroborates the closer relationship to Zhuangzi of the author of the Group I essays and the progressively more distant relationships of the Group II and Group III authors.

4) The relations within each group are more numerous than the relations between them

There are 28 points of convergence and coherence among the chapters from the Transmitter school and 15 among the chapters from the Huang-Lao school. Yet between these two groups there are only 10 points of correspondence. There are 14 clear points of coherence among the works of the Anarchists, yet these chapters exhibit only 5 points of coherence with Group I. Between the Huang-Lao school (15 points) and the Anarchists (14 points) there are only 3 points of coherence. Obviously, the relationships within the individual groups are more numerous than the relations between them. This demonstrates that our classification has, for the most part, accurately reflected both the internal similarities within the groups and the points of difference between them.

5) The relations between each group and the Inner chapters are more numerous than the relations among the three groups

As a convenience, we will refer to the number of quantifiable correspondences between groups as an "index." The highest index of relations, that between Group I and the Inner chapters, is 90, clearly higher than the highest index of relations among the three groups of Outer and Miscellaneous chapters (an index of 10, representing the relations between the Transmitter school and the Huang-Lao school). The lowest index of relations between any of the three groups and the Inner chapters is a 6 between the Anarchists and the Inner chapters. This is still clearly higher than the lowest index of relations among any of the three groups (an index of 3 between the Anarchists and the Huang-Lao school). The intermediate index of 14 between the three groups and the Inner chapters (that between the Huang-Lao school and the Inner chapters) is also clearly higher than

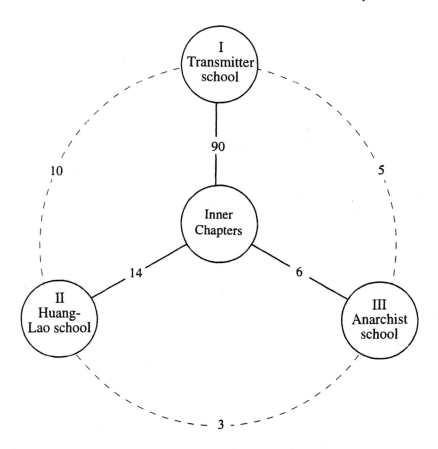

Figure 3.4. Connections among Groups I, II, and III of the Outer and Miscellaneous Chapters and Their Connections with the Inner Chapters.

the intermediate index of 5 (that between the Transmitters and the Anarchists) among the relationships between the three groups. These relations are illustrated in figure 3.4.

From figure 3.4 it is easy to see that the numbers on each radial (unbroken) line are all greater than the numbers on the two neighboring circumferential (broken) lines. This is to say that the relations between any given group of Outer and Miscellaneous chapters and the Inner chapters are greater than the relations between that group and any of the Outer and Miscellaneous chapters. This indicates that the three groups of Outer and

Miscellaneous chapters do indeed take the Inner chapters as their core. Here, the relations between the Anarchist school and the Inner chapters have a value of 6; with the Transmitter school, they are a 5—numbers seemingly insufficient to explain the problem. But, if we consider that the Inner chapters only contain 7 chapters, while the Tranmitter school is represented by 12, then the ratio of 6:7 is clearly greater than one of 5:12 (0.86 > 0.42). So then, the conclusion above can still be established. This secondarily proves that the book *Zhuangzi* is indeed a product of the Zhuangzi school that takes the Inner chapters as its core. Also, this second-arily proves that the Inner chapters should serve as a primary basis when studying Zhuangzi.

6) The position of the Transmitter school among Zhuangzi's later followers

From figure 3.4 one can also see, between the three groups of Outer and Miscellaneous chapters, that the index of relations among the Huang-Lao school, the Anarchist school and the Transmitter school separates out to 10 and 6. This is clearly higher than the index of 3 between the Huang-Lao and Anarchist schools. This shows that the Transmitter school is the most influential of the three groups of Outer and Miscellaneous chapters. Also, it is the group with the greatest number of connections to the Inner chapters (an index of 90). Hence, the Transmitter school is the main stream among Zhuangzi's later students, the orthodox branch of Zhuangzi's later follow-ers.

7) Approximate dating of the three groups of Outer and Miscellaneous chapters

In the Outer and Miscellaneous chapters of the *Zhuangzi*, the three com-pounds, *daode, xingming,* and *jingshen* appear a total of 36 times. They are distributed as follows: The Transmitter school uses them 10 times: 3 times in "Shanmu," 3 times in "Zhibeiyou," twice in "Gengsangchu" and twice in "Lieyukou." The Huang-Lao school uses them 13 times: once in "Zaiyou B," 6 times in "Tiandao," once in "Tianyun," twice in "Keyi," once in

"Shanxing," and twice in "Tianxia." The Anarchists use them 13 times: 6 times in "Pianmu," twice in "Mati," 4 times in "Zaiyou A," and once in "Rangwang." Among the works of the Transmitter school, the four essays that employ these three compounds total 33% of the group. Among the works of the Huang-Lao school, there are 6 chapters out of 7 that employ these three compounds, or 86%. Among the Anarchist works, 4 chapters out of 7 use these compounds, or 57%. Clearly, the percentage of use of these three compounds by the Transmitter school is the lowest, while the percentage of use by the Huang-Lao school is the highest. If we examine this situation according to frequency per chapter, the average use of these compounds per chapter in the essays of the Transmitter school is 0.83 times, whereas they appear 1.86 times per chapter in both the Huang-Lao works and the Anarchist works. The frequency with which these three compounds are employed is lowest in the works of the Transmitter school, and it is highest in the writings of the Huang-Lao school. If we consider that the use of these three compounds gradually expanded, then we can broadly infer that the chapters that employ these three compounds the least, the works of the Transmitter school, are the earliest group of Outer and Miscellaneous chapters. It further follows that the chapters that use these compounds the most, the works of the Huang-Lao school, are a relatively late group of Outer and Miscellaneous chapters. (Of course, this is a general conclusion; there will always be individual exceptions to this. For example, the chapter "Tianxia" in the works of the Huang-Lao school is not necessarily later than all the chapters that compose the works of the Transmitter school.

Generally speaking, within the process of the evolutionary development of one form of thought, the greater the length of time from its origination, the greater the changes. The converse is also true. From this we can infer that since the works of the Transmitter school enjoy the closest relations to the thought of the Inner chapters, they must date closest to the middle of the Warring States period. Since the works of the Huang-Lao school and Anarchist school exhibit relatively distant relations with the thought of the Inner chapters, they must date relatively late. This conclusion is consistent with the conclusion drawn from the use of compounds discussed above.

Our inference is consistent with the opinions of the majority of scholars in the world of learning. However, a good many scholars hold that the works of the Huang-Lao school are late enough to have appeared only at the beginning of the Han Dynasty, while we hold that those works were already completed by the closing years of the Warring States period.

The essential purpose of this chapter has been to conduct statistical comparisons of material from different chapters that clearly evinces similar linguistic styles or perspectives of thought. It may be objected that determining what constitutes similar linguistic styles or perspectives of thought is itself a subjective process, making objective comparison impossible. However, in our examination the similarity or consistency of the majority of examples raised would be immediately acknowledged by anyone familiar with the *Zhuangzi*. The element of possible subjectivity enters only in individual cases. While other researchers may achieve somewhat different results in terms of absolute numbers, as long as they apply their own standards consistently, the fundamental relationships of similarity outlined above will be confirmed. For example, we have adduced 90 examples of consistency between the works of the Transmitter school and the Inner chapters. We might have derived 95 or perhaps 85 examples. However, no matter how this exact total might vary, the number of correspondences will still greatly exceed the number of examples of consistency between the writings of either the Huang-Lao school or the Anarchist school and the Inner chapters. Similarly, we have found 10 instances of consistency between the essays of the Huang-Lao school and those of the Transmitter school. It is possible that someone else might uncover 12 instances or perhaps acknowledge only 8. However, no one will discover more relations between these two groups than within a single group of essays. Thus, even if we allow that the selection of individual items may entail subjectivity, it would be very difficult to overturn the numerical relationships that exist between the groups.

The demonstrations in this essay were not conducted by selecting a small number of evidentiary examples to demonstrate the relations between disparate essays. Instead, we tried our best to inclusively list examples of clear relationships in thought and linguistic style and conducted our statistical examinations and comparisons on that basis. Hence, some examples have acted as the basis of argument on their own, which seems insufficient. However, viewing this from the perspective of the entire statistical comparison, it is still meaningful. In sum, we have attempted with our method of argumentation to avoid subjectivity on a general level. Each step has obtained its required level of possibility. Striving for relatively objective proofs, our classifications have been reasonable and reliable.

Conclusion

Summarizing the foregoing three chapters, we can affirm that the Inner chapters of the *Zhuangzi* are fundamentally a product of the mid–Warring States period, while the Outer and Miscellaneous chapters are fundamentally products of Zhuangzi's later followers. These followers of Zhuangzi generally include the Transmitter school, the Huang-Lao school, and the Anarchist school. Zhuangzi and the three schools that followed him together form the Zhuangzi tradition.

In studying the thought of Zhuangzi, the man, one must rely on the Inner chapters as primary source material. Though the many stories in the book *Zhuangzi* recording Zhuangzi's activities may not necessarily be believable history, they do, however, reveal some special characteristics of the man's life and thought. These too are important sources when studying Zhuangzi. Many of the essays from the Transmitter school in the Outer and Miscellaneous chapters expound upon and expand Zhuangzi's ideas as laid out in the Inner chapters. These are important reference materials when studying Zhuangzi's thought. Generally speaking, however, it is not suitable to employ the works of the Huang-Lao or Anarchist schools from the Outer or Miscellaneous chapters to explain Zhuangzi's thought.

The essays of the schools succeeding Zhuangzi have a dual historical value. On the one hand, the works of all three schools are the fundamental materials from which one researches the evolution of Zhuangzi's theories and thought. On the other, the works of each of these three schools also have individual value. The works of the Transmitter school are important reference materials for the study of the thought of Zhuangzi, the man. The works of the Huang-Lao school are important materials for the study of the Huang-Lao branch of the Daoist school. The works of the Anarchists are important sources for the study of ancient anarchist thought.

Afterword

This English translation is based on a book completed in 1985, when I was at Beijing University. At that time, although I had written letters seeking help from scholars of Daoism in America and Japan, I had not received relevant information on the study of Zhuangzi outside China. Thus my book was addressed to the Chinese academic community, without reference to the works of Western scholars. This Afterword was written after I had seen some of the writings in English about the *Laozi* and the *Zhuangzi* that were not available in China. The first part is a comparison between my work and A. C. Graham's.

Recently, I have come to recognize that I should also investigate the date of the *Laozi*. When I was researching the *Zhuangzi* in Beijing, it did not occur to me that I should address this question, because few scholars in China considered the possibility that the *Zhuangzi* might have preceded the *Laozi*. Therefore I did not even include a footnote on the issue. However, quite a few scholars in Europe and America, as well as in Taiwan and Hong Kong, believe that the *Laozi* was completed after the *Zhuangzi*. Thus

The writer wishes to thank Dr. Zhang Hongming of the Department of East Asian Languages and Literature at the University of Wisconsin-Madison, for reading the second part of this Afterword and for his suggestions with regard to the use of phonology terms; but the writer is responsible for any errors that might occur in this essay.

Professor Shuh-sien Liu at the Chinese University of Hong Kong suggested that I address the issue of the date of the *Laozi* in my book on the *Zhuangzi*.

In my textual analysis, I presume that the *Laozi*, as well as the other four classical texts, the *Analects*, the *Mozi*, the *Mencius*, and the *Zuozhuan*, precedes the *Zhuangzi*. Even if we put the *Laozi* aside, the other four classics still prove that before the middle of the Warring States period the compounds *daode* 道德, *xingming* 性命, and *jingshen* 精神 were not in use. Thus a later date for the *Laozi* still would not effect my conclusion concerning the date of the *Zhuangzi*. However, my purpose is not only textual analysis. I date and classify the *Zhuangzi* chapters to establish solid ground for the investigation of intellectual history. If the *Laozi* was written later than the *Zhuangzi*, the classical intellectual history of China, in particular the history of Daoism, has to be revised radically. Therefore I think it necessary to discuss the date of the *Laozi* briefly here, so that we have a trustworthy foundation for the analysis of Daoism in general. Thus the second part of this essay presents a new approach to the problem of dating the *Laozi*. It also involves a further discussion of A. C. Graham's work on Daoism.

The *Zhuangzi*

A scholar planning to publish a book on the *Zhuangzi* in English cannot ignore A. C. Graham's work. I did not, however, hear of his analysis of the text until 1985, when I was told by Professor Tu Wei-ming, then teaching Confucian philosophy at Beijing University, that my methodology in textual analysis was similar to Graham's. When I arrived in the United States, I eagerly read his works and sent a copy of my book to him through a friend, Professor Leo Chang. Meeting Professor Graham at the Sixth East & West Philosophers Conference in Hawaii in 1989 was an unforgettable experience. He signed and gave me a copy of his new book, the *Disputers of the Dao*, as well as a copy of his new paper on *Heguanzi*. The volume he gave me has been one of my most important reference books. On one occasion when we had the opportunity for a long talk, he impressed me as a humble, peaceful, and friendly man. We did not talk much about the *Zhuangzi* because he told me that he had turned his interest to other subjects. I had hoped to discuss the *Zhuangzi* further with him when my book was published in English. With his death, the opportunity is forever lost.

Professor Graham had a good opinion of Guan Feng's works on the *Zhuangzi*, which were indeed orthodox and authoritative in China in the early 1960s. However, Guan's textual studies were not very original, and his theoretical analysis was a thorough negation of Zhuangzi's thought. The principles and conclusions in Zhuangzi's philosophy, Guan claimed, were totally ridiculous, reactionary, and the worst type of subjective idealism. Zhuangzi was a "negative teacher" (an enemy) who should only be attacked.[1] Graham may not have been aware that Guan worked for the Communist Party's central propaganda department, and played an active role as a kind of police officer and official prosecutor in the social sciences and the humanities. Guan's purpose in studying the *Zhuangzi*, according to his own statement, was to establish a model of Marxist critique in studies of Chinese philosophy and to "bury" Zhuangzi's doctrines, as well as to attack "bourgeois scholars," chiefly Fung Yu-lan.

The keynote of Guan's view of Zhuangzi's philosophy is the three-step formula, namely *youdai* 有待 (awaiting, depending on something, conditional situation), *wuwo* 無我 (no-self), and *wudai* 無待 (no-awaiting, depending on nothing, absolute condition).[2] Zhuangzi's philosophy, according to Guan, starts with the concept of "awaiting," goes through the stage of "no-self," and ends with realization of the state of "no-awaiting." This is good Hegelian speculation. However, neither Zhuangzi nor his students ever used the terms "awaiting" and "no-awaiting" as philosophical concepts, or discussed any similar ideas seriously. Actually the concepts "awaiting" and "no-awaiting" were first used by Guo Xiang, who flourished in the late third and early fourth century and was the most important commentator on *Zhuangzi* in ancient times.[3]

Graham started his work on the *Zhuangzi* by accepting some common views expressed by Guan Feng in the latter's article "Zhuangzi waizapian chutan."[4] In the very beginning of Graham's textual analysis, he said:

> It is now widely recognized that *Zhuangzi* is a collection of writings of the fourth, third, and second centuries B.C., in which only the Inner chapters (1–7) can be confidently ascribed to Zhuangzi himself. They are not necessarily all Daoist, and even among those which are, only the last six of the Outer chapters (17–22) need be accepted as belonging consistently to Zhuangzi's own branch of Daoism.[5]

There are three points in Graham's statement: 1) the Inner chapters can be confidently ascribed to Zhuangzi himself; 2) parts of the book, some of the Outer and Miscellaneous chapters, are writings from the second century B.C., i.e., early Han China; 3) the book is not a Daoist collection, but a mixture of writings of different schools. Graham's work, at least insofar as he regroups the Outer and Miscellaneous chapters, involves the last two points. I would like, however, to introduce some facts and discussion on these three points, and compare Graham's views with my own.

Date of the Inner chapters

It seems that the question of whether we should take the Inner chapters as Zhuangzi's own work never bothered Graham at all; he simply adopted the traditional view through Guan Feng's work without any further discussion. I wonder why Graham paid little attention to Guan's opponents, since their articles also appeared in the same book, *Zhuangzi zhexue taolunji*. Graham refers once to a different point of view expressed by Ren Jiyu,[6] who argued that we should take the Outer and Miscellaneous chapters as Zhuangzi's materials instead of the Inner chapters.[7] In the same book, Fung Yu-lan also explicitly expressed his disagreement with Guan, and claimed that we should take the first and second chapters, namely "Xiaoyaoyou" and "Qiwulun," as a basis for identifying all of Zhuangzi's other writings, whether from the Inner, the Outer, or the Miscellaneous chapters.[8] If Graham had regarded the different views seriously, he would not have been so confident in taking the Inner chapters as Zhuangzi's own work without further analysis and might have left us some remarkable arguments about this issue.

When I began working on the *Zhuangzi* in the early 1980s, the first and most important question challenging me was still which part of the book might reliably be attributed to Zhuangzi. There were four points of view: 1) the Inner chapters; 2) some of the Outer and Miscellaneous chapters; 3) chapters selected from the Inner, as well as the Outer and Miscellaneous chapters; 4) the whole book. The question is, in fact, which part of the book preceded the other parts. Obviously the early part would be Zhuangzi's writings. I found that in the Inner chapters there occur single-character terms such as: *dao* 道, *de* 德, *ming* 命, *jing* 精, *shen* 神, but not their compounds, namely *daode* 道德, *xingming* 性命, *jingshen* 精神. These three compounds occurred, however, 36 times in the Outer and Miscellaneous chapters. In texts from before the middle Warring States, *Zuozhuan, Analects, Laozi, Mencius, Mozi, dao, de, xing* 性, *ming, jing, shen* appear, but not their compounds. However, the compounds, *daode, xingming, jingshen* occur in the *Xunzi, Hanfeizi,* and *Lüshi chunqiu* of the late Warring States era. This demonstrates that the Inner chapters preceded the Outer and Miscellaneous chapters, and I was finally satisfied that the Inner chapters should be treated as Zhuangzi's works. The main part of chapter 1 in this book is concerned with this question.

Date of the Book

Regarding when the compilation of the *Zhuangzi* was finished, Graham, again through Guan Feng, adopted a stand similar to that of most leading contemporary scholars, such as Fung Yu-lan, Ren Jiyu, and my advisor Zhang Dainian. Although there are differences about which chapters belong to the early Han dynasty, most senior scholars believe that the *Zhuangzi* contains some chapters written after the Warring States, even as late as the second century B.C. Based on my examination, however, I find that opinion questionable. Actually, both detailed and more broadly based examinations show this conventional opinion to be demonstrably wrong.

According to my statistics, by the end of the Warring States period, that is, before 221 B.C., at least 30 passages from 14 chapters of the *Zhuangzi* had been quoted by the *Lüshi chunqiu* and *Hanfeizi*. These 14 chapters are equivalent to approximately 42 percent of the present 33-chapter edition of the *Zhuangzi*. This proportion is fairly high, and there is no comparable instance of borrowing in the pre-Qin philosophical classics. This would have been impossible if the *Zhuangzi* of that time had not already taken book form and been widely circulated. Among the 14 chapters quoted in the *Lüshi chunqiu* and *Hanfeizi*, there are 3 from the Inner, 6 from the Outer, and 5 from the Miscellaneous. These proportions are fairly close to those of the present edition of *Zhuangzi*, which has 7 Inner, 15 Outer, and 11 Miscellaneous chapters. This indicates that at that time the Inner, Outer, and Miscellaneous chapters of the *Zhuangzi* had fixed dimensions and that their content had fundamentally taken shape. This, then, is to say that the Outer and Miscellaneous chapters, generally speaking, had been completed before 241 B.C.,[9] when compilation of the *Lüshi chunqiu* was finished, and before 233 B.C., when Han Feizi died.

The above investigation shows that the *Zhuangzi* as a whole had been completed no later than the 240s B.C. We cannot claim that no terms and sentences were added by later writers. Nevertheless, we have found no hard evidence to indicate that any of these additions can be ascribed to Han scholars. Some seemingly serious proofs proposed and repeated by many researchers are merely conjecture.

For example, Graham particularly observed that the term *suwang* 素王 (Uncrowned King) is not attested before the Han, in support of Guan's view that chapters 12–14, the group Graham named "Syncretist," should be dated to the early Han.[10] This point was raised by Yao Nai, a famous writer of the Qing Dynasty. Scholars believe *suwang* is a term of praise used in the early Han and contains the idea that Confucius was an uncrowned emperor. However, the phrase "Uncrowned King" in chapter 13, "Tiandao," is a general term. The way of the Uncrowned King is described as "empty, still, quiescent, silent, and without action"; it has no relation to Confucius.

The *Shiji*, "Yinbenji," records of Yi Yin that "only after refusing five times did he consent to go and submit to Tang, and talk about the matter of the 'Uncrowned King' and 'Nine Lords' (九主)." The sources for the Uncrowned King and Nine Lords have never been clear. The excavation of the silk manuscripts at the Mawangdui Han tomb has proven that there were writings attributed to Yi Yin in the pre-Qin period which clearly talked about the meaning of "Nine Lords." This proves that what Sima Qian recorded really was based on fact. Hence the phrase "Uncrowned King" was not joined to Yi Yin's name on a whim. And it is possible that there were pre-Qin texts named after Yi Yin that used the phrase "Uncrowned King."

In addition to this, in *Heguanzi*, the "Wang Fu" chapter contains the phrase "Uncrowned Emperor" (*suhuang* 素皇). Both in pronunciation and in denotation "Uncrowned Emperor" and "Uncrowned King" are similar. This text is known to be a product of the pre-Qin,[11] showing that this idea did not originate in Confucian texts and is not a special appellation for Confucius. The phrase "Uncrowned King" also appears in the *Huainanzi*, in the "Zhushu" chapter, which preceded the Confucian text written by Dong Zhongshu praising Confucius as an Uncrowned King. To sum up, the phrase "Uncrowned King" was first used by pre-Qin writers; its origin has no connection to Confucius. To use the term as evidence that chapter 13 and similar chapters emerged in the Han is unfounded.

Now it is necessary to discuss the relationship between chapter 28, "Rangwang," and 6 chapters in the *Lüshi chunqiu*, with which it shares 12 similar passages.[12] The question is who copied whom. Most researchers, including Graham, have concluded that "Rangwang" was copied from the *Lüshi chunqiu*, and thus that chapters 28–31 in the *Zhuangzi*, Graham's "Yangist" documents, are the later works.

Let us take, for example, the first section of "Rangwang." This is composed of four passages in which phrases appear to be arranged in order and are connected. The first passage appears in the "Guisheng" chapter of the *Lüshi chunqiu*, and the fourth appears in the "Lisu" chapter. It is perfectly plausible that the authors of the two different chapters in *Lüshi chunqiu* selected the two passages from the *Zhuangzi* to support their own arguments. However, the reverse argument, that the authors of "Rangwang" chose two passages from the *Lüshi chunqiu* for the first and fourth passages, then independently created the second and third passages, is implausible. If the authors of "Rangwang" were able to create the second and third passages, why were they unable to create the first and the fourth passages? And in fact, the structure of these four passages is complete, their perspectives are mutually comprehensible, and they have a definite connection to Zhuangzi's school.

Next worth noting are twelve passages in "Rangwang," namely the 1st and 4th passages of the 1st section, and the 2nd, 3rd, 4th, 5th, and 6th sections, as well as the 11th, 12th, 13th, 14th, and 15th sections. In the *Lüshi chunqiu* these passages appear, respectively, in chapters 2, 19, 21, 2, 21, 2, 16, 21, 14, 19, 19, and 12. There is not the slightest discernible order. Why is it this way? It cannot be held that the author of "Rangwang" did this consciously to confuse others, because the contents of the *Lüshi chunqiu* were common knowledge: after the *Lüshi chunqiu* was completed about 241 B.C., "it was posted on the gate of the capital city [Xianyang], and it was announced that a thousand pieces in gold would be awarded to whoever could add or subtract one word from the *Lüshi chunqiu*."[13] In any case the concept of plagiarism was not known in pre-modern China. It is illogical to suppose that "Rangwang" plagiarized the *Lüshi chunqiu*.

However, the supposition that these portions of the *Lüshi chunqiu* were copied from "Rangwang" encounters no such obstacle. For example, the 1st passage of the 1st section, the 3rd section, and the 5th section of "Rangwang" appear in the "Guisheng" chapter of the *Lüshi chunqiu* in the same sequence. The 4th passage of the 1st section, the 13th section, and the 14 section, of "Rangwang" are found in the "Lisu" chapter of the *Lüshi chunqiu* in the same sequence. The same is true of the 2nd, 4th, and 11th sections of "Rangwang," which appear in this order in the "Shenwei" chapter of *Lüshi chunqiu*.

The only explanation of this uniformity is that the authors of the *Lüshi chunqiu* selected stories from "Rangwang," following the original sequence as they incorporated them into their own essays. This prodecure was easy and saved time; moreover, it was in accordance with their master's order and the editing practice of the entire book, in which every "guest scholar" (*binke* 賓客) was requested to record what he had learned. Because the "guest scholars" were not requested to create new doctrines and theories, but to collect scholarship from all over the states, they felt no compunction about quoting passages from other books and keeping the original sequence. That the *Lüshi chunqiu* quoted "Rangwang" is far more logical than that "Rangwang" copied the *Lüshi chunqiu*. In other words, it is more sensible to believe that the *Zhuangzi* preceded *Lüshi chunqiu* than to believe the opposite.

Graham also argued that chapters 8–10, his "Primitivist" documents, date from after the Warring States. His crucial evidence is a reference to the state of Qi: "Once Tian Chengzi killed the lord of Qi and stole his state . . . and possessed the state of Qi for twelve generations" (343). "Now Qi was the very last state to fall to Qin," says Graham, "so that the Primitivist must have written after the reunification of the Empire."[14] This sentence cannot be taken as a serious historian's record. Even if it were, it still might have been written before the compilation of *Lüshi chunqiu* between 264–240 B.C., when the twelfth generation of Tian family kept the rulership. Graham had correctly noted that chapters 8–10 "assume a background both of political disunity and of fierce competition between the pre-Qin schools."[15] Unfortunately, he abandoned that correct observation and followed the opinion commonly held among scholars. He supposed there was a revival of Confucianism, Yangism, and Moism during the period of civil war that lasted from 209–202 B.C., and believed the chapters could be dated "with surprising precision, within a few years on either side of 205 B.C."[16] However, we find no evidence in the historical records of a revival of the schools. In fact, the First Emperor of Qin banned the circulation of books and doctrines, which severely restricted open academic activities. The law continued in force until 191 B.C., when Emperor Hui of the Han dynasty abolished it. If the ban had been ineffective during the intervening period, it would not have been necessary formally to lift it fifteen years after the fall of the Qin dynasty. Therefore, what Graham supposed is not likely to have happened. In others words, chapters 8, 9, and 10 date from the pre-Qin period.

That there are 30 quotations in the *Lüshi chunqiu* and *Hanfeizi* from 14 chapters in the *Zhuangzi* leads to the conclusion that the *Zhuangzi* as a whole was completed before the Qin unification. Those who hold opposing theories tend to concentrate on individual words or sentences while ignoring the context of the whole chapter or group of chapters. Their arguments do not affect our overall analysis.

Nature of the Zhuangzi

Fung Yu-lan thought of the *Zhuangzi* as an anthology of Daoism, and Graham claimed it to be a compilation of works of different schools. I find, however, that the *Zhuangzi* (except chapter 30) may be taken as a volume of writings of the Zhuangzi school. The different views as to the nature of the *Zhuangzi* are shaped by the way its contents are classified. Graham seems to emphasize the differences among the Inner, Outer, and Miscellaneous chapters, while I emphasize the similarities. When scholars emphasize the differences, they tend to classify passages by date and to identify the authors by various writing styles or tendencies of thought. Thus they divide them into twelve, nine, or six groups and give them new names, such as Song-Yin school, Immortal school, Recluse school, Primitivist school, and Syncretic school, none of which are traditionally considered branches of Daoism.

In this book I use the word *Daoism* to indicate exclusively Daoist philosophy (*daojia*), as distinct from Daoist religion (*daojiao*). The term "philosophical Daoism" or *daojia* has traditionally indicated the Huang-Lao school in the second and first centuries B.C. (Han China) and the Lao-Zhuang school since the third century A.D. (Wei-Jin period). Although the term *Daoism,* like the terms *Legalism, Logical* school, and *Ying-Yang* school, appeared in the first century B.C. (early Han China), traditionally scholars have traced these thought trends back to the sixth century B.C. There is no need to seek better terminology.

In modern philosophical discourse, *Daoist* and *Daoism* refer to both the Huang-Lao school and the Lao-Zhuang school, as well as to similar doctrines. According to my understanding, *Daoism* implies these aspects: first, it emphasizes the significance of the concepts of the Way, spontaneity, non-action, and tranquillity; second, it tends to criticize traditional and orthodox values; third, it pays more attention than other schools to personal perfection, either spiritual or physical. Among these three points, the first is the most essential and radical.

As to the classifications of the Outer and Miscellaneous chapters, it is generally agreed that some chapters form apparently homogeneous groups, notably chapters 8–10, 12–14, 17–22, and 28–31, which we might call core chapters, naming them respectively Core 1, Core 2, Core 3, and Core 4 for convenience of discussion. Graham terms the authors of the chapters which center upon Core 1 the "Primitivists"; of those which center upon Core 2, the "Syncretists"; of those which center upon Core 3, the "Zhuangzi" school, and those of Core 4, the "Yangists." He adds passages from other chapters to the Inner chapters and to the above groups, then disregards the remainder.

Thus Graham not only classifies the Outer and Miscellaneous chapters, but also dismembers them. For example, he cuts out four passages from chapter 23, three passages from chapter 24, four from chapter 25, one from chapter 26, three from chapter 27, and one from chapter 32, and groups them as "passages related to the 'Inner chapters.'" He groups passages from chapters 11, 12 and 18 as "stray ideas of the school of Zhuangzi"; he also groups passages from chapters 14, 18, 19 (two), 23, and 26 as "miscellaneous of the school of Zhuangzi." He also groups one passage from chapter 14 and two from chapters 11 and 12 as "episodes related to the Primitivist essays."[17] Graham, it seems to me, goes too far, because similarities and differences are always woven together in chapters and passages, and we don't have enough information and evidence to divide them piecemeal.

The names Graham gives to the groups ignore their similarity with the Inner chapters and their links with Daoism, obscuring for readers their significance for studies of the Zhuangzi school and Daoist history. Core 2 and similar chapters, Graham's "Syncretist documents," feature a synthesis which is clearly that of the "Huang-Lao" school, another name for Daoism in Han China. Core 1, which Graham assigns to the Primitivist, obviously develops Zhuangzi's ideas, such as equalizing goodness and evil, opposing any ruler, preferring spontaneity. Core 4 (except for chapter 30), Graham's "Yangist documents," shares the criticism of Confucianism with Core 1 and shares some of the language and tendencies (mentioned above) of chapter 28, "Rangwang." We should not split these groups from the Zhuangzi school or from Daoist history. We should note that there are two types of life-prizing doctrines: the pursuit of physical immortality on the one hand, which has nothing to do with our discussion, and, on the other, the philosophical prizing of life. The life-prizing philosophies are not an independent historical school, and most scholars take these theories, including Yang Zhu's, as part of Daoism. For example, Zhang Dainian thinks of the *Lüshi chunqiu* essays on prizing life as Daoist doctrine,[18] and Qian Mu states that the doctrine of Zhuangzi comes from Yang Zhu and features prizing oneself.[19] Fung Yu-lan, too, treats Yang Zhu as an important Daoist.[20] Yang Zhu's doctrine, or the philosophy of prizing life, is commonly taken as belonging to Daoism, and it is unnecessary and groundless to separate a Yangist school from Daoism.

My purpose in classifying the chapters is to trace the development and transformation of Zhuangzi's thought as a part of Daoist history. I have found it useful to classify the Outer and Miscellaneous chapters into three groups based on the attitudes expressed towards other schools, such as Confucianism, Moism, and Legalism. Group I (chapters 17–27, 32, centering upon Core 3) follows Zhuangzi's way of denigrating and mocking Confucianists and Moists. Group II (chapters 8–11A, 28–29, 31, mainly Core 1 and Core 4) is combative and attacks them directly. In contrast, Group III (chapters 11B–16, 33, centering upon Core 2) is tolerant and adopts Confucianist and Legalist concepts into the Daoist system. More interestingly, each group is more or less influenced by the Inner chapters, or, in other words, by Zhuangzi. I found, for example, 90 textual pieces in Group I that have parallels in the Inner chapters, 14 in Group II, and 6 in Group III. At the same time, we can find similarities or relationships *among* the groups. For example, there are 10 parallel pieces between Group I and Group III, 5 between Group I and Group II, and 3 between Group II and Group III. Generally speaking, most essays in the *Zhuangzi* tend to differ from conventional and orthodox doctrines, to apply the concept or the spirit of *wu-wei* 無為, and to prefer a free, easy, careless, and romantic style. They also use analogy, exaggeration, and fable to express philosophical points of view.

The similarities and relationships among the groups demonstrate that the fact that essays of varying content were compiled together under Zhuangzi's name is not evidence that the *Zhuangzi* contains incompatible elements from other schools. This is to say, we should generally accept the *Zhuangzi* as a collection of writings of his school (except chapter 30) even though they are not strictly homogeneous. It is commonly recognized that the followers of a school differ among themselves, for instance, the socialists, Marxists and existentialists in our time. We should not expect to find that all of Zhuangzi's followers run along the lines of the master.

Adopting my classification of the three groups, we can trace an interesting transformation of Daoism. The authors of Group I, the Transmitters or expositors of Zhuangzi 述莊派, while basically interpreting the Inner chapters, applied Zhuangzi's spirit of mind-tranquillity to the creative arts, and also were the first school to propose the Daoist concept of man. The authors of Group II, the Huang-Lao school 黃老派, transformed Zhuangzi's individual interest into a social orientation, yet posited the idea that a sovereign should do nothing and the ministers should do everything. The authors of Group III, the Anarchists 無君派, turned Zhuangzi's idea of pursuing transcendent freedom towards preserving human nature and the peaceful life. Thus we find more aspects and interests of Daoism, including the Huang-Lao texts, which are typical documents of the Huang-Lao school, according to Sima Tan's definition.

Reconstruction of the Inner chapters

Obviously, Graham's emphasis on textual analysis of the *Zhuangzi* partly differs from mine. The main body of his analysis focuses on two issues. First, can we take for granted the common authorship of the Inner chapters?[21] This question also concerns me, and I have discussed it in the third section of the first chapter of this book. Although Graham's discussion refers to Fu Sinian's 1936 article, which questions the authorship of chapter 2, while mine responds to Zhang Hengshou's 1983 book, which insists that the first three sections of chapter 3 do not belong to the Inner chapters, our different approaches brought us to a similar point of view; namely, we both believe that the Inner chapters could have been written by Zhuangzi. The difference between us on this matter is just that my conclusion was milder and more conservative.

Second, Graham asks, can we fill some of the gaps in the Inner chapters with scraps from the Miscellaneous chapters?[22] This undertaking, it seems to me, is unnecessary, and in any event, impossible to realize. First, the essays in the Inner chapters are obviously not like modern essays, with a clear central idea and coherent arguments; instead they are gatherings of relevant fables, anecdotes, stories, dialogues, and debates. There is argumentation in them, but not modern reasoning and inference; there is structure, but it is not as clear and coherent as in modern essays. Therefore it is too difficult to decide where a passage is lost or what kind of fragment is lost.

Through statistical analysis and comparison of some common terms and phrases, the most we can find is similarities, which are not adequate to identify fragments as belonging to a certain essay of a single author. Disciples always imitate their masters, either consciously or unconsciously. Although some passages of the Outer and Miscellaneous chapters are very similar to the Inner chapters, there are various possibilities for explaining such similarity. The fragments could have been written by Zhuangzi's students, imitating his ideas and style; or written and then disregarded by Zhuangzi himself; or written by him but lost from the Inner chapters. If either of the first two scenarios is correct, we should not try to come to any further conclusions. Only the third scenario could justify an attempt to restore fragments to their original text, but we have no means of determining that this is the case.

Some passages seem very close to the Inner chapters, but they still fall short. For instance, Graham moved a passage from chapter 24, "Xuwugui," into chapter 3, "Yangshengzhu." There are indeed some occurrences of the same words in both, such as *youya* 有涯 and *wuya* 無涯, but the writing style is different. In the passage from "Xuwugui" we read,

> Knowing the ultimate One, knowing the Ultimate Yin, knowing the ultimate eye, knowing the ultimate adjuster, knowing the ultimate in scope, knowing the ultimately truthful, knowing the ultimately fixed, you have reached the perfect point.[24]

It mechanically repeats seven parallel sentences without any development of ideas, followed by seven equally stiff sentences. These rigid language patterns are clearly different from the general style in the Inner chapters, which are imaginative, fantastic, free, and unrestrained. Thus, Graham's judgment in this case is to be questioned.

Summing up these comparisons between my work and Graham's, both of us believe that the Inner chapters should be taken as Zhuangzi's writings. However, I do not think that we are on firm ground when we try to fill any of the gaps in the Inner chapters with scraps from the Outer and Miscellaneous chapters, as Graham tried to do. Both of us believe that the Outer and Miscellaneous chapters are later than the Inner chapters, but I believe that the Outer and Miscellaneous chapters were compiled before 240 B.C., or before the Qin Dynasty, while Graham thought some of them were works from the second century B.C., that is, early Han China. We both try to classify the Outer and Miscellaneous chapters, but Graham took them as writings from different schools, while I group them as the writings of three branches of Zhuangzi's followers.

Despite our disagreement, I sincerely appreciate Graham's scholarship, intelligence, and enthusiasm for Chinese culture. His works always present new ideas and inspire us to work more diligently.

The *Laozi* [25]

Some able senior scholars, such Graham and Anna Seidel, on the basis of their research, claim that the *Zhuangzi* is the first Daoist text and consider the *Laozi* to have come later.[26] (Benjamin Schwartz still dates the *Laozi* before the *Zhuangzi,* although he does not offer any argument to support his view.)[27]

In the Chinese academic community, generally speaking, there are three positions on the date of the *Laozi*. The "early theory" suggests that the *Laozi* reflects the thought of Laozi, who was a senior contemporary of Confucius. This is a traditional belief based mainly on Sima Qian's biography of Laozi. Recently some scholars have returned to this point of view.[28] The "middle theory" claims that the *Laozi* was written in the middle Warring States period but before the time of Zhuangzi. This is a substitute hypothesis not yet fully verified.[29] The "late theory" insists that the *Laozi* came later than the *Zhuangzi*. Qian Mu is the most important scholar supporting this view.[30] Many scholars, particularly outside mainland China, have been influenced by him, although few have offered further supportive arguments.

Many prominent scholars, such as Arthur Waley, Holmes Welch, and D. C. Lau, have discussed the difficulties of dating the *Laozi*. Welch concluded,

> The only method of dating that I personally find convincing is that based on comparison of grammar and rhyme structure with works of known date. But even here I think we are naive if we assume that the ancient Chinese author might not have been master of several styles. . . .[31]

A New Approach

Although an author might well have been master of several styles, I think that most developed their own distinctive writing styles, which constitute a reflection of both their personal characteristics and the general fashion of their age, and which differentiated them from outstanding writers of other times. If we deal with the *Laozi* as a kind of verse instead of prose, we find distinguishing features, which include some signs of its time. This is because in ancient China, poetry, as it developed from one period to another, had more differentiating features than prose. For example, most educated Chinese know the differences among the following forms of poetry: *Shijing* 詩經 from before the sixth century B.C.; *Chuci* 楚辭 (songs of the Chu state) from the fourth and third centuries B.C.; *Hanfu* 漢賦 and *yuefu* 樂府 (Han verse and folk songs) from the Han dynasties; *Tangshi* 唐詩 (regulated verse) from the Tang dynasty; *Songci* 宋詞 (lyric) from the Song dynasties; and *Yuanqu* 元曲 (dramatic songs) from the Yuan dynasty. Thus, since we have known dates for different poetic forms, the *Laozi* may be dated by comparing its poetic form with the distinguishing features of the recognized forms of early Chinese poetry.

The verse form and rhythmic style in the *Laozi* are similar to those found in the *Shijing,* which was finished before the sixth century B.C., the end of the Spring and Autumn period. They do not resemble those of the *Chuci,* which was initiated by Qu Yuan (339?–278? B.C.) in the middle of the Warring States period, namely the fourth and third centuries B.C. My point is that it is more plausible that the *Laozi* was produced under the influence of the *Shijing* than that it was written in the middle of the Warring States, when the *Chuci* represented the main trend of verse. I conclude that it is plausible that the main part of *Laozi* was written during the sixth century B.C.

Most scholars have noticed that the *Laozi* is a sort of poem or has a poetic style. Jiang Yougao, a Qing-dynasty scholar, found verse passages in 52 of its chapters.[32] Zhu Qianzhi, a former professor at Beijing University, found verse passages in more than 70 chapters.[33] I have identified 51 chapters that contain verse pieces with more than four sentences in rhyme.[34]

These 51 chapters will be compared with the *Shijing* in my textual analysis here. Although most of them are not really poems, they show similarities in verse style to the *Shijing* and obviously reflect its influence.

Before further discussion, I should like to introduce some basic information about the differences between classical Chinese and Western poetry. In Chinese poems and songs, rhyme is the most essential element, more important than in English verse. Few unrhymed lines in classical Chinese song or poetry were considered acceptable. Therefore, whether a given passage in the *Laozi* is verse should first be decided on the basis of rhyme.

In Chinese, stress is not an important component of rhythm. Every Chinese character is a single syllable, and the number of characters in a line or sentence is the primary characteristic of a rhythmic type. The second is character groups. For example, the rhythm "XX XX XX" is different from "X XX X XX," although both sets have six characters. In this essay I mainly analyze the number of characters in a sentence.

In Chinese poems, every pause is considered to be the end of a line. To save space, lines in a poem are often run together. In quoting Chinese verses from the *Laozi,* I try to format them so that readers who do not know Chinese may more easily understand what I am demonstrating. Accordingly, sometimes English translations are re-formatted in order to show my point, or to match their Chinese counterparts.

Similarities between the Laozi *and the* Shijing

Rhythm. The first thing worth noting is that the verse passages in the *Laozi* share with the *Shijing* the basic pattern of the four-character sentence: XX XX, XX XX. Of the 305 songs in the *Shijing,* 152 are pure four-character-sentence poems, 140 are based on the four-character sentence with variations of three-character, five-character, six-character, and seven-character sentences. Only 13 are not based on the four-character sentence. Thus the pattern in the *Shijing* is that of the four-character sentence with variations.

Similarly, in the traditional version of *Laozi,* of the 51 chapters containing verse passages, the main pattern in 27 of them (53%) is the four-character sentence.[35] In the Mawangdui text, the main pattern in 23 chapters (45%) is the four-character sentence.[36] Obviously, it is the basis of about half the verse passages in the *Laozi*. Although there are some three-, five-, and six-character sentences, none of these is as numerous as four-character sentences. Therefore, the main sentence pattern in the *Laozi*, as in the *Shijing*, is four-character with variations. Four-character sentences in the *Laozi* are neither as regular nor as numerous as in the *Shijing* because, after all, the *Laozi* is not a collection of poetry, and, although the author is influenced by the style of the *Shijing*, he does not imitate it consciously. Otherwise the *Laozi* would contain more regular four-character sentences.

In the middle of the Warring States period, the prevailing poetic style was that of the *Chuci:* X XX X XX X, X XX X XX. There is an ode, "Tianwen" (Questioning heaven), based on the four-character sentence pattern, but it is still different from the pattern in the *Shijing*. It is written by a poet deliberately following the four-character sentence pattern. Hence it is much longer and has less variation than the poems in the *Shijing*. Also it lacks the next two similarities with the *Shijing* that I will now discuss.

Repetition. The second similarity between the *Laozi* and the *Shijing* is the intensive repetition of words or sentences within or among stanzas. This feature is peculiar to the age of the *Shijing*, after which poets rarely repeated words in this manner and thought it poor style to do so.

My comparison between the *Laozi* and the *Shijing* is based on the work of linguists, especially that of the late Wang Li, a prominent professor at Beijing University. He distinguished two kinds of repetition in the *Shijing*: (1) words or sentences repeated within a stanza; and (2) words or sentences repeated between stanzas.[37] In the *Laozi* a typical example, chapter 28, has both kinds of repetition. (In the following Chinese quotations, underlining indicates characters or sentences repeated within a stanza, and circles indicate characters repeated among stanzas. In the English translation, bold type indicates sentences repeated within a stanza, and italics indicate words repeated among stanzas.)

知其雄，
守其雌，
爲天下溪。
爲天下溪，
恆德不離。
恆德不離，
復歸于嬰兒。

When you know the male
　　　yet you hold onto the female,
You'll be the ravine *of the world.*
When **you are the ravine** *of the world,*
Your constant virtue **will not leave.**
And when *your constant virtue* **doesn't leave,**
You'll return to the state of the infant.

知其白，
守其辱，
爲天下谷。
爲天下谷，
恆德乃足。
恆德乃足，
復歸于樸。

When you know the pure
　　　yet hold onto the soiled,
You'll be the valley *of the world.*
When **you're the valley** *of the world,*
Your constant virtue **is complete.**
And when *your constant virtue* **is complete,**
You'll return to the state of uncarved wood.

知其雄，
守其黑，
爲天下式。
爲天下式，
恆德不忒。
恆德不忒，
復歸于無極。

When you know the white
　　yet hold onto the black,
You'll be the model *for the world.*
And when **you're the model** *for the world,*
Your constant virtue **will not go astray.**
And when *your constant virtue* **does not go astray,**
You'll return to the condition which has no limit.[38]

In each stanza, the 4th line repeats the 3rd line (with rhyme); the 6th line
repeats the 5th line (with rhyme).[39] In each stanza, every sentence repeats
some words of its counterparts in the other stanzas. For example, the first
lines all share the words *zhi qi* 知其; the second lines all share the words
shou qi 守其, and so forth. This is a typical pattern in the *Shijing.* Other
instances of the repetition of words and lines are found in 48 of the *Laozi*'s
51 chapters.[40] Another example is chapter 37:

化而欲作，
吾將鎮之以無名之樸。
鎮之以無名之樸，
夫將不辱。
不辱以靜，
天地將自正。

Having transformed, were their desires to become active,
I would **subdue them with the nameless simplicity.**
Having **subdued them with the nameless simplicity,**
There would be **no disgrace.**
By **no disgrace,** they will be tranquil,
And Heaven and Earth will of themselves be correct and right.[41]

In the Chinese, more than half of the words are repeated. We rarely find this kind of intensive repetition in poetry from the middle of the Warring States period, indicating that the *Laozi* is not likely to be a product of that era.

Rhyme. The third similarity between the *Laozi* and the *Shijing* is that of rhyme. Wang Li points out that there are two main distinguishing features of the *Shijing* rhyme style: 1) the rhymes are frequent, often every line, sometimes even within a line; 2) there is no fixed or dominant pattern, and the rhythmic forms are varied. I am going to demonstrate only three points here.

(1) In the following example from the *Laozi*, chapter 52, we see that every line ends with a rhyme. (The symbols beneath the characters indicate rhyming words.)

天下有始，
以爲天下母。
既得其母，
以知其子。
既知其子，
復守其母。
沒身不殆。   （之部）
. . . .

見小曰明，
守柔曰強。
用其光，
復歸其明。
無遺身殃，
是謂襲常。 　　（陽部）

The world had a beginning,
Which can be considered the mother of the world.
Having attained the mother,
　　in order to understand her children,
Having understood her children,[42]
And returning and holding on to the mother,
　　till the end of your life you'll suffer no harm.

. . . . .

To perceive the small is called "discernment."
To hold onto the pliant is called "strength."
If you use the rays
　　to return to the bright light,
You'll not abandon your life to peril.
This is called Following the Constant.

These sentences do not rhyme in modern Chinese, because the pronunciation of classic Chinese is totally different. However, according to linguists, each of the first seven sentences rhymes with words of the rhyme class 支; each of the following six sentences rhymes with words from the rhyme class 陽.[43] The *Laozi* contains many similar examples of stanzas in which every sentence rhymes. Many passages are couplets; for example, chapter 21:

孔德之容，
　　惟道是從。　　（東部）
道之物，
　　唯恍唯忽。　　（物部）
忽啊恍啊，
　　中又有象啊。（陽部）
恍啊忽啊，
　　中有物啊。　（物部）
窈啊冥啊，
　　其中有精啊。（耕部）
其精甚眞，
　　其中有信。　（眞部）

The character of great virtue
　　follows alone from the Way.
As for the nature of the Way—
　　it is shapeless and formless.
Formless, shapeless,
　　Inside there are images.
Shapeless, formless,
　　Inside there are things.
Hidden, obscure,
　　Inside there are essences.
These essences are very real,
　　Inside them is the proof.[44]

Each is a rhyming couplet. Almost half of the 51 verse chapters of the *Laozi* contain lines of intensive rhyme, that is, ordinary end rhyme combined with internal rhyme. This intensive rhyming is not found in works from the middle of the Warring States period, such as the *Chuci*, which provides evidence for dating the *Laozi*. Historically, Chinese poetry has been dominated by a unique rhyming pattern in which the even-numbered lines (2, 4, 6 . . .) are in strict end rhyme, while odd-numbered lines (1, 3, 5 . . .) are not. This pattern originated in the age of the *Shijing* but did not become the dominant form until the time of the *Chuci*. While this rhyme scheme does occur in the *Laozi,* it is not a major pattern there, which confirms our argument that the *Laozi* substantially predates the *Chuci*.

(2) There is a special rhyme pattern in the *Shijing* in which the first line rhymes with the third, the second rhymes with the fourth, and so forth. We find similar instances in the *Laozi.* For example, in chapter 69:

是謂行無行，	（陽部）
攘無臂；	（錫部）
執無兵，	（陽部）
乃無敵。	（錫部）

This is called moving forward without moving forward,
    Rolling up one's sleeves without baring one's arms,
Grasping firmly without holding a weapon,
    Then one is unmatched.[45]

The last word in the first line, *xing* 行, rhymes with that in the third, *bing* 兵, and the last word in the second line *bi* 臂, rhymes with the last word, *di* 敵, in the fourth. A longer and more regular example is chapter 39:

天毋已清，	（耕部）
將恐裂；	（祭部）
地毋已寧，	（耕部）
將恐發；	（祭部）

神毋已靈，　　（耕部）
　將恐歇；　　（祭部）
谷毋已盈，　　（耕部）
　將恐竭；　　（祭部）
萬物毋以生，　（耕部）
　將恐滅。　　（祭部）

If heaven had not thus become clear,
　　It would soon crack.
If the earth had not thus become tranquil,
　　It would soon be shaken.
If the spiritual beings had not thus become divine,
　　They would soon wither away.
If the valley had not thus become full,
　　It would soon become exhausted.
If the myriad things had not thus lived and grown,
　　They would soon become extinct.[46]

In this quotation, the 1st, 3rd, 5th, 7th, and 9th lines rhyme with each other, as do the 2nd, 4th, 6th, 8th, and 10th. This pattern of alternating rhyme is common in both the *Laozi* and the *Shijing,* but is hardly to be found in the *Chuci* or other later anthologies.

(3) Repeating rhymes. The above mentioned chapters 28 and 39 are also good examples here, because the repeated lines are in rhyme. Yet, we have another example, chapter 59:

治人事天，
　莫若嗇。
夫唯嗇，
　是以早服。
早服，
　是謂重積德。
重積德，
　則無不克。
無不克，
　則莫知其極。
莫知其極，
　可以有國。　（職部）
有國之母，
　可以長久。　（之部）

For governing humanity and serving Heaven,
　　nothing is so good as **being frugal**.
For only if you **are frugal** can you,
　　therefore, **early submit** to the Way.
Early submission—
　　this is called to **accumulate virtue heavily**.
If you **accumulate virtue heavily**,
　　then **there is nothing you can't overcome**.
When **there is nothing you can't overcome**,
　　no one knows where it will end.
When **no one knows where it will end**,
　　you can possess the state.
And when **you can possess the mother of the state**,
　　you can last a very long time.[47]

There are also some other kinds of repeating rhymes. Like the repeating words and sentences discussed above, repeating rhymes are seldom found in the *Chuci.*

Many more examples could be cited. It is difficult to see how the *Laozi* could be a reflection of Chu culture, as many scholars have suggested,[48] when the facts presented above show that the author of the *Laozi* was strong influenced by the style of the *Shijing,* not that of the *Chuci.* Thus it is unlikely that the *Laozi* was written after the time of Zhuangzi, that is, in the middle of the Warring States period. Therefore, it is plausible to consider the *Laozi* as a work from the end of the Spring and Autumn period.

Additional Discussion

If the *Laozi* were written in the middle or late Warring States period, why would it be more similar to the *Shijing* than to the *Chuci?* There is nothing to indicate that the style of the *Laozi* was an intentional imitation of the style of the *Shijing.* In fact, it would be much more difficult to imitate the style of the *Shijing* than to imitate the style of Shakespeare's sonnets, because the former does not have a fixed pattern to follow. The *Laozi*'s language and style are coherent and natural, with no signs of conscious imitation. Further, why would anyone write a text and name it after one "Laozi" unless Laozi was already famous, in which case there would already have been a text bearing his name and no room for another! Laozi, after all, is known only for the book.[49]

If the author of the *Laozi* lived after Zhuangzi, as suggested by the "late theory," we face even more difficulties. Between about 286 B.C., when Zhuangzi died, and about 235 B.C. and 233 B.C., when Xunzi and Han Feizi died, there were approximately fifty years.[50] We have no evidence indicating that Xunzi's comments on Laozi[51] and Han Feizi's commentary on the *Laozi* were written just before their deaths. It is reasonable to suppose that their commentaries date from 10 or 20 years earlier. And if the *Laozi* was not a response to Zhuangzi's death, we can suppose that it was written 10 years after that event. This leaves a period of only 20 or 30 years between the *Laozi*'s appearance and the two philosophers' commentaries on it. The author of the *Laozi* was not a prominent person, and there are no historical documents pertaining to him. Yet, if the "late theory" is true, his five thousand characters must have attracted widespread attention among his contemporaries very rapidly. Is this likely for a little-known author at a time when books were copied by hand and there were no networks of commercial distribution? And if, as the "late theory" holds, the author of the *Laozi* was a contemporary of Han Feizi, why would the latter have felt the need to annotate it? The short texts of the *Laozi* should not have been too difficult for an audience of its own time.

Furthermore, on the basis of my textual analysis, the Outer and Miscellaneous chapters in the *Zhuangzi* were completed after 286 B.C., when Zhuangzi died, and before 240 B.C., when *Lüshi chunqiu* was compiled. Among these, chapter 33, "Tianxia," was written earlier than chapter 18, "Zhile," which itself is commonly considered to belong to the early group of the Outer chapters.[52] That means that chapter 33 was written not long after Zhuangzi's death, possibly between 286 and 270 B.C. It is commonly recognized that this chapter is not a collection of fables and stories, but the earliest document on intellectual history.[53] It comments first on officials or Confucianists, then on Moists, then on quasi-Moists Song Xing (or Song Keng) and Yin Wen,[54] then on quasi-Daoists Peng Meng, Tian Pian, and Shen Dao,[55] then on the highest Daoist, Laozi, then on Zhuangzi, the primary figure in the book.[56] The discussion moves from the Moists to Laozi, with growing approval and diminishing criticism. The author praises Laozi for having already reached the "ultimate" 可謂至極.[57] There are two points to be made in this regard. First, the author gives Laozi the highest compliment without any qualifying negative comments, a unique treatment in the chapter. Second, the author calls Laozi the "Great True Man of *Ancient Time*" 古之博大真人,[58] indicating that he believed Laozi was much older than Mozi. But if Laozi had lived after Zhuangzi's death, he would have been a contemporary of the author of "Tianxia," and would not have been discussed in these terms.

The preceding arguments do not prove that the *Laozi* contains no words or sentences of later date. But taken as a whole, it could not have been written as late as some scholars speculate. While some hold that the evidence that the *Laozi* was produced at the end of the Spring and Autumn period is inconclusive, we have even less evidence to suggest that it dates from the middle or late Warring States period. Most proponents of the "middle" and "late" theories ground their arguments on questions and doubts about the "early theory" instead of offering positive evidence for their own.

Therefore, until we find some hard evidence to fix its exact date, the best hypothesis is the traditional view, namely that the *Laozi* is a work reflecting the thought of an elder contemporary of Confucius. It seems to me that it is more logical to adhere to the traditional historical record until clear evidence suggests that it be altered, than to abandon it entirely because of doubts and speculation.

Based on this textual analysis, I am satisfied that the *Laozi* is the first Daoist classic. Containing just over five thousand characters, it is simple but carries within itself the seeds of various aspects of Daoist philosophy, metaphysics, values, methodology, and social views. It brought to later Daoism the central concepts of the Way, spontaneity, non-action, and tranquillity. Its doctrine evolved slowly until the fourth century B.C., when Zhuangzi unfolded its individualistic tendency, and originated the idea of spiritual freedom, while Huang-Lao scholars developed its social views. In other words, two hundred years later the thought of the *Laozi*, Daoism, developed in two directions: one of interest in the individual, led by Yang Zhu and Zhuangzi (and including two branches of Zhuangzi's followers, the expositors and the anarchists); the other socially oriented, represented by the Huang-Lao doctrine (and including the Huang-Lao branch of Zhuangzi's followers).[59] Thus, from examining the dates of both the *Laozi* and the *Zhuangzi,* and from classifying the chapters in the *Zhuangzi,* we can be confident in sketching out the historical development and transformations of Daoism.

Notes

All parenthetical page references in the text are to Guo Qingfan, *Zhuangzi jishi,* unless preceded by one of the following abbreviations:

    H *Hanfeizi*
    L *Lüshi chunqiu*
    S *Shiji*
    X *Xunzi*

Notes for Chapter 1

1   Ren Jiyu, *Zhongguo zhexue fazhanshi: xianqin,* 386.

2   Fung Yu-lan, *Zhongguo zhexueshi xinbian,* 367.

3   Lu Qin, 1.

4   Fung, *Zhongguo zhexueshi xinbian,* 367.

5   Fung, *Zhongguo zhexueshi xinbian,* 367.

6   Ren, "Zhuangzi tanyuan," *Zhuangzi zhexue taolunji,* 181.

7   Zhang Hengshou, 38.

8   Ren, *Zhongguo zhexue fazhanshi: xianqin,* 386.

9   Cheng Yishan, personal communication.

10   Guo Qingfan, 210. All quotations from the *Zhuangzi* are from this edition.

11   Wang Li, *Hanyu Yinyunxue,* 452.

12   For a discussion of the date of the *Laozi,* see the Afterword.

13 Page references for quotations from the *Xunzi (X)* appear parenthetically in the text.

14 This sentence is followed by another sentence containing the word *daode*. However, according to Yang Liang's annotation on the same page, *daode* might be the wrong word for *zhengzhi*. Thus it is not counted here.

15 Page references for quotations from the *Hanfeizi (H)* appear parenthetically in the text.

16 This sentence does not appear in either the *Sibucongkan* or the *Sikuquanshu* edition. It is added here according to the *Qiandao* edition for meaning and fluency. See Zhou Zhongling, 764 n. 33.

17 Page references for quotations from the *Lüshi chunqiu (L)* appear parenthetically in the text.

18 Here, what we identify as the Outer and Miscellaneous chapters does not include "Shuojian." In addition, we have divided the chapter "Zaiyou" into two parts. Hence the total of 26 chapters. See chapter 2 for a detailed discussion. The Inner chapters contain a total of 15,980 characters, while the Outer and Miscellaneous chapters contain 58,430 characters.

19 Sometimes the date of a written work is the only date known for its author. This date is based on Yan Lingfeng's *Lao Lie Zhuang sanzi zhijian shumu*.

20 The last note from Cheng's *Shu:* see Guo, 287.

21 "Someone other than myself" is added according to suggestions by Zhu Guiyao, Liu Wendian, and Wang Shumin.

22 See the first and fourth sections of chapter 3 of this book.

23 Ye Guoqing, 21–24.

24 Zhang Hengshou, 84–100.

25 Yang Shuda, 8.

26 Zhang Hengshou, 100.

27 Zhang Hengshou, 87–88.

28 Wang Shumin, preface, 1a.

29 See Yan Lingfeng, 2: 49.

30 Jiang Xichang, 153.

31 Wang Shumin, preface, 1a.

32 Wang Shumin, preface, 1b.

33 Lu Deming, 376.

34 Ren, "Zhuangzi tanyuan," *Zhuangzi zhexue taolunji*, 184.

35 Zhang Hengshou, 27–31.

36   Zhang Dainian, 69.

Notes for Chapter 2

1   Su Shi, 510.
2   See Luo Genze, *Zhuzi kaosuo*, 287.
3   Wang Fuzhi, 114.
4   Yao Nai, 154 (2:25:b).
5   Wu Rulun, 83 (5:4a).
6   Ye, 40–41.
7   Luo, *Zhuzi kaosuo*, 288–92.
8   Guan Feng, *Zhuangzi neipian yijie he pipan*, 336, 338.
9   Fung, *Zhongguo zhexueshi xinbian*, 356.
10   Zhang Hengshou, 145.
11   Page references for quotations from Sima Qian's *Shiji (S)* appear parenthetically in the text.
12   Wang Shumin, "Zhuangzi yiwen," 4b, in *Zhuangzi jiaoshi*.
13   Li Fang, 3535 (767:3a).
14   Luo, *Zhuzi kaosuo*, 307–8.
15   Zhang Hengshou, 287–91.
16   Zhang Hengshou, 288.
17   Wang Shumin, "Zhuangzi yiwen," 7b, in *Zhuangzi jiaoshi*. Li Shan, 523 (36:20).
18   Zhang Hengshou, 287, 288.
19   Ban Gu, "Jia Yi zhuan," 2228 n.15.
20   Wang Shumin, appendix, 7a.
21   Lu Jia, "Taoji," 372.
22   Lu Jia, "Siwu," 386.
23   Jia Yi, "Youmin," 410.
24   Liu An, "Qisu," 633.
25   See Zhang Zhenze, "Preface," 1. Qiu Xigui, 69.
26   Yao, 173 (3:1a).
27   Liu Jie, 57–59.
28   Jia Yi, "Liushu" 441; "Daode shuo," 445.
29   Liu An, 742.

30   Liu Jie, 60.

31   Gu Jiegang, 58.

32   Chen Guying, 347–48.

33   Wang Guowei, 7007.

34   Luo, *Zhuzi kaosuo,* 290–91.

35   Luo, *Zhuzi kaosuo,* 128.

36   Luo, *Zhuzi kaosuo,* 291.

37   Yao, 149 (2:23a).

38   Zhang Hengshou, 157–58.

39   *Heguanzi,* 223.

40   Zhang Dainian, 99. Wu Guang, 151–58.

41   Liu An, 608.

42   Ban Gu, "Dong zhongshu zhuan," 2509.

43   Yao, 154 (2:25b).

44   Lin Xiyi, 31:9.

45   Yao, 136 (2:16b).

46   Wu Rulun, 80.

Notes for Chapter 3

1   Chen Zhi'an, 25 (preface, 10a).

2   See Guan Feng, *Zhuangzi neipian yijie he pipan,* 394.

3   Ye, 39–40.

4   Luo, *Zhuzi kaosuo,* 284, 292, 299.

5   Takeuchi Yoshio, 117.

6   Guan, 324, 329, 340.

7   Zhang Hengshou, 124, 145, 180, 226, 257, 286, 296.

8   Zhang Hengshou cites this example.

9   Zhang Hengshou cites this example.

10   Chen Zhi'an, 437 (10:11a).

11   Wang Fuzhi, 138.

12   Lin Yunming, 342 (4:20b).

13   Liu Xianxin, 27.

14   Luo, *Zhuzi kaosuo,* 294.

15 Zhang Chengqiu, 294.

16 Zhang Hengshou, 183.

17 Chen Zhi'an, 473 (11:1a).

18 Lin Yunming, 354 (4:26b).

19 Hu Yuanjun, 141.

20 Zhang Hengshou, 198.

21 Gui Youguang, 396 (701b).

22 Lin Yunming, 376 (4:37b).

23 Guan, *Zhuangzi neipian yijie he pipian,* 394. Hu, 147.

24 Wang Fuzhi, 154–55.

25 Luo, *Zhuzi kaosuo,* 294.

26 Zhang Hengshou, 198.

27 Zhang Hengshou, 211.

28 Zhang Hengshou, 211.

29 Wang Fuzhi, 166.

30 Yao, 213 (3:21a).

31 Lin Yunming, 398 (4:48b).

32 Lu Shuzhi, 353 (2:92a).

33 Wang Xianqian, 235 (5:13a).

34 Zhang Chengqiu, 117.

35 Zhang Hengshou, 214.

36 Lu Xixing, 719 (5:1a).

37 Chen Zhi'an, 541 (12:1a).

38 Wang Fuzhi, 175.

39 Zhang Chengqiu, 120.

40 Zhang Hengshou, 217.

41 Wang Fuzhi, 184.

42 Zhang Hengshou, 218.

43 Wang Fuzhi, 197.

44 Hu, 187.

45 Zhang Hengshou, 244.

46 Ziqi of Nanbo, which is similar to Ziqi of Nanguo, i.e., Ziqi of South Wall. According to Guo Qingfan (848, n.1), they are the same.

47 Zhang Chengqiu, 132.

48   Zhang Hengshou, 245.

49   Lu Xixing, 917 (6:1a).

50   Wang Fuzhi, 226.

51   Hu, 217.

52   Zhang Hengshou, 257.

53   Wang Fuzhi, 226.

54   Zhang Hengshou, 271.

55   Lu Shuzhi, 509 (3:47a).

56   Zhuang Wanshou, 66.

57   Zhang Hengshou, 279.

58   Wang Fuzhi, 270.

59   Hu, 266.

60   Zhang Hengshou, 286.

61   Ye, 40.

62   Luo, *Zhuzi kaosuo,* 284. Guan, *Zhuangzi neipian yijie he pipian,* 324.

63   Yao, 121 (2:9a). Takeuchi Yoshio, 118.

64   Zhang Hengshou, 135.

65   Wang Fuzhi, 196.

66   Ge Hong, 235.

67   Ge, 234.

68   Ge, 232.

69   Ge, 233.

70   Ge, 233.

Notes for Afterword

1   Guan, *Zhuangzi neipian yijie he pipan,* 2–64.

2   Guan, "Zhuangzi zhexue pipan," 2.

3   For a more detailed argument, see Liu Xiaogan, *Zhuangzi zhexue jiqi yanbian,* 137–42.

4   Guan, "Zhuangzi waizapian chutan," 61–98.

5   Graham, *Studies in Chinese Philosophy,* 283

6   Graham, *Studies in Chinese Philosophy,* 317.

7   Ren, "Zhuangzi tanyuan," *Zhuangzi zhexue taolunji,* 160, 179.

8   Fung, *Zhuangzi zhexue taolunji*, 116.

9   Though some scholars think that the *Lüshi chunqiu* was finished later, it could not be later than 235 B.C. when Lü died, which is enough to say that the *Zhuangzi* was finished before the Qin unification.

10 Graham, *Studies in Chinese Philosophy*, 317.

11 Zhang Dainian, 99; Wu Guang, 158.

12 The six chapters are "Guisheng," "Lisu," "Shenwei," "Shenren," "Guanshi," and "Chenglian."

13 Sima Qian, 2510.

14 Graham, *Studies in Chinese Philosophy*, 305. Incidentally, Graham's translation of *yidan* 一旦 as "one morning" is incorrect. *Dan* 旦 could mean morning, but *yidan* means "once" or "one day."

15 Graham, Studies in Chinese Philosophy, 305.

16 Graham, Studies *in Chinese Philosophy*, 306–7.

17 Graham, trans., *Chuang-tzu: The Inner Chapters*.

18 Zhang Dainian, 78.

19 Qian Mu, *Zhuangzi zuanjian*, vii.

20 Fung, *A Short History of Chinese Philosophy*. ch. 6.

21 Graham, *Studies in Chinese Philosophy*, 306–7.

22 Graham, *Studies in Chinese Philosophy*.

23 Graham, *Studies in Chinese Philosophy*, 296–98.

24 To show the Chinese sentences pattern, translation is modified. Cf. Graham, trans., *Chuang-tzu: The Inner Chapters*, 62.

25 This section is based on the article, "A New Approach to the Problems of Dating the *Laozi*," in *Guogu xinzhi: Zhongguo chuantong wenhua de zai quanshi*, Tang Yijie, ed. Beijing: Beijing University Press, 1993, 494–507.

26 Graham, *Chuang-tzu: The Inner Chapters*, 5; *Disputers of the Tao*, 216, 217–8; Seidel, "Chronicle of Taoist Studies in the West 1950–1990," 229; Henricks, *Te-Tao Ching*, xi.

27 Schwartz, *The World of Thought in Ancient China*, ch. 6.

28 Zhang Dainian, 38–41. I was told that Zhang and other scholars have developed their arguments in recent years (personal communication). To my knowledge, the strongest arguments are given in Zhang Yangming's *Laozi kaozheng*.

29 Fung, *A Short History of Chinese Philosophy*, ch. 9; Luo, *Gushi bian*, 449–62.

30   Qian, *Zhuang Lao tongbian.*

31   Welch, 181.

32   See Zhu Qianzhi, 201–12.

33   Zhu, 201-12.

34   Chapters 2, 4, 5, 6, 8–10, 12, 14–17, 19–22, 24–30, 32, 33, 35–37, 39, 41, 44, 45, 47, 51, 52, 54–58, 59, 62, 64, 65, 67–69, 73, 78, 79.

35   Chapters 2, 5, 6, 9, 10, 14, 19–21, 24, 26, 28–30, 33, 36, 41, 45, 47, 51, 52, 54, 55, 58, 59, 64, 67.

36   The same listed in note 35, with the addition of chapter 1 and excluding chapters 2, 20, 24, 26, 33.

37   Wang Li, *Shijing yundu,* 87–90.

38   Most quotations in this essay are from the Mawangdui text. Translation modified from Henricks, *Te-Tao Ching,* 80.

39   In the traditional version, sentence 5 is not repeated.

40   The exceptions are of chapters 17, 62, and 79.

41   Translation modified from Henricks, 89.

42   Translation modified from Henricks, 21. Henricks did not repeat this line.

43   Zhu, 201–12.

44   Henricks, 73.

45   Translation modified from Henricks, 40.

46   The Mawangdui text does not have the last two lines. Translation from Chan, 159.

47   Translation modified from Henricks, 28.

48   Sima Qian, 2139. Zhu Qianzhi presented the relationship between the *Laozi* and Chu dialect, 213.

49   Graham proposed that before the *Laozi's* existence, a Confucian tale of Confucius inquiring about the rites from a certain Lao Tan, already current in the 4th century B.C., may be a historical reminiscence, or simply an exemplary story about the Master's humility in seeking learning wherever it was to be found. See "The Origins of the Legend of Lao Tan," in *Studies in Chinese Philosophy,* 124. However, if he had not left his work and ideas there would have been no reason for Confucianists to respect him any more than other officers in the Zhou court.

50   Zhang Dainian, 270.

51   *Xunzi,* chapter 17: "Laozi has ideas about withdrawal, instead of aggression."

52 The principle governing chapter titles in the Outer and Miscellaneous chapters is that they derived from the first two or three characters of the chapter text. Accordingly, chapter 18, "Zhile" should have been entitled "Tianxia," these being the first two words. The best explanation is that these characters had already been used as the title for chapter 33. Therefore chapter 33 is earlier than chapter 18. For details, see p. 68 of this book.

53 Zhang Dainian quotes Liang Qichao; Zhang Dainian, 70.

54 Zhang Dainian, 88.

55 Sima Qian said: "Shen Dao, Tian Pian learned the art of Huang-Lao *daode*" (*Shiji,* 2347).

56 The next to Zhuangzi is Hui Shi, but he is obviously not in this series.

57 In a few versions, this sentence is *sui wei zhi ji* 雖未至極, but this does not make grammatical sense in context.

58 Both Graham and Watson translate *gu* 古 as "old"; however, the meaning of *gu* is stronger.

59 About the doctrine of the three groups of Zhuangzi's followers, please see Liu Xiaogan, "*Wuwei* (Non-Action): From Laozi to Huainanzi," *Taoist Resources* 1,3 (July 1991): 41–56.

Glossary of Chinese Characters

Ai, Duke of Lu 哀（魯哀公）

"Aigong" 哀公

"Ansi" 安死

ba 霸

Baijia zhi xue 百家之學之時
　zhi shi

Bailun Shu 百論疏

baiyun 白雲

Ban Gu 班固

Baopuzi 抱樸子

"Beichengmen" 備城門

"Beigaolin" 備高臨

Beiyi 被衣

Bian Sui 卞隨

Bi Gan, Prince 比干

"Biji" 必己

binke 賓客

Bocheng Zigao 伯成子高

Bohun Wuren 伯昏瞀（無）人

Bo Yi 伯夷

Cai 蔡

Cao Shang, 曹商
　man of Song

"Chajin" 察今

"Changli" 長利

Changwu 長梧

Chen (place) 陳

Cheng, Emperor 成（帝）

"Chenchengma" 臣乘馬

cheng (sincerity) 誠

"Chenglian" 誠廉

"Chengxiang" 成相

Cheng Xuanying 成玄英
　(ca. 663)

Chen Zhi'an 陳治安
　(ca. 1632)

chu 樗

Chu (place, king of) 楚

Chu clan 觸氏

Chuci 楚辭

Chui, Artisan （工）倕

Chunqiu	春秋	fu (rhyme-prose)	賦
Chunqiu Guliang-		Fung Yu-lan	馮友蘭
zhuan shu	春秋穀梁傳疏	"Funiao fu"	鵩鳥賦
"Cixiong jie"	雌雄節	Fu Qian	服虔
Confucius	孔子	Fu Xi	伏羲
Cui Zhuan (fl. 290)	崔撰		
		"Gengsangchu"	庚桑楚
dadao	大道	Gongsun Long	公孫龍
dade	大德	Gongyang	公羊
"Dalüe"	大略	"Gouming jue"	鉤命訣
Danfu, king in Bin	亶父（居邠）	Guan Feng	關鋒
Dang, Prime Minister	（商大宰）蕩	Guan Longfeng	關龍鋒
of Shang		"Guanshi"	觀世
"Dangwu"	當務	*Guanzi*	管子
Dao	道	"Guigong"	貴公
daode	道德	"Guisheng"	貴生
daoshu	道術	Gui Youguang	歸有光
"Daoying"	道應	Gu Jiegang	顧頡剛
"Daozhi"	盜跖	Guo Xiang	郭象
"Dasheng"	達生	*Guoyu*	國語
"Dazongshi"	大宗師		
de	德	Han (dynasty)	漢
"Dechongfu"	德充符	Han	韓
di	帝	*Hanfeizi*	韓非子
Diankan Zhuangzi		*Hanshi waizhuan*	韓詩外傳
duben	點勘莊子讀本	*Hanshu*, "Yiwen Zhi"	漢書藝文誌
Diaoling	雕陵	*Heguanzi*	鶡冠子
"Diao Qu Yuan fu"	吊屈原賦	"He shi"	和氏
Ding, Cook	（庖）丁	He Xu	赫胥
dixiang	帝鄉	*Huainanzi*	淮南子
Dong-Guo Zi	東郭子	Huan, Duke of Qi	齊桓公
Dong Zhongshu	董仲舒	huang	皇
		Huang-Lao	黃老
fei	非	Hui	（顏）回

Hui, King of Liang	梁惠王	Kuai	噲
Hui Di	（漢）惠帝	Kuang,	（師）曠
Huizi, prime minister	惠子	Music Master	
in Liang			
Hu Yuanjun	胡遠濬	lai	來
		Lao Dan	老聃
jiang	將	*Laozi*	老子
Jiang Xichang	蔣錫昌	"Laozi Han Fei	老子韓非列傳
Jiao Hong	焦竑	liezhuan"	
jiaoyou	交遊	*Li* (Ritual)	禮
Jianhe, Marquis	監河侯	li (principle)	理
"Jianjie Shichen"	奸劫弒臣	Lianshu	連叔
Jianwu	肩吾	"Lie Yukou"	列御寇
Jia Yi	賈誼	Liezi, Master	列子
Jie	桀	Li Gui	李軌
"Jie Bao"	詰鮑	Lin Yunming	林雲銘
"Jielao"	解老	Lin Xiyi	林希逸
Jieyu,	楚狂接輿	Li Shan	李善
madman of Chu		"Lisu"	離俗
jin	今	Liu An,	（淮南王）劉安
Jin (dynasty)	晉	Prince of Huainan	
jing	精	Liu Bang	劉邦
jing	經	*Liu jing*	六經
Jingdian shiwen xulu	經典釋文序錄	Liu Xiang	劉向
Jingfa	經法	Liu Xianxin	劉咸炘
jingshen	精神	Liu Xin	劉歆
"Jingtong"	精通	Liu Zongyuan	柳宗元
"Jingyan"	經言	Li Zhu	離朱
"Jingyu"	精諭	Lu (place)	魯
"Jinshu"	盡數	"Lü Buwei liezhuan"	呂不韋列傳
"Jinting"	謹聽	Lu Deming	陸德明
Ji Zang (548-623)	吉藏	Lu Jia	陸賈
		Lunheng	論衡
"Keyi"	刻意	"Lunwei"	論威

Shangshu	尙書	Sima Tan	司馬談
"Shanguogui"	山國軌	Song, King of	宋（王）
shangxian	上仙	Song (place)	宋
Shanhaijing	山海經	Song Xing	宋鈃
"Shanmu"	山木	Sou, Prince	（王子）搜
"Shanxing"	繕性	Sui (dynasty)	隋
She, Duke	葉（公）	Sui Ren	燧人
shen	神	*Sun Bin bingfa*	孫臏兵法
shenming	神明	Sun Fengyi	孫馮翼
Shen Nong	神農	Su Shi	蘇軾
"Shenwei"	審爲	suwang	素王
Shi (in "Tiandi")	史	Su Yu	蘇輿
Shi (Poetry)	詩		
shi (often)	時	Tai, clansman	泰（氏）
shi (right)	是	*Taiping Yulan*	太平御覽
"Shiguo"	十過	Takeuchi Yoshio	武內義雄
Shiji	史紀	Tang (dynasty)	唐
Shijing	詩經	Tang	湯
Shiliu jing	十六經	(in "Rangwang")	
shishi	時勢	Tang Yao	唐堯
"Shiwei"	適威	Tiancheng, Viscount	田成（子）
Shu (History)	書	"Tiandao"	天道
Shu, the Cripple	（支離）疏	"Tiandi"	天地
Shu, "Lack-limb"	（支離）叔	*Tianren sance*	天人三策
Shu, Hobble	（滑介）叔	"Tianyun"	天運
Shun (& Yao)	舜	"Tianxia"	天下
"Shuojian"	說劍	Tianxia you zhile	天下有至樂無有
"Shuolin"	說林	wu you zai	哉
Shuowen Jiangyi	說文講義	"Tianzifang"	田子方
Si, Master	（子）祀		
Sima Biao	司馬彪	"Waiwu"	外物
Sima Biao Zhuangzi zhu	司馬彪莊子注	wang	王
		"Wangba"	王霸
Sima Qian	司馬遷	"Wang Fu"	王鈇

Ye Guoqing	葉國慶	"Yuyan"	寓言
yi	義		
Yi (Yijing or Zhouyi)	易經	zaixiang	宰相
Yi, Archer	羿	"Zaiyou"	在宥
Yi, "Lack-limb"	（支離）益	Zang, old man of	臧（丈人）
"Yibao"	異寶	Zeng	曾
"Yibing"	議兵	Zengzi	曾子
yin	陰	"Zeyang"	則陽
Yin, Gatekeeper	（關）尹	Zhang Chengqiu	張成秋
"Yinbenji"	殷本記	Zhang Hengshou	張桓壽
Yinque shan	銀雀山	Zhanzi	詹子
"Yingdiwang"	應帝王	Zhao, King, of Chu	（楚）昭（王）
Yin Wen	尹文	"Zhenglun"	正論
"Yiwenzhi"	藝文志	Zhi, Robber	（盜）跖
Yi Yin	伊尹	Zhi	之
Yi Yin shuo	伊尹說	"Zhibeiyou"	知北遊
"Yongzhong"	用眾	"Zhidu"	知度
yongju	庸距	"Zhile"	至樂
you	遊	"Zhongji"	重己
"Youdu"	有度	Zhongshan	中山
youshi	遊世	Zhou (place)	周
youshui	遊說	Zhou, Duke of	周（公）
youwan	遊玩	Zhou (dynasty)	周
Yu, Master	（子）輿	Zhou Jinran	周金然
Yulao	喻老	Zhouyi	周易
Yuanguang	元光	Zhuang Wanshou	莊萬壽
(reign period)		Zhuang Zhou	莊周
"Yuanshen qi"	援神契	Zhuangzi	莊子
Yuan Xian,		Zhuangzi citang ji	莊子祠堂記
of Lu	原憲	Zhuangzi waizapian	莊子外雜篇探源
Yue (place)	越	tanyuan	
Yue (Music)	樂	Zhuangzi waizapian	莊子外雜篇初探
"Yufu"	漁父	chutan	
Yu Shun	虞舜	Zhuangzi Xintan	莊子新探

Zhuangzi yanjiu	莊子研究	Ziqi	子綦
Zhuangzi zhangyi	莊子章義	Zisi	子祀
Zhu Pingman	朱泙漫	Zizhou Zhibo	子州支伯
"Zhushu"	主術	Zizhou Zhifu	子州支父
Zhu Xi	朱熹	*Zuozhuan*	左傳

Bibliography

Ban Gu 班固. *Hanshu* 漢書. Beijing: Zhonghua shuju, 1962.

Chan, Wing-tsit. *A Source Book in Chinese Philosophy*. Princeton, NJ: Princeton University Press, 1963.

Chen Guying 陳鼓應. *Zhuangzi jinzhu jinshi* 莊子今注今釋. Beijing: Zhonghua shuju, 1983.

Chen Zhi'an 陳治安. *Nanhua zhenjing benyi* 南華眞經本義. *Wuqiubeizhai Zhuangzi jicheng xubian* 無求備齋莊子集成續編. Yan Lingfeng 嚴靈峰, ed., vol. 26. Taibei: Yiwen yinshuguan, 1974.

Fung Yu-lan 馮友蘭. *Zhongguo zhexueshi xinbian* 中國哲學史新編. Beijing: Renmin chubanshe, 1965.

_____. *A Short History of Chinese Philosophy*. New York: The Macmillan Company, 1948.

Ge Hong 葛洪. *Baopuzi* 抱撲子. *Wenyuange siku quanshu* 文淵閣四庫全書, vol. 1059. Taibei: Shangwu yinshuguan, 1983.

Graham, A. C. *Studies in Chinese Philosophy and Philosophical Literature*. Singapore: National University of Singapore, Institute of East Asian Philosophies, 1986. Reprint, Albany: SUNY Press, 1990.

_____. *Disputers of the Tao: Philosophical Argument in Ancient China*. La Salle, Illinois: Open Court, 1989.

_____. "How Much of *Chuang-tzu* Did Chuang-tzu Write?" in Henry Rosemont, Jr., and Benjamin I. Schwartz, eds., *Studies in Classical Chinese Thought, Journal of the American Academy of Religion,* 47: 3 (Sept. 1979). Reprinted in *Studies in Chinese Philosophy and Philosphical Literature.*

Graham, A. C., trans. *Chuang-tzu: The Inner Chapters.* London: George Allen & Unwin, 1981.

Gu Jiegang 顧頡剛. *Qin Han fangshi yu rusheng* 秦漢方士與儒生. Shanghai: Qunlian chubanshe, 1955.

Guan Feng 關鋒. *Zhuangzi neipian yijie he pipan* 莊子內篇譯解和批判. Beijing: Zhonghua shuju, 1961.

_____. "Zhuangzi zhexue pipan" 莊子哲學批判 in *Zhuangzi zhexue taolunji* 莊子哲學討論集, staff of *Zhexue yanjiu*, eds. Beijing: Zhonghua shuju, 1962.

_____. "Zhuangzi waizapian chutan" 莊子外雜篇初探 in *Zhuangzi zhexue taolunji* 莊子哲學討論集, staff of *Zhexue yanjiu*, eds. Beijing: Zhonghua shuju, 1962.

Gui Youguang 歸有光. *Nanhua zhenjing pingzhu* 南華眞經評注. *Wuqiubeizhai Zhuangzi jicheng xubian* 無求備齋莊子集成續編, Yan Lingfeng 嚴靈峰, ed., vol. 19. Taibei: Yiwen yinshuguan, 1974.

Guo Qingfan 郭慶藩. *Zhuangzi jishi* 莊子集釋. Beijing: Zhonghua shuju, 1978.

Hanfeizi 韓非子. *Wenyuange siku quanshu* 文淵閣四庫全書, vol. 729. Taibei: Shangwu yinshuguan, 1983.

Heguanzi 鶡冠子. *Wenyuange siku quanshu* 文淵閣四庫全書, vol. 848. Taibei: Shangwu yinshuguan, 1983.

Henricks, Robert, trans. *Te-Tao Ching.* New York: Ballantine Books, 1989.

Hu Yuanjun 胡遠濬. *Zhuangzi quangu* 莊子詮詁. Taibei: Shangwu yinshuguan, 1967.

Jia Yi 賈誼. *Xinshu* 新書. *Wenyuange siku quanshu* 文淵閣四庫全書, vol. 695. Taibei: Shangwu yinshuguan, 1983.

_____. "Funiao fu" 鵩鳥賦, in Sima Qian 司馬遷, *Shiji* 史記, vol. 8. Beijing: Zhonghua shuju, 1962.

_____. "Diao Qu Yuan fu" 弔屈原賦, in Sima Qian 司馬遷, *Shiji* 史記, vol. 8. Beijing: Zhonghua shuju, 1962.

Jiang Xichang 蔣錫昌. *Zhuangzi zhexue* 莊子哲學. *Wuqiubeizhai Zhuangzi jicheng chubian* 無求備齋莊子集成初編, Yan Lingfeng 嚴靈峰, ed., vol. 27. Taibei: Yiwen yinshuguan, 1972.

Jiao Hong 焦弘. *Zhuangzi yi* 莊子翼. *Wuqiubeizhai Zhuangzi jicheng xubian* 無求備齋莊子集成續編, Yan Lingfeng 嚴靈峰, ed., vols. 11, 12. Taibei: Yiwen yinshuguan, 1974.

Laozi 老子. *Mangwangdui hanmu boshu* 馬王堆漢墓帛書. Beijing: Wenwu chubanshe, 1976.

Li Fang 李昉, co-ed. *Taiping yulan* 太平御覽. Taibei: Shangwu yinshuguan, 1968.

Li Shan 李善. *Wenxuan zhu* 文選注. Taibei: Yiwen yinshuguan, 1972.

Lin Xiyi 林希逸. *Zhuangzi kouyi* 莊子口義. Taibei: Hongdao wenhua shiye youxian gongsi, 1971.

Lin Yunming 林雲銘. *Zhuangzi yin* 莊子因. *Wuqiubeizhai Zhuangzi jicheng chubian* 無求備齋莊子集成初編, Yan Lingfeng 嚴靈峰, ed., vol. 18. Taibei: Yiwen yinshuguan, 1972.

Liu An 劉安. *Huainanzi* 淮南子. *Wenyuange siku quanshu* 文淵閣四庫全書. vol. 695. Taibei: Shangwu yinshuguan, 1983.

Liu Jie 劉節. "Yixiang he lu chunqiu" 《易象》和《魯春秋》, *Xueshu yanjiu* 學術研究, 1981, no. 2: 57–62.

Liu Xianxin 劉咸炘. *Zhuangzi shizhi* 莊子釋滯. Chengdu, Sichuan: Chengdu liushi shangyou shushu, 1932.

Liu Xiaogan 劉笑敢. *Zhuangzi zhexue jiqi yanbian* 莊子哲學及其演變. Beijing: Zhongguo shehui kexue chubanshe, 1988.

_____. "*Wuwei* (Non-Action): From Laozi to Huainanzi." *Taoist Resources* 3:1 (July 1991).

Lu Deming 陸德明. "Jingdian shiwen" 經典釋文. *Wenyuange siku quanshu* 文淵閣四庫全書, vol. 182. Taibei: Shangwu yinshuguan, 1983.

Lu Jia 陸賈. *Xinyu* 新語. *Wenyuange siku quanshu* 文淵閣四庫全書, vol. 695. Taibei: Shangwu yinshuguan, 1983.

Lu Qin 陸欽. *Zhuangzhou sixiang yanjiu* 莊周思想研究. Zhengzhou, Henan: Henan renmin chubanshe, 1983.

Lu Shuzhi 陸樹芝. *Zhuangzi xue* 莊子雪. *Wuqiubeizhai Zhuangzi jicheng xubian* 無求備齋莊子集成續編, Yan Lingfeng 嚴靈峰, ed., vol. 34. Taibei: Yiwen yinshuguan, 1974.

Lu Xixing 陸西星. *Nanhua zhengjing fumo* 南華眞經副墨. *Wuqiubeizhai Zhuangzi jicheng xubian* 無求備齋莊子集成續編, Yan Lingfeng 嚴靈峰, ed., vol. 7–8. Taibei: Yiwen yinshuguan, 1974.

Lü Buwei 呂不韋. *Lüshi chunqiu* 呂氏春秋. *Wenyuange siku quanshu* 文淵閣四庫全書, vol. 848. Taibei: Shangwu yinshuguan, 1983.

Luo Genze 羅根澤. *Zhuzi kaosuo* 諸子考索. Beijing: Renmin chubanshe, 1958.

_____. ed. *Gushi bian* 古史辯, vol. 4. Taibei: Minglun Press, 1970.

Ma Xulun 馬敘倫. *Zhuangzi yizheng* 莊子義證. Shanghai: Shangwu yinshuguan, 1930.

Qian Mu (錢穆). *Zhuangzi zuanjian* 莊子纂箋. Taibei: Dongda tushu gongsi, 1985.

_____. *Zhuang Lao tongbian* 莊老通辯. Hongkong: Xinya yanjiusuo, 1957.

Qiu Xigui 裘錫圭. "Mawangdui Laozi jia yi ben juan qian hou yishu yu daofajia" 馬王堆《老子》甲乙本卷前後逸書與道法家, *Zhongguo zhexue* 中國哲學, vol. 2, 1980.

Ren Jiyu 任繼愈, ed. *Zhongguo zhexue fazhanshi: xianqin* 中國哲學發展史－先秦. Beijing: Renmin chubanshe, 1983.

_____. "Zhuangzi tanyuan" 莊子探源, in *Zhuangzi zhexue taolunji* 莊子哲學討論集. Beijing: Zhonghua shuju, 1962.

Schwartz, Benjamin. *The World of Thought in Ancient China*. Cambridge, MA: Belknap Press of Harvard University Press, 1985.

Seidel, Anna. "Chronicle of Taoist Studies in the West 1950–1990." *Cahiers d'Extrême-Asie*, vol. 5, 1989–1990.

Sima Qian 司馬遷. *Shiji* 史記. Beijing: Zhonghua shuju, 1959.

Su Shi 蘇軾. "Zhuangzi citang ji" 莊子祠堂記, *Dongpo quanji* 東坡全集. *Wenyuange siku quanshu* 文淵閣四庫全書, vol. 848. Taibei: Shangwu yinshuguan, 1983.

Takeuchi Yoshio 武內義雄. *Takeuchi Yoshio zenshu* 武內義雄全集, vol. 6. Tokyo: Kadokawa syoten, 1980.

Wang Fuzhi 王夫之. *Zhuangzi jie* 莊子解. Beijing: Zhonghua shuju, 1964.

Wang Guowei 王國維. *Wang guantang xiansheng quanji* 王觀堂先生全集, vol. 15. Taibei: Wenhua chuban gongsi, 1968.

Wang Li 王力. *Hanyu yinyunxue* 漢語音韻學. Beijing: Zhonghua shuju, 1956.

_____. *Shijing yundu* 詩經韻讀. Shanghai: Shanghai renmin chubanshe, 1980.

Wang Shumin 王叔岷. *Zhuangzi jiaoshi* 莊子校釋. Shanghai: Shangwu yinshu-guan, 1947.

Wang Xianqian 王先謙. Zhuangzi jijie 莊子集解. *Wuqiubeizhai Zhuangzi jicheng chubian* 無求備齋莊子集成初編. Yan Lingfeng 嚴靈峰, ed., vol. 26. Taibei: Yiwen yinshuguan, 1972.

Watson, Burton, trans. *The Complete Works of Chuang Tzu*. New York: Columbia University Press, 1968.

Welch, Holmes. *Taoism: The Parting of the Way*. Boston: Beacon Press, 1966.

Wu Guang 吳光. *Huang Lao zhixue tonglun* 黃老之學通論. Hangzhou, Zhejiang: Zhejiang renmin chubanshe, 1985.

Wu Rulun 吳汝綸. *Diankan Zhuangzi duben* 點勘莊子讀本. *Wuqiubeizhai Zhuangzi jicheng chubian* 無求備齋莊子集成初編. Yan Lingfeng 嚴靈峰, ed., vol. 26. Taibei: Yiwen yinshuguan, 1972.

Xunzi 荀子. *Wenyuange siku quanshu* 文淵閣四庫全書, vol. 695. Taibei: Shangwu yinshuguan, 1983.

Yan Lingfeng 嚴靈峰. *Lao Lie Zhuang sanzi zhijian shumu* 老列莊三子知見書目. Taibei: Zhonghua congshu bianshen weiyuanhui, 1965.

Yang Shuda 楊樹達. *Zhuangzi shiyi* 莊子拾遺. *Wuqiubeizhai Zhuangzi jicheng chubian* 無求備齋莊子集成初編. Yan Lingfeng 嚴靈峰, ed., vol. 30. Taibei: Yiwen yinshuguan, 1972.

Yao Nai 姚鼐. *Zhuangzi zhangyi* 莊子章義. *Wuqiubeizhai Zhuangzi jicheng xubian* 無求備齋莊子集成續編. Yan Lingfeng 嚴靈峰, ed., vol. 35. Taibei: Yiwen yinshuguan, 1974.

Ye Guoqing 葉國慶. *Zhuangzi yanjiu* 莊子研究. *Wuqiubeizhai Zhuangzi jicheng chubian* 無求備齋莊子集成初編. Yan Lingfeng 嚴靈峰, ed., vol. 30. Taibei: Yiwen yinshuguan, 1972.

Zhang Chengqiu 張成秋. *Zhuangzi pianmu kao* 莊子篇目考. Taibei: Zhonghua shuju, 1971.

Zhang Dainian 張岱年. *Zhongguo zhexueshi shiliaoxue* 中國哲學史史料學. Beijing: Sanlian shudian, 1982.

Zhang Hengshou 張恆壽. *Zhuangzi xintan* 莊子新探. Wuhan, Hubei: Hubei renmin chubanshe, 1983.

Zhang Yangming 張陽明. *Laozi kaozheng* 老子考證. Taibei: Liming wenhua shiye gongsi, 1970.

Zhang Zhenze 張震澤. *Sun bin bingfa jiaoli* 孫臏兵法校理. Beijing: Zhonghua shuju, 1984.

Zhou Zhongling 周鐘靈, co-ed. *Hanfeizi suoyin* 韓非子索引. Beijing: Zhonghua shuju, 1982.

Zhu Qianzhi 朱謙之. *Laozi jiaoshi* 老子校釋. Shanghai: Longmen lianhe shudian, 1958.

Zhuang Wanshou 莊萬壽. *Zhuangzi xueshu* 莊子學述. *Taiwan shifan daxue guowen yanjiu jikan* 台灣師範大學國文研究集刊, no. 14.

Zhuangzi zhexue taolunji 莊子哲學討論集. Staff of *Zhexue yanjiu* 哲學研究, eds., Beijing: Zhonghua shuju, 1962.

Index

Printed and bound by CPI Group (UK) Ltd, Croydon, CR0 4YY

14/04/2025

14656911-0001